PROMISED LAND

SUNY Series in Religion, Culture, and Society
Wade Clark Roof, Editor

PROMISED LAND

BASE CHRISTIAN COMMUNITIES AND THE STRUGGLE FOR THE AMAZON

MADELEINE COUSINEAU ADRIANCE

STATE UNIVERSITY OF NEW YORK PRESS

Cover photo: "Ato Público" by Mev Puleo taken at a public demonstration for land reform in Marabá, Pará on July 25, 1987.

Published by
State University of New York Press, Albany

For information, address State University of New York Press,
State University Plaza, Albany, N.Y. 12246

Production by M. R. Mulholland
Marketing by Fran Keneston

Library of Congress Cataloging-in-Publication Data

Adriance, Madeleine.
    Promised land : base Christian communities and the struggle for
the Amazon / Madeleine Cousineau Adriance.
        p.   cm. — (SUNY series in religion, culture, and society)
    Includes bibliographical references and index.
    ISBN 0-7914-2649-1 (alk. paper). — ISBN 0-7914-2650-5 (pbk. :
alk. paper)
    1. Land reform—Brazil, North. 2. Church and social problems-
-Brazil, North. 3. Basic Christian communities—Brazil, North.
4. Brazil, North—Rural conditions. 5. Land reform—Amazon River
Region. 6. Church and social problems—Amazon River Region.
7. Church and social problems—Amazon River Region. 8. Amazon River
Region—Rural conditions. I. Title. II. Series.
HD499.N66A37 1995
333.3'1811—dc20   94-42607
                                                                                   CIP
                                                                                   Rev

10 9 8 7 6 5 4 3 2 1

For my father,
Edmond Cousineau,
and in memory of my mother,
Charlotte Tanguay Cousineau
(1913-1995)

CONTENTS

List of Tables   ix

Map of the Region   xi

Foreword   xiii

Preface   xv

List of Portuguese Terms   xix

List of Acronyms and Abbreviations   xxi

Introduction: Religion and Rural Conflict   1

Part I. The Context of Change

1. The Military Regime and Agrarian Policy   13

Part II. Six Cases

2. Arame: The Town Named for Barbed Wire   27
3. São Luís: The Great Aluminum Disaster   41
4. Santa Rita: Where the Buffalo Roamed   53
5. Northern Tocantins: Blood in the Parrot's Beak   63
6. Rio Maria: Tragedy and Hope in the Land of Canaan   75
7. Bye-Bye Brazil: Along the Transamazonic Highway   87
   Reflections on the Case Studies   97

Part III. Analysis

8. Help and Hindrance: The Institutional Church   101
9. Base Communities: Link between

Religion and Agrarian Activism   113
10. CEBs, Rural Unions, and the Struggle for Land   125
11. Daughters of Judith: Women in the Land Struggle   141

Part IV. Conclusion

12. Beyond the Amazon: Religion and Social Change   159

Appendix: Gaining Access and Gathering Data   169

Notes   177

Bibliography   193

Index   199

TABLES

1.1 Shares of SUDAM Funds as a Percentage of
Allocations for Legal Amazônia · 15

1.2 Growth Rates in Northern and Southern Brazil · 19

1.3 Growth Rates in Pará, Western Maranhão,
and Northern Goiás · 19

1.4 Evictions of Peasant Families · 21

9.1 Who Started the CEBs? · 117

10.1 Patterns of Emergence of Rural Unions · 130

10.2 CEB Members' Participation in Rural Unions · 131

10.3 Number of Parishes with Each Type of Land Occupation · 132

10.4 CEB Members' Participation in Land Occupations · 134

10.5 Violence against Peasant Farmers and Church People · 137

11.1 Women's Descriptions of
Husbands' Responses to CEB Participation · 149

11.2 Care of the Children · 152

MAP OF THE REGION

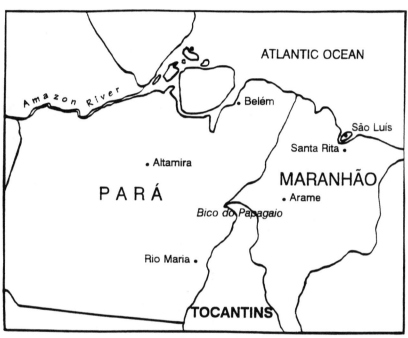

Map of the Region

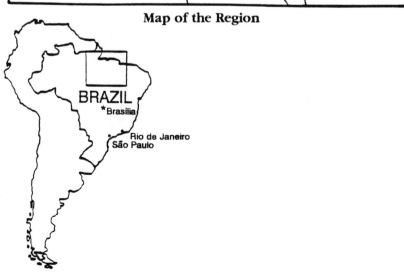

FOREWORD

We can be very grateful to Madeleine Adriance for the book *Promised Land: Base Christian Communities and the Struggle for the Amazon*. It brings together her many years of experience in Brazil and gives us an understanding of the Amazon region which we have never before had. In the first place, her central thesis is important: The social activity of the *comunidades de base* is religiously inspired. Their members are deeply committed religious people acting out of religious motivation when they either intervene to protect their own interests in the land or act as advocates for the peasants who are beaten off their land and sometimes killed by powerful ranchers. The idea that the *comunidades* are a form of Christian Marxism or have become nothing but revolutionary bands, if it is true anyplace, is certainly not true of the situation that Dr. Adriance describes. The complicated relationship to the larger ecclesiastical establishment is very interesting and important. The small communities—explicitly Catholic—function effectively even in situations of opposition by some of the hierarchy.

In the process, she gives us a vivid and harrowing description of the life of the peasants. They have established rights to their land according to long-standing Brazilian traditions, but they are violently displaced by powerful people who want the land. Peasants' development of organizations to protect themselves takes place largely through the *comunidades de base*, and the process as described by Dr. Adriance is high drama. The number of martyrs who have died in the struggle for the rights of the peasants is appalling and constitutes a national disgrace. Priests and sisters are among them. It is surprising that the world knows all about the martyred priests of El Salvador but we rarely, if ever, hear of the priests and sisters who have been dying in northern Brazil. The picture should be of great interest to the government of the United States and to the United Nations, both of which are concerned about human-rights violations in Brazil. The story of the atrocities must be made more widely known, and Dr. Adriance's book will help substantially in that effort.

Her description of the involvement of women is most important. While women in the United States struggle for equality in employment and wages, the women of northern Brazil face death regularly in the peasant struggle. The problems women must face with their families in order to participate represents a moving story of patience on the part of husbands and children as well as great courage on the part of these women. Certainly their involvement is shaping a new society in which the traditional role of women in this section of Brazil will have changed radically. One complicating feature of this is transportation; simply getting to a meeting miles away represents a major challenge.

The ability of Dr. Adriance to establish contact with these people and gain their confidence is a tribute to her. Peasants who are struggling with their lives to protect their rights are generally suspicious and distrustful of strangers, even those who, like Dr. Adriance, have long experience in Brazil. Dr. Adriance succeeded in winning their confidence, and thus her personal experience with the peasants constitutes an important feature of the book.

The book has an added value as an important study in the sociology of religion. Dr. Adriance reviews all of the important literature related to the theme of her study. She evaluates these works and relates them to her own theory of the relation of religion to political action, and her conclusion—namely, the primacy of religious motivation for the political action of the base Christian communities—is a substantial contribution to sociological theory.

Joseph P. Fitzpatrick, S.J.

PREFACE

My decision to do the research on which this book is based was influenced both by a curiosity about the relationship between grassroots church groups and social activism and by a personal concern for issues of human rights. This does not mean, however, that the information in this book is distorted by bias, at least no more than is usually the case with research conducted by people of any political or religious persuasion. We all have conscious or unconscious notions regarding, for example, how societies should be structured, what form of government would be best, whether changes should come from the top or from the bottom of a society, and what the role of religion in that process should be. It is when such notions are allowed to interfere with the gathering and the analysis of data that they are most likely to produce distortions. Distorted data are counterproductive for most purposes, including the promotion of human rights. So, for this reason, along with a commitment to intellectual honesty and an interest in contributing to the literature on religion and social change, I have been careful in the gathering and analysis of the data, which were derived from in-depth interviews supplemented by documentary research. (The details of my method may be found in the Appendix.) I have had to put aside some of my cherished theories because they did not fit the reality. For example, I had hoped that all of the rural parishes I visited would have precisely the same connections between religion and mobilization that I found in the first one, as described in chapter 2. Many of them did not. I was also trying, right from the beginning of the project, to find evidence that the pastoral style of sisters who work with base communities was demonstrably different from that of priests. Although I did find some differences, there was nearly equal evidence that a number of priests and sisters were developing similar approaches to pastoral work. I also began with the assumption that, since base communities play a strong role in helping to mobilize peasant farmers, Pentecostal Protestant sects were not gaining converts in the countryside at the same rate that they were in the cities. Yet every place that I visited had its Assembly of God and usually several other sects as well. Throughout the study, I tried to remain open to information that would challenge my assumptions.

My sympathies on the side of peasant farmers actually worked to my advantage in the conduct of this research. As church people and other activists got to know me and became familiar with my sociopolitical and religious attitudes, they began to treat me as something of an insider. In two locations in which it appeared that the parish priests did not completely trust me (likely because my sources of contact with them were not as direct as in most places), I had to work harder to gain the trust of others. In most of the parishes, however, the sense of trust was strong. I inferred, through the way that my contact persons spoke with me, that their willingness to help me gather information in their parishes and to make contacts in other areas was related to their perception of my point of view. Because of the potentially dangerous situations in which these people work, their trust in me was vital to the completion of this research.

This study could not have been done without the help of countless people and several organizations. Since I could not have even thought of traveling to Brazil without a considerable amount of financial support, I would like to begin my acknowledgments with the organizations that provided research grants: the Society for the Scientific Study of Religion, the Association for the Sociology of Religion, the National Endowment for the Humanities, the Small Grants Program of the American Sociological Association/National Science Foundation, and the Faculty Development Committees of Mount Ida College and the University of Massachusetts at Boston. The final five-month phase of the project was made possible by a Fulbright Lecture/Research Award. From Fulbright I received not only a generous stipend but also a tremendous amount of information, practical help, and moral support in the persons of Ralph Blessing in Washington, Carmen Ramos in Recife, and, in Brasília, Marco Antônio da Rocha, Terry McIntyre, and Ruth Chandler.

The conduct of the research itself was greatly facilitated by my initial contacts in the state of Maranhão: Sister Judith Clemens, Sister Íria Presotto, and Venina da Costa Bezerra, coordinators of base communities at the state and diocesan levels, helped me map out the first stage of the project and, even more importantly, encouraged people in all the parishes to cooperate with me. Sister Barbara English had an even earlier and later influence on this research, for it was she who, during my first trip to Brazil in 1983, persuaded me to begin my project in Maranhão and sent me to live for a few weeks in the interior of the Island of São Luís. It was there, in the village of Igaraú, that I learned firsthand of the importance of people's access to land as a means of survival. Years later, Barbara submitted to yet another interview to fill me in on more details needed for this book, as well as responding to last-minute requests for information when the manuscript was in progress.

Friends and colleagues who provided helpful feedback on the manuscript or on specific passages include Ruth Wallace, Phillip Hammond, Father Joseph Fitzpatrick, Gelma Coelho, Paula Ford, Carol Drogus, Sister Barbara English, Sister Dorothy Stang, Tanya Gardiner-Scott, Danilo Fonseca, and Jay Demerath. Stephen Haas of the Healy Library at the University of Massachusetts at Boston provided invaluable bibliographic assistance. I would like to thank Christine Worden of SUNY Press for her help and encouragement throughout the preparation of the manuscript and for her prompt e-mail replies to all my questions. I would also like to thank Jay Demerath for including northern Brazil in his recent comparative research project, since, in the process of accompanying him for a week, I had occasion to spend time with people whom I would not likely have interviewed for my own study. One particularly unforgettable person was Bishop Patrick Joseph Hanrahan of Conceição do Araguaia, who died shortly after I completed this research. I treasure the memory of this kind, gentle man, with his Irish accent, quiet sense of humor, and firm support of priests and other church workers who defend the rights of peasant farmers.

One of the special bonuses of doing research in Brazil is the network of warm, supportive friendships that one acquires. I am grateful to the students and faculty at the Federal University of Pernambuco for making me feel like part of their department during my semester there; to the Sisters of Notre Dame de Namur, the Sisters of Saint Joseph, and the Daughters of Divine Love for their kindness and hospitality; to Vanise Araújo, Cecília Mariz, Lila Rayol, Solange Rodrigues, Father Ricardo Rezende, and Pedro Ribeiro de Oliveira for their friendship and for helping me with academic or church contacts. I am especially grateful to Father Clodovis Boff for encouraging me in this research and for sharing insights during helpful and lively discussions.

The people in the national, regional, and diocesan offices of the Pastoral Land Commission who were helpful are far too numerous to mention, and, in any case, I do not know the full names of all of them. I am especially grateful, however, to the coordinator of the regional office in Pará, Jerónimo Treccani, and to the former regional coordinator for Maranhão, Father Aléssio Moiola, who made their archives available to me, to Franciney Carreiro de França at the national headquarters in Goiânia, and to all the people at the regional offices in Maranhão and Tocantins who responded by fax and e-mail to my requests for updated information. Also far too numerous to mention are all the people who granted me interviews, put me up in their homes, and provided contacts with others. Since most of the interviews were granted with a promise of confidentiality, they would probably prefer not to be named. I hope that this general acknowledgment will suffice to let them know of my deep gratitude.

PORTUGUESE TERMS

Amazônia Legal. (Legal Amazônia) Region which includes all of the states in the north of Brazil presently or formerly covered by tropical rain forest, plus portions of Maranhão, Goiás, and Mato Grosso; this was the area designated by the Brazilian government, as of 1966, for over a billion dollars in tax credits to be offered to individuals and companies that would propose development projects.

assessoria. Consultation and advising, such as is provided to grass-roots groups by middle-class professionals.

babaçu. A palm tree which grows in Maranhão and Tocantins; its nuts are harvested by rural women and sold to supplement the family income.

Bico do Papagaio. (Parrot's Beak) The northernmost portion of the state of Tocantins (formerly Goiás), known for violence in relation to land conflicts.

desobriga. Traditional practice of the annual visit by a parish priest to a rural area, usually on the feast day of the village's patron saint, to celebrate Mass and perform baptisms and weddings.

grilagem. The taking over of public land by ranchers or speculators, who either expel any peasant farmers who may be on it or demand the payment of rent or a substantial share of their crops.

grileiro. A land robber.

herdeiro. A peasant farmer who has inherited the right to use public land (see *posseiro*).

machista. (adjectival form of *machismo*) Sexist; patriarchal; favoring the dominance of men over women.

pelego. (noun) A government spy in a labor union; (adjective) refers to a union that does not fight for the rights of the workers.

posseiro. A peasant farmer who has gained the legal right to a plot of land by having cultivated it for a year and a day.

ACRONYMS AND ABBREVIATIONS

ACR   (*Atuação Cristã no Meio Rural*) Christian Action in the Rural Milieu; formerly called *Ação Católica Rural*, Rural Catholic Action. A church-based movement for the training of rural leaders.

CEBs   (*comunidades eclesiais de base*) Base ecclesial communities, or base Christian communities. Small groups of Catholic lay people who study the Bible and apply their reflections on it to their everyday experiences.

CIMI   (*Conselho Indígena Missionário*) Missionary Indigenous Council. A church-based agency that defends the rights of indigenous peoples.

CNBB   (*Conferência Nacional dos Bispos do Brasil*) National Conference of the Brazilian Bishops.

CPT   (*Comissão Pastoral da Terra*) Pastoral Land Commission. Church-based agency that defends the land rights of peasant farmers and rural workers, documents rural violence, and supports agrarian reform.

GETAT   (*Grupo Executivo de Terras de Araguaia-Tocantins*) Executive Land Administration of the Araguaia-Tocantins Region. Agency which was established by the military government and which, from 1980 to 1987, tried to suppress rural unrest in the south of the state of Pará, the west of Maranhão, and the north of Goiás.

INCRA   (*Instituto Nacional de Colonização e Reforma Agrária*) National Institute of Colonization and Agrarian Reform. The federal agency responsible for resettling peasant farmers and processing requests for the expropriation of land.

ITERMA   (*Instituto de Terras do Maranhão*) Land Institute of Maranhão. State agency that deals with land issues.

MST   (*Movimento dos Sem Terra*) Movement of the Landless. An
             organization begun by church people in the south of
             Brazil (now autonomous) which aims at bringing about
             agrarian reform by actively organizing land occupations.

PC do B   (*Partido Comunista do Brasil*) Communist Party of Brazil.

PT   (*Partido dos Trabalhadores*) Workers' Party.

PMDB   (*Partido do Movimento Democrático do Brasil*) Party of the
             Brazilian Democratic Movement.

PSB   (*Partido Socialista Brasileira*) Brazilian Socialist Party.

STR   (*Sindicato de Trabalhadores Rurais*) Union of Rural Workers.

SUDAM   (*Superintendência de Desenvolvimento da Amazônia*)
             Superintendency for the Development of the Amazon.
             Federal agency which oversaw the development of mines
             and cattle ranches in Legal Amazonia, administering a
             system of tax credits for large enterprises.

UDR   (*União Democrática Rural*) Democratic Rural Union.
             National organization of large landowners and ranchers.

INTRODUCTION:
RELIGION AND RURAL CONFLICT

On April 15, 1985, Sister Adelaide Molinari was killed by a bullet intended for the union leader with whom she had been conversing in a rural bus station in the eastern Amazon region of Brazil. Thirteen months later, Father Josimo Morais Tavares was gunned down on the stairway to his office at the Catholic Church's Pastoral Land Commission. In February 1990, Expedito Ribeiro de Souza, poet, peasant, president of a rural union, and friend of the local parish priest, was shot to death in the town of Rio Maria. In August 1991, shots were fired near the window of the room in which Father Ricardo Rezende was sleeping, adding to the long list of verbal death threats and actual murder attempts he had experienced. One year later, Nivaldo Vieira de Nascimento, a Catholic layman working for the Pastoral Land Commission, was wounded in an attempt on his life. In May 1993, Arnaldo Ferreira, the union leader with whom Sister Adelaide had been talking when she died, was finally killed, after four assassination attempts. All of these attacks are believed to have been the work of gunmen hired by wealthy ranchers. Their victims were people who defended the right of peasant farmers to work the land.

The Context of the Conflict

The conflict going on in the Amazon is one more manifestation of the complex dynamic between religion and politics that is taking different forms all over the world: the violence between Protestants and Roman Catholics in Northern Ireland, the process leading to cautious hopes for peace in Israel, the tensions and tentative alliances between Christians and Communists in Cuba, the pressure politics of various religious groups in the United States, and the different spheres of influence of Protestant Pentecostalism and Catholic liberation theology throughout Latin America. This last case is especially relevant in relation to the murders of people like Sister Adelaide and Arnaldo Ferreira.

Why have church people and union leaders in Brazil become the targets of assassins? And why, if Brazil and other Latin American countries are becoming urban, is so much of this particular type of violence taking place in rural areas? So far, these questions have not been clearly addressed in the social science literature on the Brazilian Catholic Church, which is based mostly on research in cities.[1] This book provides answers and calls attention to the religiously inspired revolution going on in the countryside.

There are at least two reasons why it is important to study the relationship of religion to social activism in rural areas:

1. Land is a key issue in the Third World. Conflict over land has led to widespread hunger and malnutrition, massacres of indigenous people and peasant farmers, and massive rural-urban migrations that have aggravated problems of unemployment, homelessness, crime, and violence in the cities.
2. The relationship between religion and activism is clearest in rural areas of Brazil. In the cities in the center-south of that country, such as São Paulo, this relationship is more indirect. In urban areas religious groups are among several sources of mobilization, and they overlap in membership with various activist groups. Political organizers may try to infiltrate church organizations in order to strengthen their base of power. In rural areas in the north of Brazil, however, the relationship is direct. There is seldom any question of infiltration, since church groups and groups that mobilize peasants around issues of land reform are usually composed of the same people. There are very few activists who do not have religious roots, because most people's activism is a consequence of their religious commitment.

This last point plunges this book into the midst of two controversies regarding the roots of the contemporary relationship between religion and political activism in Latin America. One debate concerns the apparent affinity between liberation theology and Marxism, particularly in their critical analysis of social inequality, sympathy with oppressed classes, and call for structural change. While Gustavo Gutierrez and other liberation theologians insist on the biblical roots of their belief system, with Marxian sociology entering simply as a tool of analysis,[2] critics such as Michael Novak and Andrew Greeley seem to suggest that priests and sisters who identify with the struggles of the poor are well-meaning but naive individuals who have been duped by leftist agitators.[3] The data I gathered in the Amazon lead me to question the latter position. Many of the "agitators" themselves began as active members of the Church. My interviews with lay people as well as with priests and sisters show that their activism, far from being a product of external Marxist influence, emerged from their involvement in religious groups.

The other debate is less visibly ideological, although there may well be political biases behind the intellectual arguments.[4] It concerns the source of religious change—specifically, the question of why the Brazilian Catholic Church abandoned its centuries-old alliance with wealthy landowners to take a position advocating the empowerment of poor people in the process of transforming unequal social structures. An important means which the bishops promoted for bringing about this transformation was the encouragement of base ecclesial communities (*comunidades eclesiais de base*, or CEBs), small groups of lay people who study the Bible and apply their reflections on it to social activism.

It is a common belief among people who do pastoral work with CEBs that change in the Church resulted from a groundswell movement of the laity of the poorer classes, and this belief has been articulated by Latin American religious writers, among them Cussianovich and Libânio.[5] The opposite position, held by North American social scientists Bruneau and Hewitt, is that change comes from the bishops and that base communities flourish only where the bishops encourage them.[6] My recent research, as well as my earlier studies, shows that both of these extreme positions are inaccurate, since the change in the Church came about through a combination of factors at both the grassroots and the hierarchical levels.[7] Although the actions of the hierarchy did help to accelerate a growing consciousness among the poor of their potential place within both Church and society, the development of this consciousness was already being facilitated by religious sisters and priests who were organizing base communities. I will return shortly to the question of whether CEBs can flourish without the support of bishops, but would first like to elaborate on some characteristics of the communities themselves.

Base Communities

Base ecclesial communities, also called base Christian communities, are groups ranging from ten to sixty people, primarily from the poorer classes, who gather for Bible study, usually on a weekly basis. A large rural parish may have as many as fifty such groups. They are led by lay people, although they are frequently organized by religious sisters or priests. According to a recent nationwide statistical study done by Rogério Valle and Marcelo Pitta, there are approximately 75,000 base communities in Brazil.[8]

While it is a common notion among North American observers that base communities are alternatives to traditional parishes, my own research in several regions of Brazil has revealed that they are actually subdivisions of parishes. In this regard, I would like to emphasize the term "ecclesial" in the phrase "base ecclesial community." The CEBs are first and foremost church-based groups, and their social activism should be understood in that context. They are not political groups seeking to gain religious legitimation in order to increase their power but rather religious groups whose political role derives from their faith commitment.

At the same time, the social activism of base community members is not accidental. The sisters and priests who organize CEBs usually invite participants to take Bible courses, where they learn a specific method of Scripture study—the combination of reflection and action that was developed in the Brazilian Church during the 1960s and later articulated by Paulo Freire.[9] Through this process, people are encouraged to take a critical look at their everyday experiences in the light of biblical messages of love and justice. Since most CEB members are poor, this critical reflection often leads to activism. Furthermore, the experience of having middle-class people, such as priests and sisters, listening to and giving value to their viewpoints is something new for poor people in Latin America, and gives additional encouragement to their activism. Finally, the lay leaders who emerge within the church groups tend to transfer their newly acquired leadership skills to the larger community. Thus, it is not surprising that Valle and Pitta's study revealed that more than half of the base communities in Brazil are involved in social activism.[10]

Origin of the Study

As mentioned earlier, the relationship between base communities and activism in urban areas is often indirect. In cities, CEBs are not the only source of activism. Rather, they are one factor contributing to a climate of mobilization around such issues as labor, housing, sanitation, health care, and women's rights. Since I had not done intensive research in rural areas before 1990, I assumed up to that time that the relationship between base communities and activism was not a direct one. That year, however, I began a study of the roles of religious sisters and priests in organizing base communities. I did not specifically seek out rural communities but was looking for a variety of research sites in the state of Maranhão. I chose that particular state in the north of Brazil because of its twenty-five-year history of strong CEBs and because of the absence of studies there by other North Americans. I also wanted to refute the position of those who were insisting on the primacy of the role of bishops as agents of change. I knew from previous field research that Maranhão had hundreds of active base communities and very few bishops who were inclined to encourage the kind of lay initiative and political militancy that they embody. In fact, at a statewide gathering of CEBs in 1983, I met people from a diocese whose bishop had taken strong measures to discourage the communities, without success. So in 1990 I went back to Maranhão.

The first two parishes that I studied were on the periphery of São Luis, the state capital. Then I went to the town of Arame.[11] In this remote rural outpost on the eastern edge of the Amazon, certain religious-social connections immediately captured my attention. Several years earlier, three Italian missionary priests had arrived there and begun organizing base communities. These CEBs organized a rural union, the union organized land occupations, and more than a thousand families gained plots of land. In my interviews with CEB members, it was evident that their activism was integrated with and supported by their religious beliefs.

In Arame the focus of my project began to shift to the connection between base communities and rural mobilization. Although I did complete the study originally planned, of the roles of priests and sisters,[12] I also took advantage of the flexibility in the interview format that I was using for that study to start preliminary work for the new one, asking questions about land problems and related church activity in the regions where the subjects were living. On my return home between field trips, I added materials on agrarian activism to my readings. During two subsequent trips, I revisited Maranhão and expanded the study into the neighboring states of Pará and Tocantins, selecting fifteen rural parishes, five in each of the three states, and conducting 107 in-depth interviews with members of base communities, priests, sisters, lay church workers, and non-religious activists. I also participated in regional and national gatherings of base community representatives.[13]

Religion and Social Change: Theoretical Perspectives[14]

The central theme around which I have organized this research is the classic question of the relationship between religion and social change that has been debated by sociologists for the last hundred years. My specific application of this question is the impact that a progressive form of Roman Catholicism is having on rural organizing in the Amazon region. At the same time, it is important to note that CEB members' interpretation of their religion was developed within a specific social context. Thus, in order to understand the relationship between base communities and activism, we need to look at both social structures and religion. In other words, we must first ask what has happened in the political-economic context of the north of Brazil that has made peasant farmers open to mobilization in favor of agrarian reform. Then we may examine the religious factors which have facilitated that mobilization. This type of combined structural-religious analysis is found in the work of the Latin American sociologist Otto Maduro.[15] Maduro's approach is a synthesis of two seemingly contradictory theories—that of Karl Marx, which presents religious belief as conditioned by inequality and conflict, and that of Max Weber, which emphasizes the potential of religion to change an economic system.[16]

Maduro draws from Marx for an understanding of class conflict and of its consequences for religious belief and practice. For example, Roman Catholicism, as it developed in Latin America, was woven into the fabric of societies in which a tremendous social and economic distance between rich and poor people was considered to be legitimate. This would explain why the Church identified with the large landowners and taught the poor that their position was the will of God.

For sources of change in this situation, Maduro looks to Weber, using his analyses of religious organization and of the role of the prophet as religious innovator. In terms of organization, Weber's concept of the religious division of labor helps to explain the fundamental differences in power between clergy and laity. Maduro integrates the Marxian perspective into this concept by further dividing these two categories along the lines of social inequality: higher clergy (bishops), lower clergy (priests), laity of the dominant classes, and laity of the subordinated classes. The Church's new emphasis on lay leadership and its involvement in the struggles of the poor could thus be interpreted as a shift in the religious division of labor, with an increase in the power of the laity of the subordinated classes in religious decision making.

Maduro has also adapted Weber's concept of the prophet by proposing that not only individuals but also religious movements may produce prophetic innovations—that is, those that come from "the periphery of ecclesiastical power" and that call the established order into question.[17] By this definition, base communities could be considered a prophetic movement.

Finally, Maduro draws together these various elements of Weber's theory by noting that religion influences society through belief, practices, and organizational structures. As will be shown in subsequent chapters, these specific components of religion have been having an impact on rural mobilization in the Amazon region.

For the purposes of this book, rural mobilization should be understood to mean the organizing of peasant farmers into unions, political parties, community associations, or church groups that do any or all of the following: (1) support the right of the people to stay on the land where they are living and working or to gain new land, (2) work toward creating a program of agrarian reform or pressure the government to implement an existing program, and (3) develop an ideology oriented toward systemic social change.

The literature on Third World rural social movements provides a means for specifying the relationship between political-economic change and the development of critical social consciousness among peasant farmers.[18] I will give a brief summary of themes found in that literature and then suggest how the development of peasant consciousness is further influenced by religious factors. The themes are as follows:

1. Peasants live at or near the level of subsistence, and hence are not inclined to take risks. Even when they do become mobilized, their immediate goal is to restore their traditional right to work the land.
2. Peasants are most likely to become mobilized when there is a threat to their subsistence.
3. The modernization of agriculture, which results in the replacing of the traditional estate with profit-oriented enterprises and of semi-autonomous peasant farmers with underpaid wage laborers, poses a fundamental threat to the security of the rural working class.

Figure 1 integrates these themes by illustrating the relationship among the factors leading to rural mobilization, with the peasants' need for land as the central factor and with the addition of the influence of religion and the outcome of agrarian reform, both of which are explained below.

From this we may infer that changes in the broader social context—which, as will be shown in chapter 1, may result from a combination of government policy and the demands of an international market economy—will threaten peasant farmers' material security, resulting in their being open to mobilization. The word "open" should be emphasized. Peasants do not normally get organized on their own. They are too accustomed to the relative powerlessness of their situation, whether in semifeudal economies or under capitalism. Furthermore, their passivity is usually reinforced by a religiously based fatalism. The social structure as it exists is seen as the will of God, who will give the poor their reward in the next life or in some millenarian utopia to be established on earth through supernatural means.[19]

FIGURE 1

Process of Peasant Mobilization

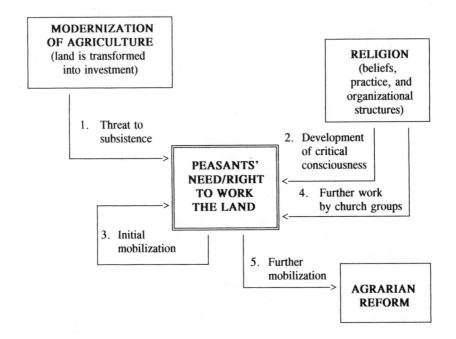

Much of the literature on agrarian activism does not give a great deal of attention to religion as a source of change. Yet there is repeated reference to the need for some form of organization to enable rural workers to break out of their passivity and to confront the prevailing system of land tenure. This may take the form of progressive political parties, cooperatives, credit societies, or community-development projects.[20] Some authors, however, do note the role of the Catholic Church as a source of rural organization, particularly in Latin America.[21]

Church, Change, and Contradiction

At this point it is important to emphasize a certain element of inconsistency, even contradiction, in relation to religion and social change. I do not wish to present the Roman Catholic Church on the global or national level as a specifically progressive organization. As several social scientists with an ideological range from Bruneau to de Souza Martins have shown,[22] the Church in Brazil initially adopted progressive positions for conservative reasons—that is, the attempt to prevent a loss of membership to socialist groups or to Protestant sects. At the same time, as has been pointed out by Maduro,[23] much of what goes on in the social world is beyond the conscious intentions of the actors. The Brazilian Catholic Church is a case in point. As will be shown in chapter 8, its motive of self-preservation—which in the past had led bishops to form alliances with wealthy classes, the government, and the military—would later lead them to form a new alliance with the poorer classes and to advocate social change.

This does not mean, however, that all of the actions of religious leaders support democratization of church and society. When the laity become militant to the point of challenging ecclesial authority structures, the motive of self-preservation leads the bishops to attempt to reassert their control over the institution. This is presently occurring in Latin America. The actions of the Vatican in its efforts to regain power have ranged from the replacing of retired progressive bishops with conservative ones, who generally try to thwart grassroots initiatives in their dioceses, to the censuring of liberation theologians, such as Gustavo Gutierrez and Leonardo Boff.[24] So, although the activism of base community members in the rural milieu was originally a result of Church policy, it is now continuing despite the efforts of the Vatican and some priests and bishops to pull back from the consequences of that policy.

I would also like to acknowledge the unevenness of the success of base communities themselves as a Church policy. There is a growing body of literature indicating that many poor people prefer Pentecostal churches and syncretist religions to base communities and that this trend may be increasing.[25] Because my research focuses on the consequences of CEBs rather than on comparative numbers, I have not done an analysis of participation in these other religions, which generally tend not to mobilize people on social issues, although I was aware of their presence throughout the period of my research. It is clear that base communities are not the only religious units of people of the poorer classes. They are, however, the ones that generate the most activism toward agrarian reform.

Conclusion

In summary, the relationship between base communities and rural mobilization can be understood in terms of the motivating factor of religious belief, facilitated by religious organization, within a broader social context that has increased the economic insecurity in the lives of the rural poor. In order to show all the dimensions of this process, I have divided this book into four parts. The single chapter in Part I explains the roots of the land problem, showing the effects of government policy in relation to the Amazon, which resulted in violence against peasant farmers, as well as large-scale destruction of the rainforest. Part II presents six case studies that show variations in the relationship between religious belief and rural activism. Part III provides analyses of data from all fifteen parishes visited during the course of this project in terms of specific categories: the institutional Church, base communities, rural unions, and the causes and consequences of activism among women. Part IV, which contains the final chapter, discusses the generalizability of this analysis beyond Brazil.

Before concluding, I would like to mention a biblical element that appears both in the theoretical literature and in my field notes. Recently, while rereading Weber's theory,[26] I was struck by the similarities between his analysis of events in the history of the ancient Israelites and the experiences of migrant peasant farmers in the Amazon. Weber showed how the later biblical prophets were concerned not only with religious matters but with social ones as well. They condemned those who oppressed and enslaved the poor, took over large tracts of land, subverted justice through bribery and, in doing these things, increased social-class inequality. Like the contemporary theologian Roy H. May,[27] Weber understood the conquering of the land of Canaan in terms of struggles between peasants and large landowners. Not surprisingly, I have discovered that certain biblical texts, particularly Exodus through Joshua and the Prophets, are especially meaningful to members of base communities, as reflected in their discussions of Scripture, their liturgical celebrations, and the songs and poems they create. This was part of the reason for the use of "promised land" in the title of this book. There is an additional level of meaning, however, that is related to a political factor at the root of rural conflict. As will be shown in chapter 1, the Brazilian government encouraged impoverished peasant farmers in the northeast region to migrate to the Amazon, promising them land. At the same time, the same government sold huge tracts to wealthy individuals and companies for the purpose of installing cattle ranches. When the farmers attempted to settle on land and cultivate it, they were evicted by the ranchers, frequently suffering violence at the hands of hired gunmen and military police. Hence, for thousands of farmers the promise of land has yet to be fulfilled.

PART I

THE CONTEXT OF CHANGE

1

The Military Regime and Agrarian Policy

On April 1, 1964, the army took over the government of Brazil and held it for twenty-one years. Although all sectors of society felt the effects of the coup, there were particular consequences for rural people. In the northeast region, where a strong peasant movement had begun in the 1950s and had grown and spread to other areas, the repression was especially severe. The army headquarters in the city of Recife became notorious for the severity of torture practiced there. Francisco Julião, the socialist lawyer and congressman who had organized a peasant movement in the northeast, fled the country and, like many other activists, remained in exile until the easing of the repression after 1978 permitted his return. The rural movement was effectively quashed. Meanwhile, the military government, in its drive to reduce an enormous national debt, was planning projects that would eventually result in the emergence of new conflicts in the countryside.

Military Modernization

The generals, inspired by neoliberal economic theory, decided to accelerate the movement of Brazil into the modern world. Their plan included rapid economic development in both the industrial and the agricultural sectors.[1] Development of the Amazon was justified by the doctrine of "National Security," with the rationale that the sparsely populated northwest region left the country vulnerable to border infringements, guerrilla movements, and the entry of foreign economic interests. The latter concern intensified after the appearance, in the mid-1960s, of a proposal from the United States-based Hudson Institute which called for the flooding of the Amazon valley in order to provide easier access for transnational mining companies to the mineral wealth of the region.[2]

In October 1966, just two and one-half years after the military takeover, the government created the Superintendency for the

Development of the Amazon, or SUDAM, for the purpose of integrating the region into the national plan for modernization. Its main activity was to be the stimulation of the Amazonian economy through a system of credit and tax rebates to private developers. Companies and individual entrepreneurs could deduct up to 50 percent of the income tax payable on all of their enterprises throughout Brazil, provided that they invested the money in the Amazon. The rebates could constitute up to two-thirds of the total cost of the project. Since the military regime's overall plan for the economic progress of Brazil was oriented to the demands of the world export market, production was to meet those demands. This would result in an emphasis on large-scale commercial agriculture, cattle raising, extractive activities, industry, and mining. Because Amazônia was still too isolated in the 1960s to provide markets for commercial farming, the regime gave special incentives for cattle ranches.

The region for which the government offered the tax incentives was not limited to what had traditionally been known as the Amazon. A new designation, Legal Amazônia, was created to include, in addition to the states and territories covered by tropical rain forest, the portion of the state of Maranhão west of the forty-fourth parallel, the part of Mato Grosso above the sixteenth latitude south of the Equator and the upper half of Goiás, north of the thirteenth latitude, which now comprises the state of Tocantins. Legal Amazônia would cover five million square kilometers, or 60 percent of the total area of Brazil.

The government's system of fiscal incentives resulted in the rapid occupation of the rural north by companies from the industrial south of Brazil and by multinational corporations. Many companies started cattle ranches as subsidiary investments, such as in the case of the Vale do Rio Cristalino Ranch, owned by Volkswagen, in the state of Pará.[3] The largest ranch in the entire world, Jari, was also located in Pará. It was owned by North American millionaire Daniel K. Ludwig and was about the size of Belgium. In order to gain access to the tax concessions, businessmen would present proposals to SUDAM, detailing planned expenditures for a term of four or five years. If a project was approved (as virtually all of them were), SUDAM would pay out rebates in yearly installments, also granting an exemption from income tax on the project for ten years and freedom from tariffs on imported equipment. If a project was reformulated after the initial term expired, further tax concessions could be approved. Some companies reformulated their projects three or four times.[4]

From 1966 to 1977, SUDAM approved 549 projects, the majority of which were for cattle ranches, authorizing over a billion dollars in tax rebates.[5] Table 1.1 shows the share of the funds obtained by the three states that are the focus of this book—Pará, Maranhão, and Tocantins (then part of Goiás)—during the first eleven years of SUDAM's operation, when the greatest number of projects was approved. Since the value of Brazilian currency is constantly changing because of rapid inflation, the table shows each state's share as a percentage of the total funds allocated to Legal Amazônia rather than the amount in cruzeiros, along with its rank among the eight states or territories that received funds from SUDAM.

TABLE 1.1

Shares of SUDAM Funds as a Percentage of Allocations for Legal Amazônia

State	Cattle	Industry/Mining	Services	Total Share	Rank
Pará	26.5%	54.1%	31.5%	39.5%	1
Maranhão	1.5%	7.8%	1.8%	4.3%	4
Goiás	4.4%	2.8%	0.1%	2.9%	6

Source: Octavio Ianni, *Ditadura e agricultura: o desenvolvimento do capitalismo na Amazônia (1964-1978)* (Rio de Janeiro: Civilização Brasileira, 1979), 232.

Clearly the state of Pará was the target for the largest investment. The southeastern part of the state was the location of both the greatest number of cattle ranches, mostly in the valley of the Araguaia River, as well as of the mining projects in the Carajás Hills.

SUDAM, which became notorious for corruption, was lax in monitoring the projects. Many of the businessmen received the tax rebates while actually investing very little in their ranches. The typical entrepreneur had little interest or expertise in cattle raising. So, although SUDAM poured large amounts of money into the Amazon, the region did not produce signs of self-sustaining economic growth.[6]

SUDAM ignored warnings from environmental experts about possible ecological damage resulting from the ranchers' large-scale burning of the rain forest, and about the unsuitability of much of the Amazon soil for agriculture or cattle grazing. Instead, the government found a scientist, Henrique Pimenta, who justified the destruction of the forest, and they incorporated his theories into official thinking. Pimenta claimed that the Amazon forest was "senile" and that, if the businessmen did not conquer it, it would disappear by the force of its own nature.[7]

SUDAM failed to provide technical advice to ranchers who were attempting to work with a physical environment that was very different from what they were accustomed to in the south. Fewer than one-third of the ranches it funded ever produced anything. After 1976, SUDAM stopped approving new projects, but did continue funding existing ones for a few more years, including those that had not proven to be productive.[8]

It is interesting to recall that a large part of the military regime's motive for developing the Amazon was to prevent foreign control, particularly in reaction to the Hudson Institute's proposal to assist mining companies. Once SUDAM was in place, however, some of the beneficiaries of its tax incentives were the mining companies, including such international giants as Bethlehem Steel, Alcoa, Alcan, Kaiser Aluminum, Reynolds, Union Carbide, International Nickel, and W. R. Grace.[9] In 1967, U.S. Steel announced the discovery of a huge deposit of iron ore, along with gold and a wealth of other minerals, in the Carajás Hills in the south of Pará. Bauxite was found in several places, with its largest deposits further north in the same state, near the Trombetas River. The Brazilian government, after initiating the development of the Amazon to keep it out of foreign hands and to improve the national economy, delivered it right into those same foreign hands, depriving the public coffers of billions of dollars that went instead into tax exemptions and other subsidies for the large multinationals. One rationale for the exploitation of the mineral deposits had been to reduce the national debt and to curb the high rate of inflation. However, as a consequence of the tax rebates and the funds spent to provide roads, electric power, and other elements of infrastructure specifically for the mining companies,[10] the national debt and the rate of inflation increased even more.

The Arrival of the Impoverished Farmers

Meanwhile, ranchers and other wealthy investors were not the only ones coming to the Amazon. The migration of peasant farmers from the northeast, which had been occurring sporadically since the nineteenth century, began intensifying in the 1960s. A combination of social and environmental factors were driving the northeasterners westward. Land in the northeast was mostly titled and held by large owners. These owners would allow the peasant farmers the use of small plots in exchange for free labor. In addition to the poor quality of the land usually allotted them, the farmers suffered because of frequent droughts. When they began migrating, many northeasterners went first to Maranhão,[11] the westernmost state of their region, where there was more rain, as well as large expanses of fertile land that was considered public. By law, people could gain the right to this land by occupying it and using it productively for a year and a day. They could obtain titles this way, but only by paying fees and going through a bureaucratic procedure that was incomprehensible to the average peasant farmer. As long as land was plentiful, however, the farmers saw no need for titles. If a poor rural family was evicted by someone claiming to be the owner of the land, they would simply move on to available land elsewhere. Since Maranhão was immediately adjacent to the Amazon, some of the peasant farmers moved into that region.

In the 1960s there was a sudden increase in spontaneous settlement along the Belém-Brasília Highway and other roads that had been constructed to facilitate the development projects.[12] This caused concern to the leaders of the military regime. If there was to be any large-scale rural migration, the generals wanted to be in control of it. An uncontrolled migration of peasant farmers, who lacked capital and technical expertise, could interfere with their plan to encourage large-scale commercial agriculture. In 1970 the government took action.

That year President Médici visited the northeast, which was going through one of its frequent droughts, and was apparently concerned about the level of starvation and misery that he witnessed. It is likely that he saw the possibility of a resurgence of peasant activism if something were not done to relieve the situation. Rather than proposing agrarian reform for the region, since that would have been opposed by the large landowners, Médici decided to launch a program of colonization, relocating peasants from the northeast. "Land without people for people without land" became the government's slogan, in apparent disregard of the personhood and of the land rights of the indigenous people and migrants who already populated Amazônia. In June 1970, a federal decree created the National Institute for Colonization and Agrarian Reform (Instituto Nacional de Colonização e Reforma Agrária, or INCRA), whose purpose would be resettling peasant farmers. An important component of INCRA's role was "social necessity." This meant that the agency could expropriate the land of large owners in order to prevent civil unrest, although in fact it did so only when peasants became organized and filed a petition for expropriation. INCRA received jurisdiction over all land within 100 kilometers on each side of the roads. Under this plan, it gained control of 30 percent of the land in Brazil and 50 percent of Legal Amazônia.[13]

The Transamazonic Highway was constructed in the early 1970s specifically to facilitate colonization. It was the only one of the new federal roads that went from east to west, extending from the town of Estreito in Maranhão to Humaitá in the state of Amazonas. The other roads were designed to encourage migration from the south. Although to this day the Transamazonic remains a narrow dirt road, it was sufficient to provide a means of travel for thousands of impoverished migrants from the northeast.

The colonization program was doomed to fail. It was badly administered and did not involve explicit measures to provide infrastructure, adequate technical assistance, or local markets for the small farmers. Neither did it have any provisions for protecting the lands of the farmers against invasion by speculators. Even more significant was the fact that this colonization was in conflict with the government's own policy of opening up the region for wealthy elites who would produce goods for the international market. Businessmen from the south put pressure on the government to prevent the colonization from becoming too extensive.[14] Because support from the government was minimal and market prices for crops were kept low, many of the small farmers were unable to survive on the land, and later sold their plots for very low prices to cattle ranchers.[15] In any case, the government provided very little support to INCRA. Not surprisingly, the agency fell far short of the goal of settling two million people, as had been proposed by Transportation Minister Mário Andreazza, succeeding in settling only about five thousand.[16]

Although most of the government's colonization efforts failed, the effect of Médici's encouragement of migration was an acceleration of the spontaneous occupation of land by people who did not wait to be chosen for a colonization project. The population of the Amazon region grew in the 1960s and 1970s at a rate above the national average. Table 1.2 shows the growth rate for Brazil as a whole, for the south/southeast (which is where many of the largest cities are located), and for Legal Amazônia. Table 1.3 focuses on the region of the present study—Pará, western Maranhão, and northern Goiás.

Table 1.3 demonstrates that Pará was clearly the state with the fastest growth, roughly parallel to Legal Amazônia as a whole (see table 1.2). The figures are a little less dramatic for the west of Maranhão and there was even a slight decrease in the growth rate for the north of Goiás (now Tocantins), because these were areas of spontaneous migration for northeasterners even before the colonization program. Maranhão had roads in the 1950s, before many were built in the south of Pará. After the Belém-Brasília Highway was completed in 1960, the east-west roads in Maranhão were improved and extended—particularly BR 222, which connected the Pindaré-Mearim valley to the city of Açailândia, where it met the Belém-Brasília. This connection also explains the rapid growth of the north of Goiás during the 1960s. From Açailândia it was a short trip south on the Belém-Brasília to Imperatriz,

TABLE 1.2

Growth Rates in Northern and Southern Brazil

Region	1960-1970	1970-1980
Brazil as a whole	33.1%	28.2%
South/southeast	32.6%	26.2%
Legal Amazônia	38.5%	56.5%

Source: Johan M. G. Kleinpenning and Sjoukje Volbeda, "Recent Changes in Population Size and Distribution in the Amazon Region of Brazil," in *Change in the Amazon Basin, Volume II: The Frontier after a Decade of Colonisation*, ed. John Hemming (Manchester, U.K.: Manchester University Press, 1985), 14-15.

TABLE 1.3

Growth Rates in Pará, Western Maranhão, and Northern Goiás

State	1960-1970	1970-1980
Pará	41.7%	59.6%
Western Maranhão	24.3%	37.4%
Northern Goiás	57.6%	42.5%

Source: Johan M. G. Kleinpenning and Sjoukje Volbeda, "Recent Changes in Population Size and Distribution in the Amazon Region of Brazil," in *Change in the Amazon Basin, Volume II: The Frontier after a Decade of Colonisation*, ed. John Hemming (Manchester, U.K.: Manchester University Press, 1985), 14-15.

which was just across the Tocantins River from Goiás. Since land in the north of Goiás at that time was 98 percent untitled and sparsely inhabited, it was very attractive to migrants, who were being pushed out of Maranhão by land speculators. In any case, although the effect of Médici's colonization effort was most visible in the state of Pará, all three areas showed growth rates above the national average for the 1970-1980 period.

The Big Projects

At the same time that the president was encouraging colonization programs, he was taking measures that would lead to their demise. In 1972, as part of his attempt to reform the corrupt SUDAM, Médici brought in more technocrats. These reestablished priorities that favored wealthy developers at the expense of the peasant farmers. Even INCRA, in its second stage of the colonization project in early 1973, began to abandon its concern for small producers and to sell plots of 2,000 to

3,000 hectares (about 5,000 to 8,000 acres) to larger owners, with an explicit goal of forming a rural middle class. In the third stage, after July of that same year, INCRA began working jointly with SUDAM and selling plots as large as 50,000 hectares (about 135,000 acres), justifying this as a means of attracting more capital and greater agricultural expertise to the Amazon.[17] There was a definite favoring of the large companies, which continued when General Geisel became president in 1974. During his administration, the emphasis shifted completely from colonization by northeasterners to the large projects in mining, forestry, and cattle raising.

Under Geisel's plan, particular importance was placed on mining, and this became increasingly evident in the 1980s. SUDAM backed mineral enterprises in various regions of the state of Pará, particularly for bauxite in the Trombetas region in the north, and for a wide variety of minerals, including iron, in the rich deposits in the Carajás hills. One of the justifications for these large-scale ventures was that they would create jobs. In 1967 SUDAM estimated that more than 680,000 jobs would be generated by the big projects, but by 1985 only one-seventh of that number had been created.[18] Both ranching and mining initially appear to provide employment, in the clearing of the forest and in the construction of mines and refineries. Once these enterprises are in operation, however, they are not labor intensive. The wealth generated in the state of Pará did not benefit the average resident or migrant worker. Most of the profits flowed to businessmen in the south and to corporations based in foreign countries.

Violence Against the Farmers

The combination of big projects in mining and cattle and mass migrations of poor people set the stage for violent conflict in Pará, Maranhão, and Northern Goiás. Many peasant families were evicted several times by speculators claiming to own what was actually public land or by owners who were not using the land productively. Estimates for the rate of eviction in the Amazon during the late 1970s run as high as 30,000 families per year. Data from recent annual reports of the Pastoral Land Commission (Comissão Pastoral da Terra, or CPT)[19] show that this trend has continued up to the present time. These data are presented in table 1.4. Both illegal and court-ordered evictions are included in the figures. The CPT figures are more conservative than the above estimate because they include only those evictions that are actually reported to the organization. The wide fluctuations in the figures from year to year suggest underreporting at various times for each state.

TABLE 1.4

Evictions of Peasant Families

Year	Pará	Maranhão	Tocantins	Legal Amazônia
1988	280	939	12	1,952
1989	218	440	24	882
1990	1,026	779	25	2,120
1991	595	8	393	1,083
1992	1,401	639	107	2,147
1993	277	497	466	2,036

Source: Annual reports of the Pastoral Land Commission. Reports of the Pastoral Land Commission in the early 1980s were mimeographed and can be found only at the CPT itself and at some of its regional offices. Later reports have been published by Edições Loyola, São Paulo.

Traditionally, land could be titled if it was purchased from the government. In the northern states, however, where the land system was corrupt and badly organized, titles could be obtained through bribery. The state of Pará became famous for "two- and three-story land," that is, multiple titles for the same area. It has been said that if all the presently existing land titles of Pará were to be added up, the area on paper would be at least double the actual geographic reality. Demarcation of properties was further complicated by the fact that many owners never saw the land to which they held title, since their intention was to hold it for speculation, rather than to use it productively.

In addition to legal ownership of large holdings, there is the problem of *grilagem*, or land robbing, which has become particularly widespread in Maranhão. Before the establishment of SUDAM, land in Maranhão was considered to be virtually worthless in terms of monetary value. Even the peasant farmers placed no value on land itself but rather on the crops produced on it. They saw land as a free and plentiful resource, like water or air. They would clear an area, farm it until it was exhausted, then move on to another area. Large landowners had little interest in this state, which had even less infrastructure than the rest of the northeast. With the inclusion of more than half of Maranhão in Legal Amazônia, however, speculators suddenly perceived the land as valuable. In addition, the governor of Maranhão, José Sarney (who became president of Brazil in 1985), waged an advertising campaign in newspapers of the center-south region to attract cattle raisers. In 1968 he established the State Reserve of Lands, with local

offices whose goal would be the granting to ranchers and other agricultural entrepreneurs titles to most of the public land. The resultant
sudden increase in land values in Maranhão attracted hundreds of
grileiros (land robbers/speculators), who fenced in and claimed ownership to large areas. Since these areas were already occupied by peasant
farmers, the newcomers would charge them rent or would demand a
share of their crops. They also began to control extractive activity, such
as the harvesting of the babaçu nuts.[20] Grileiros who wanted to transform the farm land immediately into cattle ranches would evict the
peasants, with the help of hired gunmen, the Military Police, or both.

The chaotic system of conflicting land claims, combined with a
lack of law enforcement that enabled large owners and land robbers to
use violence against anyone who got in the way of their economic plans,
created the context in which impoverished peasant farmers arrived in
the Amazon. The government gave no assistance to most of them, not
even indicating where they could or could not settle. Consequently,
the farmers came into conflict with large landholders, who hired armies
of gunmen to protect their claims, even if they did not legally own the
property.

The impunity of the wealthy ranchers in their violence against
peasant farmers is common in the Amazon, particularly in the south of
Pará. This violence is usually carried out with the support of the state
and local governments, either by their failure to prosecute the perpe-
trators or by their calling on the Military Police to assist the ranchers in
evicting people. The farmers and those people who organize them are
accused of being Communists and, hence, a threat to national security.
During the 1980s, the military government set up a special federal
agency to control rural unrest, the Executive Land Administration of
Araguaia-Tocantins (Grupo Executivo de Terras de Araguaia-Tocantins,
or GETAT).

The Institutionalized Violence of GETAT

GETAT was established by decree in February 1980 and continued
until 1987, after the transition to civilian government. During that
period, it took over the functions of INCRA for the region which happens to be coextensive with the areas of this study—western Maranhão,
northern Goiás, and southern Pará. The official objectives of the agency,
according to Decree Number 87095, Article 5, were stated as follows:

a. the regularization of the properties in the region
b. the linking of use of land to conditions of social integration

c. the promotion of the just and adequate distribution of property
d. the settling of farmers, respecting the land occupations that were
    characterized by habitual residence and effective cultivation of the
    land
e. the social and economic recovery of the region.[21]

The benign appearance of these objectives contrasted with the actual operation of GETAT. Because of the presence of the mines in the Carajás Hills in this region, GETAT officials were instructed to ensure that nothing went wrong in the government's development plans. Unrest was to be eliminated by whatever means were necessary, whether political or repressive. The general pattern of action for GETAT agents was to move in wherever there was a serious land conflict, impose a repressive solution, and treat as criminal anyone who refused to accept that solution.[22]

It is likely that the jurisdiction over land issues in this one region was placed under the direct control of a military agency both because of the mineral wealth in the Carajás Hills and because of the high degree of agrarian conflict in the valleys of the Araguaia and Tocantins Rivers. Just a few years earlier, the army had sent in 10,000 soldiers to crush a movement of about seventy guerrillas in Xamboiá, a town on the Araguaia River in northern Goiás. Lieutenant-Colonel Sebastião Rodrigues de Moura (nicknamed "Major Curió"), who had become famous as a torturer of guerrillas, was likely instrumental in the creation of GETAT.[23] Since the military regime was claiming that the Catholic Church was inciting the peasants to revolt against the government, one of Major Curió's aims was to undercut the influence of the Church in the region. He was involved in the arrest and imprisonment of two French missionary priests, Fathers Aristide Camio and François Gouriou, on charges of inciting guerrilla activity in their parish of São Geraldo do Araguaia,[24] just across the river from Xamboiá. He also worked at building his own political base among gold prospectors by blocking the mechanization of one of the major mines in the region, and thus succeeded in getting elected to Congress.

The presence of GETAT in the eastern part of Legal Amazônia did nothing to decrease the violence there. More than 300 people, mostly peasant farmers, died in land conflicts in that region between 1980 and 1994. In fact, GETAT actually helped increase this violence by making decisions that favored newly arrived ranchers over peasant farmers with longer time on the land and by ignoring abuses of the former, such as sending in gunmen to evict the farmers.[25] This favoring of the ranchers, who often did not have legal titles, suggests that a hidden objective of GETAT was the concentration of land and the transformation of the region into cattle ranches.

There were cases in which GETAT's participation in acts of repression against farmers, particularly union activists, was more direct, such as in illegal arrests and public beatings. GETAT agents were also seen traveling in the company of known gunmen and heard making death threats.[26] Evidence of the harsh treatment of unionists by agents of GETAT emerged in my interviews with peasant farmers:

> We were attacked in '84 by the government agency GETAT, together with the rancher's gunmen and the police. . . . We were all arrested. Tortured.

> I argued with an agent of GETAT, and he didn't want to give me land. So he brought in the Federal Police. And then when they came it was to kill me, but I was in a meeting with a lawyer.

A priest who is a former regional coordinator for the Pastoral Land Commission also spoke about serious problems with GETAT:

> I received death threats many times because of land issues. And the period when there was the greatest incidence of threats was during the imprisonment of the [French] priests, because I went to São Geraldo a lot, to try to undo that farce. The agents of the government, of GETAT, tried to kidnap me, to kill me.

Although, despite the accusations of the military regime, there was no evidence that clergy in the region controlled by GETAT had ever incited people to insurrection (in fact, they have consistently advocated nonviolence), people representing the Catholic Church have, through beliefs and organizational structures, provided support for the farmers' struggles. The role of the Church will be evident in the case studies and will be further discussed in chapters 8 and 9.

Part II

Six Cases

2

ARAME: THE TOWN NAMED FOR BARBED WIRE

High, green hills completely surround Arame. They are the first thing one sees when getting off the bus in this town in the western region of Maranhão. Next one sees the dust, the mud-and-wattle houses, the backyard privies, and other signs of poverty in a place where the majority of people are peasant farmers. The hills then become a point of jarring contrast, a symbol to suggest that this was meant to be a place of beauty, not misery.

Arame is the Portuguese word for wire, specifically, fencing wire, often barbed. Before Arame became a town it was called the "region of wire," because of the cattle drives that came through it. The cattle owners built long fences to create a pathway for the drives. Some people say that that was to keep the cattle from straying. Others say that it was to keep out the Indians. In the context of land conflicts, *arame* has come to have another meaning. *Cortar o arame* (cutting the wire) is associated with the act of occupying land. Peasant farmers may cut through wire fencing in order to enter an area that they wish to claim, or they may destroy the fences put up by ranchers who arrive after the peasants have already settled a piece of land. In any case, the town is well named, since it has been the site of numerous agrarian conflicts.

Land Problems in Arame

In terms of the land situation, Arame is typical of western Maranhão, which is the easternmost section of Legal Amazônia. It was settled by people from other parts of the state and of the northeast in the 1970s, when the government's promise of land raised the hopes of impoverished peasant farmers, who began to migrate to previously unsettled areas. Arame grew so fast that it officially became a municipal district in 1988. It is also typical of western Maranhão in terms of the specific kind of agrarian conflict found in frontier regions: Peasants arrive from some other place, settle on a piece of land, and soon find themselves in conflict with big ranchers whose claims to the land may or may not be legal but who have access to the services of both private gunmen and Military Police to help them enforce their claims.

The Priests of Arame

The timing of the arrival of clergy in Arame resulted in a strong role for the Catholic Church in relation to the land conflicts. In December 1980, three young Italian priests—Claudio Zannoni, Luís Pirotta, and Gian Zuffellato—arrived to establish the parish of Saint Francis of Assisi. These priests may have been somewhat unusual. First of all, although not members of a religious order, they wanted to live in community, in contrast to the frequent pattern of an individual priest with sole responsibility for a huge parish. Second, while still seminarians in Italy, they had made a conscious decision to prepare themselves to work in Brazil, and they waited until arriving in the diocese of Grajaú, of which Arame is a part, to be ordained. Third, before making a commitment to work in the diocese, they had presented their pastoral plan to the bishop, a plan based on their commitment to the theology of liberation. One of the priests summed up the process in an interview:

> We were ordained here in 1980. We had been prepared in the Theological Faculty of Turin. And afterward, on the invitation of the bishop of Grajaú, we came here, to get to know the realities here. And the bishop accepted our pastoral plan.

He explained their pastoral approach:

> Here a new form of Church is being born—birth by means of friendship and not by teaching with authority. We need to give value to work that is developed together with the people.

It was clear that these priests wanted to start something new. A parishioner with whom I spoke several years later told me that the three young men had been offered a choice of several parishes. When someone asked them why they had chosen Arame, one of them replied, in his characteristic Mediterranean manner, that they saw their mission as a kind of marriage and Arame was still a virgin.

Immediately upon arriving in Arame, the priests began to organize base communities. They visited all the distant parts of the parish, sometimes traveling as much as seventy kilometers on foot because of the absence of roads that would have allowed the passage of their four-wheel-drive Toyota. Eventually they organized more than forty communities.

> One of the first types of work that we developed was that of sitting with and, above all, listening to the people—the rural people, the people crushed by the large landowner, crushed by the oligarchy—and, from this, learning what the people were feeling.

Each year the priests invited peasant farmers from all of the base communities to a large meeting in town. They also sent delegates to the annual statewide CEB gathering, thus providing external sources of strength to the isolated rural groups.

The Union and Land Occupations

Within a year, people in the CEBs were discussing the need for a union. In May 1982, they founded their union as a branch of the one in Grajaú, since Arame was not yet a separate town.[1] One of the base community leaders described how the union came into being:

> It began in 1982. When the priests got here in 1980 there was no union organization, nor were there base communities. They came from Italy and began to work with the Church, with the farmers, organizing the base communities. In '82 the union was born out of the communities. The people were already organized, and they began to have this concern to create a union here. . . . So through the base communities, there was born this concern, and a branch of the union was created here.
> *From whom did the idea of creating the union come?*
> It began with the farmers.
> *And did it have the support of the priests?*
> It had the support of the church, of the base communities.
> *Wasn't it the idea of the priests?*
> (Laughs) No, it wasn't.

The first focus of the work of the new union branch was the refusal by peasant farmers to pay rent to grileiros (land robbers). The latter responded by prohibiting the farmers from planting their crops. In 1983 a group of peasant farmers organized the first land occupation. It was followed by another in 1984 and two larger occupations in 1985, along with others in 1987 and 1988. The large landholders responded with violence. Two union leaders described this situation:

> In 1983 seventeen workers occupied an area. In 1984 there was another occupation. Hired gunmen and military police came here, both against the peasant farmers.

> During the first occupation, there were strong conflicts, there were murders of peasant farmers, there was the burning of houses of peasant farmers. The rice was completely destroyed.[2] And there were also death threats.

More Violence

From 1983 to 1985 there was a particularly high degree of violence against the peasant farmers. In May 1985, a band of hired gunmen invaded Arame, initiating a period of terrorism, shooting people at random, injuring several, and killing two.[3] Neither the local nor the state authorities took any action in relation to these murders or assaults, allowing the gunmen to act with complete impunity. In October, one of the gunmen began to boast about their hit list, and people learned that the list included all of the offices of the union, all of the leaders of the base communities, and the three priests. This information stirred to action people who did not normally resort to violence. Without the knowledge of the priests (two of whom were away at the time), some of the union leaders went into the countryside and came back with eighty men who hunted down the leader of the gunmen and killed him. All of the other gunmen fled the area, as did some of the grileiros, who then complained to government authorities about the violence of the peasant farmers. After the killing of the one gunman, 200 men went to the top of a hill at the edge of town and occupied it from October 13 to November 3. Although this particular piece of land was of no agricultural value, the men used the occupation as a means of calling attention to the government's stalling in the expropriation of two large properties (Pedra Negra and Viamão). The occupation may have also been a means for the men to keep together in the face of retaliation by the authorities for the murder of the gunman. The retaliation came in the form of 130 military police who surrounded the hill and held it under siege. At one point they entered the occupied area, searching for weapons, but they did not find any. For three weeks, the police did not allow any men to leave or enter the occupied area except for the priests, who came in and celebrated Mass. When the federal government finally agreed to move on the expropriation of the two properties, and the state government called off the police, the union organized a massive victory demonstration through the streets of the town. This demonstration was attended by more than two thousand peasant farmers, as well as church people, progressive politicians from other parts of the country, and journalists. The case of the dead gunman was not dropped, however. The Military Police opened an inquest that never found anyone guilty (it was impossible to determine who among the eighty men had fired the fatal shots) but was never closed. People have been questioned sporadically, with intervals of years between interrogations. As late as 1992, suspects, including the three priests, who were named as accessories, were still being called to give testimony. This keeping open of the inquest is believed by the priests to be a form of harassment against those who organize the poor.

Accusations of Guerrilla Activity

Another form of harassment was the accusation that the priests were bringing Sandinista guerrillas into Maranhão and stockpiling weapons. As one of the priests explained it:

There was a point at which the people became conscious of their exploitation. They were discovering the root of their suffering. At that point there began that litany that everyone knows: "Be careful, the priests are Communists. Be careful, the priests are terrorists." They were saying that we were Sandinistas, and that we had gone to Managua for training. They had "documentation" in the newspapers, on the front page: "Presence of Sandinistas in the Interior of Maranhão!"

Newspaper articles from March 1986 report that President Reagan had told the citizens of the United States that there were Sandinistas in Brazil and that, even though the president of Brazil had denied it, Luíz Rocha, the governor of Maranhão, was saying that they were in Arame and that they were linked to the Catholic Church there.[4] Later the governor admitted that he did not have proof of a Sandinista presence in Arame. The priests attributed the accusation to the fact that a lay person from the parish had gone to a church meeting and had come back with ten Nicaragua solidarity buttons, which were common in church circles at that time. Regarding the charge that the Catholic Church in Arame had connections with Managua, Father

Zuffelato was later quoted in one of the newspapers as having dryly replied, "We don't even have the means to get to Manaus, let alone Managua!"[5]

The Gaining of Land

The land struggle in Arame brought positive results. Occupations resulted in the expropriation of four large properties (Pedra Preta in 1985, Citusa and Viamão in 1986, and Lagoa da Onça in 1990) and the granting of land to about 1,500 peasant families, although they have never received titles. The occupations also resulted in a change in the attitudes of many of the women who were members of base communities. The initial occupations had been completely organized by men. The change came with the occupation of the hill after the killing of the leader of the gunmen. One of the officers of the union talked about this occupation:

> In 1985 we occupied the land at the top of the hill where the women's center now stands. It lasted from October 13 to November 3—twenty days of occupation, women and men together. . . . One hundred thirty police came from São Luís.

The Mothers' Club

At first the women had not been part of the occupation. However, when the police surrounded the hill, members of the mothers' club connected with the base communities became concerned that their husbands, fathers, and sons would starve. So the women gathered up their pots, pans, rice, beans, and cassava meal and headed for the hill. They were able to pass through the police lines without difficulty, likely because most rural Brazilian men, including those who go into the Military Police, do not take women seriously. After cooking for the men, they decided to remain in the encampment. Since it was evident that the women could get past the police while the men could not, they began serving as couriers between the organizers of the occupation and some of the union leaders who had remained in town, concealing messages in their bras and panties. One of the women explained their participation:

> The women and the men are part of the same struggle, because we are all farmers. During the encampment, when the gunmen came, everyone was threatened, women as well as men.

Although the first land occupation in which women participated was in 1985, their experience in base communities had already been leading them to rethink their traditional feminine roles. One of the priests talked about how this happened:

In 1983, they had a desire to know more about the presence of women in the Bible. And I remember well that the first book that they asked me to explain was the book of Judith. And when they saw, in the Word of God, that a woman could be active, they began to wake up.

The men who had been involved in the occupation showed their gratitude for the women's contribution by constructing a building for the mothers' club. They built it on top of the hill, which was now called the Thirteenth of October Hill, in commemoration of the occupation. The women's center is a more solid building than many of the houses in the town—with a tiled roof, cement floor, and walls built of ceramic bricks covered with clay and painted yellow. During my first visit to Arame, several people, both women and men, told me about the women's center and insisted that I climb the hill to see it.

Continued Problems

The case of Arame is not one of all happy endings. There are serious problems that continue to plague the peasant farmers of this town: the lack of infrastructure, persistent poverty caused by low prices for crops, the vast properties still held by large landowners—and unavailable to the approximately 2,500 families who are still landless—and difficulties caused by the higher levels of the institutional church.

The lack of infrastructure is problematic because of the enormous distances encompassed by the municipal district. Those few farmers who have been fortunate enough to gain land within a few kilometers of town have access to roads, schools for their children (although the quality of education is poor), and a health center staffed by a person with paramedical training. There are, however, many families whose land is as much as seventy kilometers outside of town, in areas without access to any kind of road, schools, or medical care.

Low prices for crops guarantee the continuation of poverty, even for those who have land. The government sets the price of rice, the main cash crop of the peasant farmers, but this price does not become operational until after the harvest season. Since poor farmers cannot wait that long to sell their crop, they sell it at a very low price. This problem is further aggravated for those who live a great distance from town. Because they lack transportation to get their crop to the market, they have to sell to middlemen.

As difficult as these problems are, the situation is worse for the 2,500 families in Arame who have no land at all. They continue to work as tenant farmers or as peons on the land of others, with the former paying rent that eats away at the small amounts they get for their crops and the latter being paid very low wages.

Problems with the Institutional Church

The fourth problem listed above brings this analysis back to the role of the Church. As mentioned earlier, the three Italian priests had submitted their pastoral plan to the bishop, who accepted it and ordained them. Within a short time after their arrival, this bishop died of cancer. The bishop who replaced him did not interfere with the work of the priests in Arame, but he did not remain in the diocese for long. After a few years he asked to be transferred elsewhere. In 1987 the present bishop, Dom Serafim Spreafico, arrived in Grajaú. His pastoral style was the complete opposite of the priests of Arame, and he began to take measures to make it difficult for them to continue working. One of the first actions was to remove two sisters who had recently begun working in the parish. When word got out, however, that he was planning to remove the three priests as well, the other priests of the diocese spoke out in support of them, even threatening to resign if their colleagues were expelled. Finally, the priests of Arame themselves came to the decision that, in light of their constant conflict with the bishop, it would be best for all concerned if they left the diocese. Before doing so, however, they organized the lay people to continue the work that they had begun and appointed a young married couple to serve as caretakers of the church, for which they received a small salary from the diocese. These caretakers, a former school teacher and his wife, who was the director of religious education for the parish, in effect functioned as parish administrators, living in the house formerly occupied by the sisters and coordinating the work of the other lay people. A sympathetic priest from a neighboring parish came once a month to celebrate Mass. This situation continued for fifteen months, beginning in December 1990. Meanwhile, Dom Serafim traveled to Italy to recruit priests who would limit their pastoral approach to spiritual matters. In March 1992, two new priests arrived in Arame. Shortly afterward they were joined by four sisters.

I returned to Arame in August 1992 to learn what had transpired, and talked with the new priests, one of the sisters, and three of the lay people who are active in base communities. Because of the sensitive nature of the present situation, I did not tape-record these interviews, but I did ask specific questions and took notes. In the case of the new pastor I postponed note taking until after talking with him, since he seemed nervous about meeting with me. He had tried more than once to avoid doing so—telling me during a telephone conversation that he would not be in Arame when I arrived because he had to visit the rural communities. He was in town when I got there but said that he was leaving immediately on some other errand. When one of the lay people later insisted on taking me to the parish house unannounced, the pastor appeared surprised to see me. He then agreed to talk but kept looking at his watch. He also tried to prevent me from meeting the sisters, saying that they were too busy to talk with me.

The interviews with the lay people revealed complete dissatisfaction with the new situation. A repeated complaint was that the new pastor did not take the time to talk with people, did not want to listen to them, and kept the door to the parish house closed at all times (his predecessors had usually kept this door open during the daytime). I asked each of the lay interviewees three questions with three subareas: (1) How did the parish as a whole function? (2) How did the base communities function? (3) How did the union function? The three subareas were (1) with the three original priests, (2) during the subsequent period without priests, and (3) with the new priests.

The responses in relation to the first subarea—with the three original priests—were uniformly positive. For example, in relation to the first question—How did the parish as a whole function with the three original priests?—the three lay interviewees said:

> The three priests worked very well. The door of the parish house was always open. They took the time to visit sick people.

> They were united. They came here with goals already formulated. They gave the people every opportunity. The lay people were responsible for tasks. . . . The priests used the see-judge-act[6] method to avoid hindering the action of the people.

> We always felt at home in the parish house, together as brothers and sisters. The people felt supported.

When I asked specifically about base communities, responses were similar:

> They were animated. The priests knew how to work [with the people]. They helped the people to participate in meetings out-

side of Arame. They invited some of the people in town to go with them to visit base communities in the interior. They had an attitude of equality. They learned with the people. They worked together with the people.

With the three priests, the base communities functioned well.

They organized those annual parish meetings in which everyone was invited to participate. One year there were 300 people.

With regard to the question of the union, all three respondents said that the priests had been supportive. One of them was very specific in explaining how the previous priests had helped:

The union was united with the church in working for agrarian reform. The priests helped in the construction of the union hall. They encouraged this effort. They helped raise funds needed by the officers for transportation for union-related matters [such as to make reports to the Pastoral Land Commission about current problems].

Regarding the fifteen-month period when there were no priests in Arame, responses to questions about the three areas—the parish as a whole, the base communities, and the union—again were similar. People felt sadness at the departure of the priests, but were able to continue functioning without them because of the foundation that they had built. This was particularly true with regard to the base communities.

People were very sad. They knew that the bishop was not supportive. But the CEBs continued. The seed had been planted.

Without the priests they continued to function well. Good seed does not die.

One of the interviewees added that the people in the base communities did not feel that they had been abandoned by the priests, because communication with them continued, even after they had gone to work in another diocese. However, another person said that, without the presence of the priests, it was more difficult to arrange for transportation for union business. He mentioned a recent situation in which one of the union leaders needed to go to the state capital (more than five hundred kilometers away) to speak with a labor official but was unable to do so because of the lack of a means of transportation.

Responses to the third set of questions—related to the experience with the new priests—were uniformly negative. Regarding the functioning of the parish as a whole, the respondents said:

They never have time for the people. And the Mass is different. There is no longer a Kiss of Peace. It feels colder.

The priests don't want the lay people to be involved. The door [to the parish house] is always closed. They don't even like the kinds of hymns that we sing at Mass—songs of the struggle. They seem to want Mass in silence.

[The new pastor] asked us how to do things, but then did them his own way. He says one thing but does another. Several people have already had conflicts with him. During Mass he won't allow spontaneous prayers.

People talked in some detail about the conflicts that had already emerged in their interaction with the new pastor, such as over the running of meetings and the relationship of the Church to the union. One person pointed out that the new pastor had stated that he wanted to be supportive of the union, but abruptly withdrew that offer when one of the officers asked for his help with the annual rural workers' festival, which had always had religious components.

Although base communities are continuing to meet, they seem to be losing energy. According to the lay people interviewed, the new pastor has been trying to minimize their importance to the parish, claiming that the CEBs do not represent everyone and that a parish must be all-inclusive. At the time of my visit, people were upset because the priests were planning to remove from the walls of the church the banners representing seven of the annual parish CEB gatherings. The most recent gathering had only 120 participants, and no one from Arame attended the statewide meeting, because they could not afford the bus fare. (Previously, one of the priests would usually attend the state wide gatherings, and would take several lay delegates along in his Toyota.) The new pastor even indicated his dislike for the presence inside the church of the poster for the national base community gathering, a poster displayed in churches and church organizations throughout Brazil. One of the interviewees was particularly upset about the coming "Land Pilgrimage," an annual event that is organized by the Pastoral Land Commission and attended by members of rural base communities. In previous years, the parish had helped the lay people with funding for the bus fare to attend this pilgrimage. This year the priests told the lay people that the priests and sisters should be the ones to go as representatives of the parish.

One of the interviewees had specific complaints about the way the pastor related to base community leaders:

A catechist organizes something, and the pastor tries to undo it. [The pastor] is the worst offender in this respect, although [the other priest] is more modern. [The pastor] obeys the bishop.

The pastor's strict obedience to the bishop seems to be a key factor in explaining what has happened in Arame. My interviews with the two priests and one of the sisters revealed that the situation was not simply one of different pastoral approaches but rather of complex authority relations. The three original priests, whom the lay people still refer to as "the priests of Arame," ran the parish as a cooperative effort, with equal decision making among themselves and a practice of sharing power with the laity. Their relationship to the original bishop was characterized by an attitude more of mutual respect than of total submission, evidenced in their decision to be ordained for his diocese only after he had accepted their proposed pastoral plan. The new structure is clearly hierarchical, with a pastor who has authority over the second priest and the four sisters as well as a strong sense of obedience to the bishop.

The interviews with the sister and with the curate (i.e., the second priest) led me to believe that their pastoral approaches might have been compatible with the original priests of Arame. The sisters are from an Italian congregation with missions in Africa and South America, working primarily with peasants and other poor people. Although the pastor had told me that the sisters were too busy to speak with me, one of the lay interviewees took me to the sisters' house when the pastor was out of town. The first sister we met did not appear to be busy, and she took time to speak with me, although she was hesitant at first. It was not clear whether her hesitation was due to her difficulty in speaking Portuguese or because the pastor had gotten to her before I did. The conversation with this sister revealed that she was open to learning from the people and to taking time to find out what their needs were. She also spoke positively of the base communities, noting that they had remained strong despite the absence of priests in this parish for over a year.

While the pastor was out of town I went to speak with the curate. Unlike the pastor, this priest seemed eager to talk with me. He also seemed very willing to spend time talking with the parishioners. I noted that, during our conversation, he left the door of the parish house open after the first caller came in. He expressed the desire for living closer to the poor, and said that he hoped to proceed slowly in establishing his work here, so as not to impose things on the people. He also acknowledged that the Gospel is not purely spiritual and that the Church needs to help people deal with the problems they face. This priest spoke positively about base communities, saying that they are the wealth of the Church in Brazil, the Church emerging from the people, and that the laity have a key role to play in this process.

In my conversation with the pastor, he also spoke positively about base communities. My interviews with the lay people, however, suggest that he is not as open to working with them as is the curate. What was particularly clear, both from my conversation with the pastor and from comments made by lay people, is his strong sense of obedience to the bishop. When I asked how he came to choose this particular diocese, he said that the decision was made by the bishop in his home diocese in Italy. He also mentioned that he had been interested in working in the diocese of Picos, in the state of Piauí, and that he greatly admired the bishop there, but his bishop had decided to send him here instead. This statement was particularly interesting, given the fact that the bishop of Picos has a reputation for being progressive; he encourages base communities and lay initiative, which do not seem to be the present policy in Arame. Thus, the key to understanding the situation there would appear to be not so much this priest's pastoral philosophy as his devotion to a hierarchical structure of authority. He apparently takes his cues exclusively from his bishop, whether a progressive or a conservative, and expects to wield authority over the other priest and the sisters. Admittedly, this is in keeping with the standard power structure in the Roman Catholic Church, but it is not the practical approach found in many parishes in Brazil. In twelve out of the fifteen parishes of this study, for example, I found priests who seemed inclined to share power with sisters and lay people and to work *with*, rather than under, the bishop.

In any case, the attitude of the new pastor in Arame seems to be one of submission to the bishop. Since the bishop of this particular diocese is unfavorable toward lay initiative and the insertion of the Church in the land struggle, the tone has been set for a pastoral style that is in contradiction to everything to which the lay people in this parish have been accustomed.

I inadvertently came close to becoming a focus of conflict between the pastor and the lay leaders. During my previous visit to Arame, all parish activities had been open to me. During my recent visit, the lay people assumed that I would attend the parish meeting that was to take place that Sunday afternoon. When the pastor learned of this plan, however, he sent a message informing me that that would not be possible. This was a meeting of the parish, he said, and it would not be appropriate for an outsider to attend.

When the news of this decision spread among some of the lay people, they became angry about not having been consulted, and wanted to challenge the pastor's action. After thinking about this, I asked them not to do so, explaining that my purpose as a researcher was to observe situations, not to create them. I then left Arame a day earlier than originally planned, so as not to be in town at the time of the meeting.

Conclusion

The experience of Arame is instructive in at least two ways. First of all, the first ten years provide a virtually pure case of the type of relationship between religion and agrarian activism that is the subject of this book. The priests organized base communities, lay members of the communities organized a rural union, the union organized land occupations, and 1,500 peasant families gained land.

The present difficulties of the lay people in relation to the new priests is also instructive. It shows the importance of the pastoral agent, particularly the local pastor, as a source of support for the CEBs. The bishop alone could not stop their momentum. During the period when there were no priests in the parish, the lay people continued the work that the original priests had begun. The present challenge to the power of the base communities seems to be coming not directly from the bishop but rather through the new pastor, who is acting on the bishop's wishes.

Although CEBs in Arame are experiencing severe difficulties, this situation does not spell doom for all base communities in Maranhão. There are many parishes in which progressive priests, sisters, and lay leaders have found ways to function in dioceses run by moderate bishops and, in some cases, by conservative ones. (It is the moderates, not the progressives or conservatives, who constitute the majority of the Brazilian episcopate). These priests and sisters continue to give support to base communities and to the struggle for land.

3

SÃO LUÍS:
THE GREAT ALUMINUM DISASTER

São Luís, the capital of Maranhão, boasts the presence of one of the world's largest aluminum refineries, the result of a cooperative venture of the Brazilian government and Alcoa that was financed by a consortium of North American banks.[1] A crowning achievement of the government's design for the development of the Amazon, the plant is part of a mining-industrial-export project that brings bauxite ore from mines owned by Alcoa in the Trombetas region of the neighboring state of Pará. The ore is transported by means of a newly constructed railroad, is refined in São Luís, and is shipped to other parts of Brazil and abroad through the recently expanded Port of Itaqui. Behind this seemingly impressive development, however, is a story of human tragedy, of lost land, of growing poverty, of false promises, of the manipulation of peasant farmers by both church and state, and of threats to people's health and livelihood created by massive pollution.

The Base Communities of São Cristóvão

To understand the complex role played by the Catholic Church in relation to this process, it is important to know about the history of the parish of São Cristóvão on the periphery of the city of São Luís. In the 1960s, São Luís was a quiet provincial capital located on an island within an indentation in the north coast of Brazil. Much of this island consisted of fertile farmland occupied by peasant farmers, many of whom had inherited the right to work the land from their ancestors. In some of the villages in the rural sector of the municipal district, these inherited land rights went back more than two hundred years.

In 1967 two missionary priests from the United States, members of the Redemptorist order, arrived in São Luís with a plan similar to that of the priests in Arame. They were interested in starting a new parish, but only if the archbishop, Dom João José da Mota, would allow them to do work in keeping with the renovative spirit of the Second Vatican Council. Dom Mota accepted their proposal. He authorized them to establish a parish in the rural sector, with the church to be located in a neighborhood at the southern edge of the city. The original name of the parish was Christ Redeemer. The priests asked the Sisters of Notre Dame de Namur, whose North American provinces had recently begun sending missionaries to Brazil, to help them with their new project. In January 1969, four sisters arrived in the parish, with the understanding that their priority would be organizing base communities.

The priests and sisters began working within the traditional religious custom of *desobriga* (discharge of religious obligation) that had long existed in regions with a scarcity of priests. That meant visiting each rural village once a year, usually on the date of the feast of its patron saint, and "catching up" with the religious practice—celebrating Mass, baptizing all the babies born during the past year, and performing marriages. The new missionaries used this opportunity to begin suggesting to the people a different way of expressing their faith, of being responsible for organizing their own religious life. Some of the people responded immediately to this suggestion. Within a year eight base communities had sprung into existence. Over the next two years the number reached twenty: nineteen in rural villages and one in the immediate neighborhood of the parish church. About half of these were started by lay people from other communities. Sister Barbara English, who was on the pastoral team of Christ Redeemer at that time, described the process by which they worked:

> We started out in a reflection-action mode: life and Gospel. We paid attention to the Word, the living Word in the life of the people. Then we used the biblical Word to shed light on that reality and to motivate people to respond to it. They immediately began to see the implications of their Gospel reflection, and began to move into action that would improve their lives.

The lay people in the base communities were integrated into the parish decision-making process by means of parish assemblies. This experience helped people to look beyond religious matters.

> There was an assembly of the communities. These communities assembled every two months, and they discussed their problems and which way the parish was going. It became the lived experience of the parish, but in another sense it also became the rehearsal

grounds for their role in the world, no matter whether it was in the parish or outside of the parish, no matter whether it was civic or social, religious or political.

One of the problems that people were discussing at that time was the disappearance of available land. Increasing areas of public land were being taken over by speculators, and barbed-wire fences were appearing around areas to which peasant farmers had previously had access. People were also aware that the government had plans to convert a portion of the interior of the island into the industrial belt of Maranhão. They talked about adapting to this situation by diversifying their market crops. Until then, their chief cash crop had been cassava. Now they were talking about growing a wider range of vegetables, in order to become part of a "green belt" that would provide food for the industrial belt.

The New Pastor

Changes were coming, however, over which the people would have little control. The first change occurred in the Church. In 1974 the Redemptorist order made the decision to close their mission in Maranhão, and recalled the priests. The people of the parish asked the archbishop to send them a replacement. Dom Mota's initial reply was that there was no priest available. He appeared to be encouraging the lay people to continue in their leadership roles. Two of the sisters continued working as resource persons with the base communities. Each CEB had already developed a wide range of social and religious ministries: community outreach, care of the sick, catechetical preparation of children and adults for the sacraments, biblical reflection, and liturgical celebrations. Together they had also developed a system of regional networks of mutual support. After the departure of the priests, they selected a coordinating team of four lay people to organize activities for the communities and for the parish as a whole. In 1976 the archbishop apparently became concerned about all this nonclerical initiative, and did send a priest—an extremely conservative one who began working to put an end to lay leadership. For two more years the sisters attempted to continue working in the parish, which the new pastor renamed São Cristóvão (Saint Christopher). However, they found themselves under increasing constraints from this pastor, who apparently wanted to restore a pre-Vatican II structure of ministry and authority, in contrast to the collaborative spirit of his predecessors. Finally, the priest informed the archbishop that he could not work with these sisters, and either they would have to leave the parish or he would. The archbishop pressured the sisters to conform to the pastor's vision of a centralized parish structure. Sister Barbara explained that vision:

> He had very traditional ideas about "I'm the pastor. My voice is authority. And I represent God. . . . I'm the one in charge." His church structure was an authoritarian, hierarchical parochial model, over against the prior model, which was communitarian and collegial. . . . By 1978 we realized that the situation in our parish was causing a lot of confusion, because the priest was accusing people like us of being subversives and nonreligious. He was denouncing us at Mass. We figured that this wasn't helping in any way. So we resigned from the parish team, and continued working with the communities on an informal basis, through a community association that they had formed in 1977.

After resigning, the sisters remained in São Luís, working through various archdiocesan structures in community organizing and education. My conversations with parishioners twelve years later revealed that many of them still felt special affection toward the sisters, but were confused about their sudden departure. One woman told me that she never knew where they went or why. A man told me that the pastor had informed the people of his village that the sisters had had to leave because they were Communists. Sister Barbara continued to find herself in opposition to the pastor, in relation to the arrival of Alcoa, since she became a key actor in the resistance against the aluminum refining project, which the pastor supported.

The Arrival of Alcoa

In 1980 the governor of Maranhão, João Castelo, ceded about 27,000 acres[2] of public land in the southern section of the island of São Luís to Alcoa for the purpose of constructing an aluminum refinery. Opponents of this transaction claimed that it was illegal because it bypassed the consent of the state legislative assembly and of the senate, as required in the state constitution, for the turning over of public land exceeding 3,000 hectares. It did, however, have the full support of the federal government.[3] The company was granted ten years of exemption from income taxes. In addition, the government financed the building of the railroad to transport the bauxite ore from Pará as well as the expansion of the Port of Itaqui. The proposed plant posed a serious environmental threat because aluminum refining badly pollutes air and water and produces hazardous waste. Environmental scientists consulted by the state government had already judged the plan of an aluminum refinery in this particular location to be nonviable. Dr. Raul Ximenes Galvão, a chemist and economist from São Paulo, cited United Nations guidelines that specifically warn against building an aluminum refinery close to a waterway.[4] Since São Luís is on an island that is cut through with numerous streams, it was the worst possible place for the plant. In addition to the danger to public health, there were other human costs. The sale of this land threatened the existence of the farming and fishing villages in the southern section of the island, including those where the sisters had organized base communities. Some of them were directly threatened because they were located where the company planned to build its plant or because they were in the path of the new railroad. Residents of these villages began receiving notices informing them that they would have to leave their land. There were other villages that did not receive such notices but whose residents would eventually feel forced to abandon them because of severe pollution. One village, Igaraú, was located on the site of a proposed toxic waste dump.

A group of citizens in São Luís became outraged both because of the environmental threat and because of their suspicion that there was political corruption involved in the land deal, which had been negotiated in secret. In August 1980, they organized the Committee for the Defense of the Island, which began a campaign to inform the public, through both the national and the international press, of the hazards of an aluminum refinery in that particular location. It also provided legal defense for the villagers, challenged Alcoa in court three times for illegal actions, promoted television debates, generated discussion on radio programs and in newspapers, and worked in solidarity with international environmental organizations. At the same time that the committee was urging the villagers to resist eviction, the pastor of São Cristóvão was encouraging them to cooperate with Alcoa. He even sold the corporation a large tract of land belonging to the Church, and also appeared in Alcoa's television advertisements, which drew protests from several church groups.

Although *posseiros* (long-term squatters) do not have title to the land on which they are working, they are considered to be the owners of the improvements they make to the land, such as clearing and cultivation, as well as the simple houses they build on it. So, although they cannot sell the land itself, they can be compensated for these improvements. The pastor strongly urged the people to accept the meager compensation that the company was offering them and to leave the land that their ancestors had settled.

Most of the 20,000 people who were in the affected region decided to leave. Beyond the urging of their pastor, they knew that the project had the support of the federal government, and thus believed that they could not fight it. In addition, most of these people had never seen much cash, and so, at that time, the offers they were receiving appeared to be good. Some of them, advised by an agronomist working for one of the church organizations, did demand and receive fair compensation. Within two years, however, many of these same people, who were now living in poverty on the periphery of São Luís, were telling Sister Barbara that they wished they had not left their villages. Because of poor employment opportunities, they were much worse off than when they had had land. There were people in other villages who, because of their proximity to the plant under construction, felt pressured to leave. The amount of dust and smoke was so great that many people were experiencing eye irritation and inflammations of the throat. Infants and children were becoming ill with respiratory problems. Crops were failing. As a result of these difficulties, combined with pressure from the state government, seventeen of the nineteen rural villages were abandoned.

Igaraú Resists

In Igaraú, where the company was planning to put its toxic waste dump, thirty-seven families decided to resist eviction.[5] Sister Barbara described the company's reaction to this resistance:

Alcoa courted the people of Igaraú, took them on buses to different places, saying, "Wouldn't you like us to remove you from Igaraú to here?" To encourage them in any way. But nothing that the people saw could equal their village, and so they refused to go.

In 1981 the people of Igaraú began working with the Committee for the Defense of the Island. They also attempted, with the help of two attorneys, to gain title to the land in the names of four people, two women and two men, members of the Baldez family, who were known to be direct descendants of the original settlers. They never succeeded in obtaining the titles. At one point, the possibility was raised of having the village declared a national historical site, but that tactic did not succeed either.

Throughout the 1980s, Alcoa tried various ways of dealing with Igaraú, ranging from friendly gestures, such as giving construction jobs to some of the residents and organizing a soccer match in the village, to more confrontational tactics, such as sending thugs to demolish houses (the latter did not succeed because the villagers congregated to block the access of the thugs to their homes). Igaraú continued to resist. Sister Barbara kept in touch with the villagers, visiting them on weekends and later receiving the backing of Cáritas, a church organization dedicated to community development, to work full-time to help organize the resistance. In addition to supporting the efforts of the people of Igaraú by her presence and helping them in their attempts to establish their legal ownership of the land, she publicized the plight of the village outside of Brazil, inviting foreign visitors to visit Igaraú and writing articles for publication in the United States. After Sister Barbara left Brazil in 1985, the people of Igaraú continued to resist eviction.

I had spent a month living in Igaraú while doing field research in 1983, and revisited the village in 1990 and in 1991. In 1983 it was a seemingly isolated place, although it took less than an hour to reach it by automobile from São Luís. Without a car, one had to travel there on a crowded, uncomfortable bus, and then walk for a mile-and-a-half on a dirt road, crossing a small stream by means of a wobbly log. There was no electricity or running water. People bathed in natural springs, and the women washed clothes in the same. Houses were built of mud and wattle, with roofs that were either thatched with palm branches or covered with clay tiles. The main form of entertainment was visiting one another's homes and chatting. In the evening this socializing was carried on by the light of tiny wicks stuck into oil cans. In contrast to the low technological level of the village was its natural beauty. It was a very green area, even during the long drought that plagued the rest of the region in the early 1980s, and was filled with all kinds of palm trees. Although the standard of living was generally poor, the people appeared to be healthy. Infant mortality was low. The census that I took of the village revealed that only five babies of the present generation of children had died, and three of these had the same mother, suggesting an individual, rather than public, health problem. There were several people in their seventies who still took an active part in community life, helping to care for their grandchildren and, in some cases, even working in the fields. The basic diet of rice, beans, and cassava meal was supplemented by meat from the chickens and pigs that were all over the place, fish from the nearby bay—including large quantities of shrimp that people ate several times a week—and a wide variety of fruit that grew on the trees in everyone's back yards.

I returned to Igaraú in 1990 to find that the village was still there, although the neighboring ones had all been destroyed, and that the conservative pastor had been replaced by an energetic Dutch

Missionary of the Sacred Heart, Father John Joseph Koopmans. Father Koopmans was traveling by motorcycle all over the vast area of the parish, which included many more villages than the ones where the sisters had worked, in his efforts to organize base communities. The conservative archbishop, Dom Mota, had been replaced by Dom Paulo Ponte, who was showing support for CEBs. A negative change, however, was in the villagers' diet. They were getting less fish, because the water pollution from the aluminum refinery was killing them, and the shrimp had disappeared altogether. A lot of the fruit were falling from the trees without ripening, and the juçara, a local favorite, was not appearing at all. Neither were there any mangoes, avocados, cashews, or guava. The few remaining fruit were much smaller than they used to be.

The Governor's Solution

Toward the end of my stay in Maranhão in 1990, an article appeared in a local newspaper,[6] reporting on a settlement negotiated by Governor João Alberto. This settlement was between the people of Igaráu and Alcoa. The article did not go into much detail, except to state that the company had agreed not to invade the 800 hectares (about 2,000 acres) designated as belonging to the village, and that there would be a fence constructed between the properties of Alumar and Igaraú. It also included statements about Governor João Alberto's commitment to being "always on the side of the weak," about his promise to send a school teacher to the village, and about all the jubilation, applause, and gratitude on the part of the villagers.

When I returned to Igaraú once more in 1991, I nearly did not recognize the place. The access road of one-and-a-half miles that joins the village to the road to São Luís, while still unpaved, was not as uneven as it used to be. A rough bridge had replaced the log across the stream. In the village itself there was now electricity, with the result that there was a television in every home. There was also an artesian well, connected to water pipes terminating in a single tap in each house. Women were no longer washing clothes in a water hole, but had a community laundry with running water and sinks. New houses were being built, both by older residents and by their grown children, who were returning to settle in the village. The father of the household where I had always stayed during my visits proudly gave me a tour of the improvements to the village, ending with the health center, a small, attractive, brick building, which was locked, because there was no doctor or any other staff. On the front of the building was a plaque, expressing the gratitude of the people of Igaraú to Alcoa and Governor João Alberto. There was also a new soccer field. I asked my guide where all these improvements had come from, especially the water pipes and the electricity. He replied that they had come from the government and Alcoa. He also said that the people of the village had been promised titles to the land (although, as with almost everywhere else in the rural north of Brazil, the titles were yet to be seen). I kept asking him what the company had gained in return. He evaded the question. Finally he admitted that the villagers had promised not to prevent the construction of an underground industrial waste tank on land adjacent to theirs. He also said that one of the prominent members of the Committee for the Defense of the Island would probably tell me that Igaraú had sold out to Alcoa, but that was not the case; rather, they had negotiated. My friend then told me that the pollution in the area had diminished. Other villagers with whom I later spoke said they were not so sure about that— they still did not have much fish and fruit.

Two days later I spoke with the man from the Committee for the Defense of the Island and discovered that he was, indeed, angry with the people of Igaraú and did believe that they had sold out, adding that they had not consulted anyone on the committee before entering this negotiation. I also visited a lay church worker in the parish of São Cristóvão, who told me that she believed that the villagers had been manipulated by the governor. Even though she was visiting Igaraú regularly, meeting with the base community and encouraging people to discuss local issues, the villagers had never mentioned anything to her about the process of negotiation with Alcoa. She would ask them how things were going, and they would reply "Fine," but would say nothing more. She found out about the settlement only after it was all over. Later, after I had left São Luís, Father Koopmans wrote to tell me that he had spoken recently with the people of Igaraú and that they seemed happy about their situation because they apparently did not understand the risk to their future health posed by the presence of the industrial waste tank. They did not seem to think that it could ever leak or overflow during a particularly heavy rainy season.

And yet, despite the health hazards posed by air and water pollution, toxic waste, and the loss of important features of the local diet, the people of Igaraú may be considered to be the lucky ones, if their situation is compared to that of the other 20,000 people from the rural sector who no longer have any land at all. São Luís has gone from being a small, picturesque city, surrounded by productive farmland, to a troubled urban area with widespread unemployment and a swollen periphery filled with people living just at or below the level of subsistence. The new industries that are poisoning the air, water, and soil of the island have produced very few jobs for local residents beyond the temporary employment resulting from the process of constructing the plants. Instead, by throwing people off the land, the companies have taken away their livelihood.

Reflections on Church Policy

This case may lead one to wonder whether there would have been a different scenario had Church policy been consistent. The hiatus of twelve years between the departure of the North American Redemptorists and the arrival of the Dutch missionary coincided with the period in which Alcoa arrived and destroyed seventeen villages. While this is not to suggest that there was any deliberate Church or government policy that led to the removal of the Redemptorists, beyond the internal decisions of their own religious order, the change in parish administration turned out to be very helpful to the interests of the corporation. Instead of being faced with priests who, like the sisters whose pastoral approach they supported, might have been inclined to encourage people in all the villages to question the company's right to evict them—especially after having acquired the land without the proper, legally mandated process—Alcoa encountered a pastor who was willing to side with the company in urging all the farmers to leave. Given the trust in the Church that had already been cultivated by the North American missionaries, the farmers were understandably swayed by this pastor. The people of Igaraú, however, did not fully trust him. Unfortunately, after Sister Barbara, whom they did trust, returned to the United States, it appears that they did not transfer that trust to the new church personnel who came along a few years later. This would explain why they did not confide in the new pastor and in the lay church worker who were visiting the base communities in São Cristóvão in 1990 before making the decision to permit the construction of the toxic waste tank.

Conclusion

This case is illustrative of certain religious and social dimensions of base communities. The first is the importance of the pastoral agent, especially the priest. The sisters were able to work at organizing base communities when the parish was administered by priests who supported that type of work, but were not able to continue under a priest who opposed it. The archbishop, on the other hand, could not himself stop the work of the sisters, but he was able to do so through a priest. In the late 1980s the base communities began to be revived by another priest, who was assisted in this work by a lay church worker.

The second dimension that is important to note is the role of the church in social processes. The Redemptorist priests and the Sisters of Notre Dame had been working for one kind of change, specifically, the empowerment of the peasant farmers through the base communities. With the replacement of the progressive priests by a more authoritarian one, the Church played an important role in a different kind of social change—the industrialization of São Luís in a manner that has not been beneficial to the majority of the people there. The sister who remained in São Luís after being pressured to resign from the parish of São Cristóvão was able to exert influence on a smaller scale, by providing support for the village that resisted. It seems possible that if the parish had had a pastor who supported Sister Barbara's efforts, Alcoa would have encountered much stronger resistance. While it is not likely that the government would have permitted the complete loss of the plant, it could have required that the plant be built farther from waterways, with equipment to reduce the amount of pollution emitted and after a democratic process of decision making to give attention to the needs and viewpoints of people already living and working on the land.

This situation, like that of Arame, provides a negative case, showing the results of a pastoral policy aimed at thwarting the religious and social consequences of base communities. The cases in the chapters which follow show a variety of more positive outcomes.

4

SANTA RITA: WHERE THE BUFFALO ROAMED

The social conditions in the town of Santa Rita, named for the parish of Saint Rita of Cassia, are both similar to and different from those in Arame and Igaraú. Santa Rita, which is located about fifty-five kilometers south of São Luís, is an area of old settlement. Many of the peasant farmers there inherited the right to work the land from their parents and grandparents who were posseiros.[1] Nevertheless, they have suffered many of the same difficulties as people in regions of newer settlement, with grileiros attempting to throw them off the land or charging them rent. In addition, farmers in Santa Rita have experienced serious problems and conflicts that have resulted from the decision of ranchers in the area to replace cattle with buffalo.

Base Communities

Before going into detail about that story, however, it is useful to begin with a brief history of the parish, since the church has been involved in the campaign against the buffalo. The parish of Santa Rita dates back only to 1978. Prior to that, the area was part of the century-old parish of Our Lady of the Rosary, in the neighboring town of Rosário. The process of the founding of the new parish was different from that in Arame and São Cristóvão, both of which represented the introduction of an innovative pastoral approach. Santa Rita is part of the Archdiocese of São Luís, and by 1978 the archbishop, Dom Mota, had already revealed himself to be opposed to lay initiative. Thus, it is not likely that he encouraged the first pastor of Santa Rita to organize base communities. What is worth noting, however, is the presence of CEBs prior to the founding of the parish. The first one was begun in 1967 by a French priest whose role in the process was explained by a union leader and base community member:

In 1967 the CEBs began in the village of Venezia.
How did they get started? By whom?
By Father Servat, who lived in Recife. He went to the region of
Coroatá, then to Caxias. And after that he came here. . . . Then
lay people got involved in this work of organizing communities
and regional gatherings.

Although Father Servat was based a thousand miles away in the
city of Recife, he spent time in Maranhão in the 1960s, organizing nuclei
of *Atuação Cristã no Meio Rural* (ACR), an outgrowth of the Catholic
Action movement which had been brought to Brazil from France in the
1950s. The focus of this movement was to develop lay leadership to
help evangelize a specific social milieu—for example, factories, univer-
sities, or rural areas. In those parts of Maranhão where ACR took root,
its members were especially active in organizing rural base communities. As a result, there were areas, such as Santa Rita, where numerous
communities were started by lay people, rather than sisters or priests.
According to one of the CEB leaders in Santa Rita,

There were people linked with ACR who were the creators of
communities here. . . . They visited other villages as well.

In addition to members of ACR, there were lay people who had
migrated from other areas, bringing the CEB idea with them. A woman
who had organized one of the communities talked about this:

That was the way we started [the CEB] in 1984 . . . just ourselves.
There was a man here who had already participated in another
community. He began to work with us.

This woman also mentioned that for a five-year period, from 1980
to 1985, there was no priest in Santa Rita. This may provide at least a
partial explanation for the high level of lay initiative. If there had been a
pastor who was opposed to CEBs, he likely would have found ways to
undercut the organizing efforts of the lay people. If there had been one
who was favorable toward CEBs, he might have organized them himself.

It is likely, however, that the main stimulus to lay initiative was
ACR, since the period of the greatest growth of CEBs in Santa Rita was
in the 1970s. In addition, people in this parish speak of the influence on
the base communities of some North American sisters who visited the
area in the early 1980s, during the time when there was no pastor.

There were nuns, too. Sister Lúcia. Later Sister Carolina. We studied the Bible, and we connected the Bible with our reality. . . . I
worked a lot with Carolina. We worked together coordinating the
statewide gathering of CEBs several times.

It is important to note that although these base communities did
not receive any encouragement from the archbishop, they still flourished because of the influence of a foreign priest from another state,
foreign sisters from another parish, and a strong core of lay organizers.
There are now twenty-four CEBs in Santa Rita.

Members of base communities were instrumental in transforming the union, which was previously controlled by people who favored
the large landowners, to a militant one that struggles for the rights of
peasant farmers.

The Union of Rural Workers

The Union of Rural Workers of Santa Rita, which dates back to
1971, was started not by peasant farmers who were CEB members but
rather by medium-sized property owners and right-wing politicians.
As one of the present union officers explained:

When the union began here it was a *pelego* union, started by the
politicians with farmers who were not engaged in the struggle.
From 1972 to 1986 the union was controlled by people who were
put there by the political oligarchy.

The word *pelego*, which literally means "sheepskin," figuratively
refers to a wolf in sheep's clothing, or a government spy planted in a
labor organization. A "pelego union" has come to mean one controlled
by the government or, in rural areas, by people who favor the large
landowners. During the 1960s and 1970s, unions were part of a corporatist structure in which occupational categories were organized vertically, rather than by social class, in order to provide for tight control by
the military regime.[2] In Santa Rita, as CEB members began to develop a
critical social consciousness, they formed an opposition group within
the union, and began trying to gain control of it through the election of
officers and the board of directors. In 1986 they finally succeeded. Today
the leadership and the most active members of the union are mainly
people from base communities.

*Are the people who are in the union today part of the base communities as
well?*

Yes.
All of them?
All of those who are now in the union directorate are part of the communities and do the work of the communities. It is a direct connection.
Are there members who are not part of the communities?
Yes, but they are a small group.

Although in many municipal districts the union membership is predominantly male, this is clearly not the case in Santa Rita. Women are a visible presence, not only in the base communities but also in the union and in the local chapter of the Workers' Party (Partido dos Trabalhadores, or PT). In my interviews with union men, they expressed particular appreciation of the participation of women.

The women of the base communities are very important in relation to the land struggle. . . . Almost half of the union members are women.

The women are completely together with us. They give the greatest support. We feel that strength. . . . The union can trust that the women will work equally with the men.

One of the union officers had special praise for a woman who is part of the union directorate:

She is very active. We feel that she has will and courage. She is part of the struggle.

An important motivating factor in the takeover of the union by women and men from the CEBs was conflict over land. Since peasant farmers had already settled in this area prior to the creation of SUDAM, their mobilization took a different form from that in Arame and areas farther to the west. When speculators began, in the 1970s, to perceive property in Maranhão as valuable, the action of the farmers in Santa Rita consisted not of entrance into new land but rather of organized resistance to eviction from land on which they were already living. The problem of land robbing has continued to the present time. One of the union officers explained the typical practices of grileiros in Santa Rita:

In an area of public land they buy directly from some farmers. If they buy ten hectares they fence a hundred. If there is a group of posseiros in that area, they expel them and plant grass [for cattle].

Since the base communities in this area date back to the 1960s, some of them were already organized at the time that this land robbing began. Wherever there were base communities, their members resisted eviction and, in many cases, gained the right to the land. Some people even received titles.[3]

A Priest on the Side of the People

In 1985 the peasant farmers of Santa Rita gained an important ally when a newly ordained priest, Father Osvaldo Fernandes Marinho, became their pastor. One of the women who is a leader in her base community and in the union talked about his arrival:

When Father Osvaldo came here, thanks be to God, he was a priest on the side of the people, on the side of the suffering. And he was very much slandered and very much persecuted by the big landowners. But he has a very great faith in God and he resisted. So now we have this pastor who is interested in his flock.

A native of Maranhão who was born into a poor rural family, Father Osvaldo quickly became a thorn in the sides of the large landowners. Although soft-spoken in conversation, this priest is a powerful preacher. In his sermons he does not hesitate to combine biblical reflection with a hard-hitting analysis of local problems. Before entering the priesthood, he was a member of the Brazilian Democratic Movement, or MDB, which, after opposition parties were once again allowed to emerge in the early 1980s, became the PMDB. He later shifted his support to the more radical Workers' Party (PT), whose presidential candidate carried Santa Rita in 1989. The PT of Santa Rita was organized by members of base communities after they gained control of the union. One of the base community leaders described the relationship between the PT and the Church:

All of those who are in the party are linked with the Church. They are the people of the base community. Thanks be to God, Lula[4] won here in the first and second vote.

Around the time of Father Osvaldo's arrival, a new problem emerged in Santa Rita: the buffalo.

Free-Roaming Buffalo

The animal that has a prominent place in North American folklore has had a destructive impact on the ecosystem in the lowlands of north-central Maranhão, to which it is not native. Although some accounts indicate that buffalo raising has been carried out by ranchers in the region for about twenty years, there was a sharp increase in this practice between 1985 and 1991, adding about 48,000 head per year.[5] The main reason usually given to explain the increase is that ranchers have found buffalo more profitable than beef cattle. Church people and unionists also suggest that the buffalo have been used as a means of pushing out the small farmers, when grilagem was not successful. This explanation is plausible, since the numbers of buffalo began to increase right around the same time that the peasant farmers were taking control of the union.

This explanation is also plausible in light of all the problems the buffalo caused for the small farmers, making them an effective form of harassment. Because they were being raised in a free-roaming manner, they threatened the lives, safety, and livelihood of the local peasantry. At least five farmers were killed by buffalo and several people were injured, including children. In addition, the buffalo trampled crops and other plant life, and killed small game and domestic animals. Their excrement polluted the lakes and streams, killing the fish and rendering local water supplies undrinkable. Many families in Santa Rita went hungry because of this destruction of their food sources.

When it became evident to the farmers that the government was not going to do anything about this situation, they began killing the buffalo. In some instances, they killed one of the animals after it had attacked a farmer. At this point the police did take action—against the farmers, arresting them, beating them, and destroying their food supplies. On one occasion, twelve farmers who had been arrested were released on the demand of a crowd of people led by Father Osvaldo.[6] In addition, gunmen hired by the ranchers began threatening the lives of union leaders and church people. According to a union officer,

> Father Osvaldo was attacked and I was attacked, and we received death threats from the ranchers who raise buffalo.

From 1989 through 1991, Father Osvaldo was receiving death threats as often as every week. On December 21, 1989, a group of people believed to be linked to the UDR (União Democrática Rural—the national organization of ranchers and other large landowners) set fire to his house, and succeeded in damaging the roof and wooden window frames.[7] At that point, the archbishop of São Luís, Dom Paulo Ponte, spoke out publicly against this attack and in support of Father Osvaldo, even defending his radical political image, stating that no priest should be condemned when, as a citizen, he supports a particular political candidate. A local newspaper quoted the archbishop as saying:

If Father Osvaldo has gone so far at some times as to say that he is a PT militant, that is an internal matter for the Church. Now, personally, I admire the work that he has done in Santa Rita, a town where, until a short time ago, the population served as an electoral bloc for bad politicians.[8]

Dom Paulo went on to say that the example of Santa Rita serves to show that people need to struggle for their rights. This strong support from the archbishop, both for the peasant farmers and for Father Osvaldo, is especially significant, since Dom Paulo is considered by Catholics in his diocese to be more of a moderate than a progressive bishop.

There are still buffalo in the lowlands of Maranhão, but, as a result of the mobilization of the farmers by the Church and the union, they are no longer roaming freely. In order to conform to public pressure to contain them, without really restricting the movement of the animals, the ranchers attempted to fence in large areas of public land. However, people from the communities went to court to get an order preventing them from doing so.

A New CEB in an Old Village

A conflict that began more recently than the buffalo problem occurred between the residents of the village of Sítio Novo, where most of the families settled the land over eighty years ago, and the new owner of neighboring land, a rancher named Wady Sauáia.[9] One of the base community leaders in Sítio Novo described the origin of the conflict:

All this area was surrounded by land owned by Wady. He thought that he would take this part and throw us out to increase his territory. So his hired thugs took the responsibility of getting rid of us.

In September 1990, gunmen hired by Sauáia began harassing the villagers. They destroyed a house, a school, and some of their produce. After the villagers complained to the local police, the gunmen intensified the harassment, shooting at people in the woods and saying that they were following the orders of the landowner.

Although there had been base communities in Santa Rita for many years, there was none in Sítio Novo. The lay people decided to organize one, in order to strengthen their resistance against the attempts of their powerful neighbor to evict them.

It began with this conflict, when they tried to throw everyone out. The guy who lives in that house over there came up with the idea. . . . He had already been part of a community in São Luis. So we formed this group, during this struggle for the land, because without the community we would not have been able to do what we did.

The gunmen continued to threaten the villagers and to destroy some of their fields. They set fire to two houses, one of which belonged to a base community leader. The word got around that they were looking for the community leaders and intended to kill them. On one occasion Sauáia himself threatened the life of a seventy-three-year-old man, accusing him of trespassing. Since Sauáia's land surrounded the village, the only access road was through his property.

Finally, in November, the gunmen, following orders of Sauáia's son, forcibly evicted the residents, burning their homes and destroying their household goods. The rancher later tried to claim that the farmers had set fire to their own houses. The following day, Father Osvaldo, the president of the union, and representatives of the Pastoral Land Commission, of Cáritas, and of the Maranhão Society of Human Rights went to the area, along with representatives of the state land agency, ITERMA, to conduct an investigation. They were met by Wady Sauáia's son, Savigny, who was accompanied by armed gunmen and who accused the investigators of invading his property. The government agents insisted on being allowed to enter. Savigny finally permitted them to do so, but without any of the people from the various organizations who had accompanied them. These people were surrounded by the gunmen, who harangued them with vulgar language and threats.

One day later, the peasant farmers, accompanied by the human-rights and church organizations and representatives of the union and the parish, had an audience with the state governor, João Alberto. He ordered the state Military Police to disarm the gunmen and to accompany the people back to their land. This event was significant, because the usual pattern is for the police to be used on the side of the ranchers. When the peasant farmers returned to their village, they found that all but one of the houses had been destroyed, along with the chapel. They built a large shelter of palm branches, to provide a place for everyone to eat and sleep. After a few weeks, they began building shelters for individual families.

Two weeks after the return of the farmers to Sítio Novo, one of Sauáia's gunmen was killed. Right after the murder, the death threats against Father Osvaldo intensified. Sauáia accused him of the murder, along with the president of the union, Cloves Alves de Souza. However, church people suspect that the landowner ordered the death of the gunman himself, with the specific intention of blaming it on the priest and the union leader. It is also possible that the gunman was killed by a peon, since he had hired men to clear land but had not paid them.

The role of the base community in this conflict is demonstrated in the farmers' awareness that they needed a CEB to help them face this crisis. After it was organized, it strengthened the farmers' determination to resist Sauáia's efforts to evict them. Twenty-four families returned to the area accompanied by the Military Police, although some people admitted that they were frightened. Their fear was not only of the gunmen. People in this area have not had positive past experiences with the Military Police, who sometimes join forces with hired gunmen against them. Five of the families did not return. Among those that did, their participation in the base community influenced their decision.

Were those who returned all members of the CEB?
Yes, they were. All from the community.

For some time after the resettlement of the farmers in Sítio Novo, Sauáia continued to insist that the land belonged to him and continued to threaten the lives of base community leaders, one of whom was nearly killed in an ambush by three men identified as Sauáia's hired gunmen. Then the rancher went to court to request an eviction order. It was at that point that the archbishop again proved himself to be on the side of the peasant farmers. When the people appealed to Dom Paulo for help, he went to talk with the governor, who promised that he would not send the Military Police to enforce an eviction order against the people of Sítio Novo. Unfortunately, he said this near the end of his term of office. The following year (February 1992), the Commandant General of the Military Police of Maranhão, at the request of Sauáia, sent thirty-eight men to evict the villagers. The police were accompanied by the rancher's thugs, who used tractors to demolish the houses. Then they brought in 450 head of buffalo to devour all the crops. Three weeks later, the district judge determined this action to have been totally illegal, since the Military Police acted without judicial order. The people once again returned to their land.

The conflict was finally resolved in June 1992, when ITERMA purchased 700 acres of nearby land and offered it to the farmers. After determining that the land was good, the farmers accepted the settlement. They named their new village the Father Josimo Community, after the priest who had been assassinated in western Maranhão in 1986. (The story of Father Josimo will be told in the next chapter.)

Conclusion

The case of Santa Rita is instructive because, unlike Arame, the parish did not begin with ten years of consistent effort by priests to start and support base communities. The influence came from outside the parish—in fact, largely from outside the diocese. The efforts of Father Servat to organize the ACR in Maranhão resulted in a strong group of lay people with a sense of their own religious/social mission. These lay people organized the base communities that would receive further support from sisters from other parishes and from the courageous young priest who finally became their pastor. When the land problems intensified, members of these CEBs, along with the union that they had taken over and made responsive to their needs, were ready to take action to defend the rights of peasant farmers. In one area where there were no CEBs already existing at the time that the conflict broke out, people knew that they needed to organize a base community to help them resist the efforts of the grileiro to evict them. The fact that those who were members of that community returned to their land twice after being evicted, and persisted until the state government arranged for a satisfactory settlement, shows the power of religious organization in strengthening people's activism.

5

NORTHERN TOCANTINS: BLOOD IN THE PARROT'S BEAK

The parrot is a symbol of the Amazon. These beautiful, multicolored birds appear on travel posters and in the arts and crafts sold in souvenir shops. The parrot also appears in figures of speech in everyday language. One such expression—*o Bico do Papagaio* (the beak of the parrot)—refers to the north of the state of Tocantins because the geographic formation created by the confluence of the Araguaia and Tocantins Rivers is tapered and curved like a parrot's beak. For many people in Brazil, however, there is another symbolism in this phrase: It has come to be synonymous with rural violence because of all the blood shed over land conflicts in northern Tocantins.

The Migration

The Bico was settled by an overflow of the migration to western Maranhão, just across the Tocantins River. Some early settlers came in the 1950s, using the primitive roads created by lumber companies. However, my interviews with farmers in three of the parishes in the region (Itaguatins, Sítio Novo, and São Sebastião) indicate that the greatest number of migrants arrived in the 1960s and 1970s. As shown in table 1.3, the most rapid growth of this region (which was previously part of the state of Goiás) pre-dated the mass migrations to other parts of the Amazon. This was likely a consequence of two patterns occurring in Maranhão during the 1960s: (1) the expulsion from public lands of peasant families by grileiros, a result of the increase in land values after the creation of SUDAM, and (2) the extension of east-west roads which connected Maranhão and its neighboring state of Piauí with the Belém-Brasília Highway. This enabled peasant farmers from both states to reach the city of Imperatriz, on the western border of Maranhão, from which they had only to cross the river to reach the northernmost part of the state of Goiás (which is now Tocantins). Those who arrived in the 1960s found a sparsely populated area with a great deal of public land and no large owners.

There were very few people and a lot of forest when we came here.

We were living in Maranhão, near Imperatriz, and we came here. Everything was forest.

I left Piauí because it was difficult to live there. Lack of rain. There was new land in Goiás.

One of the folk-religious traditions of the northeast may have provided further encouragement for the farmers to cross the Tocantins River. Northeasterners have a special devotion to Father Cicero,[1] a priest from the state of Ceará who was the focus of a millenarian religious movement beginning at the end of the nineteenth century. His prophecies are still repeated by the rural people. According to one of these prophecies, those who wish to be part of the millennium at the end of time must cross the great river in search of the path of the green flags. Peasant farmers who migrated to Goiás and Pará understood the great river to be the Tocantins and the green flags to be the forest. They believed that when the end came, those who had not crossed would be unable to do so because the river would become incandescent. De Toledo, in her research in the Bico do Papagaio, discovered this factor by accident.[2] The peasant farmers whom she interviewed gave a variety of explanations for their decision to migrate to the region, but none of them mentioned the prophecies. However, when she asked one interviewee whether he had ever heard of Father Cicero, the man replied that it was because of Father Cicero that he was there. He went on to say that the legendary priest had said, "When the situation gets worse, the faithful should leave, cross the great river, and look for the green flags."[3] In subsequent interviews, she included a direct question about Father Cicero, and discovered that all of the people from certain regions acknowledged that the prophecies were a factor in their coming to the Bico. Those people included natives of Piauí, their descendants in Maranhão, and others from the center and northeast of Maranhão. Since they believed that, having arrived on the other side of the great river, they should not leave, De Toledo suggests that this belief strengthened their resistance to eviction from the area.

The Conflicts Begin

The threats of eviction came only a few years after the first migrants arrived. By 1973, land speculators, aware of the federal government's plan to develop the Amazon, were beginning to fence in areas of public land in the Bico do Papagaio in order to claim owner-ship. Some would try to charge rent to the people who were already on the land, such as 50 percent of their crops, but most of the speculators would simply evict the occupants. One of the migrants who came to Itaguatins around that time described the situation that he found:

> At the time that I got here, a lot of people were leaving. We were already having this problem of "owners" of the land. And people had already lived on this land for many years. It did not belong to anyone. It was public land. At the time that we got here, we saw that many posseiros were being evicted.

This pattern repeated itself across the seventy-eight-mile length of the region. Many farmers did not resist eviction. They had little educa-tion and little information about their legal rights. Neither did they have a sense of ownership, since, for people from Maranhão, land had always appeared to be a free natural resource. These farmers were accustomed to migrating. Consequently, many of them responded to the arrival of the grileiros by leaving and seeking land elsewhere. They also were not inclined to question the validity of the claims of men who had more wealth and power than they did and who were supported by the Military Police and, after 1982, by GETAT as well.

> The ranchers said, "This land is ours and those who are within it have to leave." And the police removed us. . . . They always helped the ranchers.

In the context of this conflict, the base communities would serve an important function. Because CEBs encourage people to develop an awareness of their rights, they enabled hundreds of peasant farmers to stay on their land.

The Base Communities

The role of the Catholic Church in helping to generate resistance to eviction in the Bico do Papagaio has been a strong one, although the institutional support has been uneven among the six parishes of the region.[4] De Toledo, in the course of her research in the Bico from 1982 to 1986, noted the importance, for the organization of the land struggle, of small groups of Catholics who reflect on the Bible, as well as the con-nection between leadership in the rural chapels and leadership in the union.[5] She also noted the unevenness in institutional support. This unevenness, characterized until recently by differences among priests as to their perception of land issues as relevant to their pastoral work, was somewhat counterbalanced by a multiplicity of religious influences— missionary sisters and priests from at least four different countries, the Pastoral Land Commission (CPT), and a legendary Italian lay mission- ary who worked in the area for only a brief period but left his influence in the base communities and unions. There is, however, some dis- agreement among residents of the region as to the strength of base com- munities in the region. The priests and sisters whom I interviewed told me that the CEBs in their parishes are weak, although most of them did acknowledge that they were strong in some parts of the parish and that there had been base community activity in areas where unions were organized. On the other hand, lay people whom I interviewed revealed that they participate in small groups that study the Bible and discuss its relevance to their lives and that these groups enable them to persist in the land struggle. In some cases, they made a specific link between CEB experience and resistance to eviction.

Why did you resist eviction here and not resist when you lived in Sítio Novo?
Because we didn't have acquaintance with the reality.
And how did you gain knowledge of this reality?
I gained knowledge of this reality because I was participating in the base community, in the union. And from there I learned that you have to struggle for those things to which you have the right.

Do you think that the decision to occupy land emerged in the discus- sions of the base community?
Yes, it did. The decision emerged in the community itself, through our discussions.

In interviews and discussions with people who had past and pre- sent experience with pastoral work in the Bico do Papagaio, I tried to understand the contradiction between what the pastoral agents had told me and what I learned from interviews with lay people and from De Toledo's research. I concluded that while the relationship between CEB formation and rural activism may not have been as clear-cut in this region as it was across the river in Arame, the relationship is still there. The different opinion on the part of the pastoral agents may be the result of the weakening or disappearance of some CEBs since the period of the greatest number of land struggles in the mid-1980s, affect- ing the perceptions of priests and sisters who arrived after that time (who constitute more than half of those presently there).

On the other hand, there was a certain inevitable bias in the selection of the lay interviewees. It is likely that I was conducting interviews in villages where the CEBs were strong, because I had specifically asked my contact persons to introduce me to CEB members. This does not reveal the overall strength of CEBs in the region. As in any other part of Brazil, there are variations in the concentration of CEBs, even within a single parish. What is important to note, however, is that in those parts of the region where the militant union movement got started in the early 1980s, there were at that time base communities, and members of those communities were leaders in organizing the unions. That was a connection acknowledged even by people who said that the CEBs in their parish were weak.

Some of the migrants from Maranhão had already had experience of CEBs, since they had come from a state where the communities had developed and multiplied before they were being encouraged in other parts of Brazil and where in some parishes the church was already beginning to focus on social issues. One man talked about the experience of church that he had brought with him:

Where were you living when you decided to come here?
I was living in the town of Santa Luzia, in Maranhão.
Did you have contact with the church in Santa Luzia?
It was in Santa Luzia that I reached the point of having more consciousness about the work of the church. The priests there already had a different program. The church today. That church with the work of organizing around the land struggle.
Did you begin to participate in a base community there?
Yes. We got together in a group . . . and we studied the Gospel, and studied the life of the people.

Some of the people who arrived in the region from Maranhão in the 1960s and 1970s were dismayed at not finding the same type of church that they had left behind. One woman, who eventually became a strong leader in both the church and the union, described her experience upon arriving in the Bico:

The priest would only celebrate Mass, and would not talk about community. People got angry when I would talk about community, because they thought that to talk about community was Communism. . . . So I started to suffer, because I didn't have that support that I had had in the community. . . . I felt lost here.

This particular woman was so unhappy that she was thinking about returning to Maranhão, when she met another woman who was trying to get a CEB organized. After this she heard about two French sisters who were organizing communities and about a lay missionary named Nicola who was going around talking about unions.

The Union of Rural Workers

Those peasant farmers who had come from parishes where they had already been exposed to base communities and to rural unions were less likely to move in response to orders from grileiros, more likely to stay and resist, attempting to organize others to do so as well. One man talked about how he began trying to persuade his neighbors to resist eviction and to recognize their right to stay on the land. He and other interviewees talked about the help given by the Italian lay missionary, who was mentioned by several people in the Bico as having been influential in the formation of base communities and in the organization of a union of rural workers.

> In '72 there appeared a man here by the name of Nicola. He appeared here, gathered the people, organized meetings, and explained to the people what a base ecclesial community was.

> After I got here in '73, we had two big meetings at which Nicola was present. He lived in Imperatriz and traveled here, organizing meetings. Afterwards he came more often. . . . He gave me a book, in which I studied the movement of union organization.

Nicola was apparently an unusual person. Although he was part of a organization of lay missionaries, this organization gave him a great deal of freedom in developing his work. During the 1970s, he was providing health care to poor people in the city of Imperatriz, and had developed a reputation for having special healing abilities. Some interviewees indicated that he was almost a mythical figure. During that same time he began crossing the river and visiting the farmers in the Bico do Papagaio, laying the groundwork for base communities. By 1979 Nicola was working full time in the rural areas, traveling the whole distance of the Bico on foot. He was teaching the people a new interpretation of the Bible and encouraging them to think about organizing a union. A priest who worked with him described his method:

He would read some texts of the Bible about the fundamental rights to land, food, salvation, liberation. . . . But he did not speak much. He would listen a lot. . . . He became a key person in the Bico do Papagaio.

The reaction of the ranchers and of the local authorities to these union-organizing efforts was strong. In 1979 Nicola was arrested, although he was soon freed because of the efforts of a large group of women in Imperatriz who were permanently grateful to him for having cured their illnesses and those of their children. The day that he was arrested, soldiers surrounded a church in the town of Sampaio, where a group of people was gathered, discussing their rights in relation to information that Nicola had given them. The soldiers surrounded them, threatened to kill them, and arrested three.

In another town, the local police were instrumental in delaying the formation of the union.

There were people [in the town hall] . . . who said that in order for us to found the union, the majority of rural workers who lived in the municipal district had to sign up. When it was the day [to sign up members] the police came. They said that they would arrest people.
So that they couldn't get a majority?
Yes. So that it wouldn't happen. . . . That was in '82. Then we tried again.
Do you have any idea who sent the police?
These police here belong to the town of Itaguatins. At the time the mayor was [one of the ranchers].

The following year, the union organizers succeeded in getting the number of signatures needed.

By the time the unions were beginning to become established in the Bico do Papagaio, Nicola had moved on to a different region. Some interviewees expressed puzzlement about his disappearance. One priest who had spoken highly of him suggested that Nicola's charisma may have taken up so much space that some other church people found it difficult to work beside him.

In addition to Nicola, base community members also talk about the help they received in organizing unions from three French sisters, a former sister from the south of Brazil, and two lawyers from the CPT (one of whom was a French Dominican priest, the other, a Brazilian layman).

Then the sisters arrived in '80. . . . And when they arrived, they began to visit the communities. The first time that I met them was in the house of a man who was talking about a union.

The interviewees also established the connection between the founding of unions and the base communities:

The union was started after the communities. The first union that was started was in São Sebastião. That was in 1981. At that time we organized a meeting in the church in Augustinópolis. And there, on the day of that meeting, the ranchers, together with their thugs, fired shots inside the church, where there were more than 300 people. . . .
Were there people participating in the founding of the union who were not of the base communities?
No. There was no one who was not of the communities.

In some parts of the Bico, it is difficult to establish the chronology of union formation after CEB formation. It appears that Nicola was laying the groundwork simultaneously for the two. One thing that is clear, however, is that people who became active in the CEBs were the same ones who became active in the founding of the unions. As a result of these efforts, an increasing number of people began to become aware of their rights to the land on which they had been living and working. Across the whole region, poor farmers were getting organized.

Father Josimo

An important figure who emerged at that time was Father Josimo Morais Tavares. The only son of a poor black family from Goiás, Father Josimo began working in the region in 1983 as pastor of the parish of São Sebastião, continuing the work among the peasant farmers that Nicola and the sisters had begun. He also worked as coordinator of the Pastoral Land Commission for the Bico do Papagaio. Since Father Josimo arrived after the land conflicts had begun and just as people were organizing unions, he quickly became a central figure in the conflicts, beloved by the small farmers and hated by the land robbers and the police. In interviews in different parishes, people spoke with affection for Father Josimo. They talked about how he visited the rural communities, celebrated Mass in areas of struggle, taught a new interpretation of the Bible, and organized the poor to struggle for their rights. One woman described him as follows:

He was a person who for his whole life defended the class of [rural] workers. He was struggling together with the suffering class, with the poor class. For instance, there was a time when thirteen farmers were arrested, and he along with them. He took workers to Brasília. And he struggled, step by step, side by side, together with the workers. Many times the big landowners would try to say that he wasn't a real priest because he went around in rubber sandals.

Another peasant farmer, a union leader who is the victim of ongoing death threats, had this to say about Father Josimo:

The landowners found him strange, because in every needy area, when we would go into the countryside, he would celebrate Mass there. And he would explain about the rights that we didn't have. He didn't only celebrate Mass in church. Wherever there were farmers, he would celebrate Mass.

With the help of Father Josimo, the sisters, and other people who worked for the CPT, thousands of farmers in the Bico successfully resisted eviction and gained the right to the land. The ranchers responded with violence, killing many of the settlers. Father Josimo received several threats on his life. On one occasion, he was shot at as he sat in his pickup truck. The only thing that saved his life was the second layer of metal in the door of the truck, which stopped the bullets from reaching him. After that, representatives of the CPT asked the Brazilian government to provide police protection for Father Josimo, but it was never granted.

On May 10, 1986, as Father Josimo was climbing the stairs to his office at the Pastoral Land Commission in Imperatriz, Geraldo Rodrigues, a gunman hired by the ranchers, shot and killed him. After Rodrigues was convicted and sentenced to prison, he was allowed to escape twice. During his trial, Rodrigues had named the rancher who hired him, Nazaré Teodoro da Silva, known as "Deca." Deca was not indicted at that time, although he was also suspected of involvement in the murder of a union leader in 1992, and is believed to be continually threatening others.[6] Only in December 1993, after church groups gathered 9,000 signatures demanding justice in this case, were Deca and another rancher summoned for questioning in the district court in Imperatriz. In August 1994, two other suspects were arrested. As of this writing, the judgment is still pending.

The tragedy of the death of Father Josimo has been turned into an important religious symbol in relation to land conflicts. Each year there

is a Father Josimo pilgrimage, which reinforces the participants' sense of
the religious legitimacy of their struggle. A poster with the priest's picture and an excerpt from a tribute written to him by the poet Pedro
Tierra hangs in many parish houses, union offices, and homes, not only
in the Bico do Papagaio, but throughout Tocantins, Maranhão, and
Pará. This excerpt from the poem, "The Announced Death of Josimo
Morais Tavares," reads as follows:

> Who is this black boy
> who challenges limits?
> Only a man.
> With scuffed sandals.
> Patience and indignation.
> Clear laughter.
> Sweet darkness.
> Inescapable dream.
>
> He struggled against barriers.
> All the barriers.
> The barriers of fear.
> The barriers of hatred.
> The barriers of land.
> The barriers of hunger.
> The barriers of the body.
> The barriers of the landowner.
>
> I have in the palm of my hand
> a fistful of the earth
> that covered you.
> It is fresh.
> It is black, but it still is not free
> as you wanted it to be.[7]

After Father Josimo's death, the land struggles in the Bico began to
meet with success. However, few of the farmers who were granted land
have received titles. In addition, they are still faced with the difficulties
seen throughout the north of Brazil—the lack of roads, technical assistance, schools, and health care, as well as low prices for crops.

The Violence Continues

Although the intensity of the violence in the Bico do Papagaio has
decreased in recent years (relative to neighboring regions in Maranhão

and Pará), it has not stopped. In Father Josimo's parish of São Sebastião, which today is staffed by Jesuit priests from Spain, there has been an average of one murder of a rural activist per year for the years 1987-1992. Although no one was killed in 1993, that may have been because Amnesty International organized a letter-writing campaign near the end of 1992 on behalf of a union leader who said that he was receiving death threats. Even though the local police claimed that he was not in danger, the letters, which came from as far away as Japan, may have served to make the local ranchers aware of vigilance by human-rights advocates outside of Brazil.

There is also a local effort to stop the violence—the Father Josimo Human Rights Commission—organized in 1992 by representatives of each of the Catholic parishes in the Bico. The first two actions of this commission were to hire a full-time attorney to defend the rights of the peasant farmers and to organize a Human Rights Week to make people aware of the issues. Its most significant achievement was with regard to pushing the judicial system to action toward prosecuting the ranchers responsible for Father Josimo's death. The gathering of signatures that led to the indictment of Deca was a result of the combined efforts of the Father Josimo Human Rights Commission and the Pastoral Land Commission.

The existence of this new organization also illustrates the unity that now exists among the six parishes of the region. In addition to the coordination of pastoral approaches—in particular with regard to the ongoing problems of the peasant farmers—there is a strong sense of community among the church people, mostly foreign missionaries, who work in the region. One priest described the joint pastoral effort in which the clergy, the sisters, and lay people from the CPT participate:

We meet every two months, evaluating the work and thinking together. The problems of the region are always discussed. And we have more or less a similar attitude. Each of us takes positions according to his own conscience . . . but there is at least this strength, this unified work.
So you don't see a problem of differences between priests here, as exist in other regions?
No. And as was the case here five years ago, during the time of Josimo. . . . There was opposition. There was resistance. There were accusations on the part of other priests. I'm not judging anyone. I'm just relating the facts.
How did the situation change?
There were changes in priests. Almost all the priests of this region are different from those who were here before.

Interestingly, this unity did not come from deliberate action on the part of the bishop, who, according to the interviewees, is just beginning to show support of people engaged in the land struggle, but rather from the Pastoral Land Commission. The CPT agents who work in the region seek out pastoral teams with whom to coordinate their efforts. It was with their encouragement that the priests and sisters began to meet on a regular basis.

Conclusion

The Bico do Papagaio provides a case of multiple levels of church action in relation to land problems: the somewhat idiosyncratic figure of Nicola, who imparted to the poor farmers a new interpretation of the Bible and a knowledge of their legal rights, thus preparing the way both for base communities and for unions of rural workers; the attorneys from the CPT, who defended the rights of the farmers and helped them organize the union; the sisters who have continued the work begun by Nicola in a more structured way, organizing base communities and helping the unions to become a reality. At the present time, two of the French sisters are still working in the parish of São Sebastião, as is the former sister, and three German sisters now work in the parish of Itaguatins. At another level of church action is the growing uniformity in support of the farmers among the priests in the region, which is a very different situation from when Father Josimo was working there.

Father Josimo, in addition to doing direct pastoral work in one of the parishes, brought in the institutional support of the CPT. His murder by a gunman hired by ranchers demonstrates the extent to which the church, on both the institutional and the grassroots levels, had a real impact on the land situation of the region. Father Josimo was clearly identified by the ranchers as a source of opposition to their plans to take the land away from the posseiros. He also became an important religious symbol to the farmers who continue to struggle for land, in the image of a martyr who died because of his dedication to the Gospel and to the poor. Finally, the new human rights commission that bears his name is a sign of an organized effort to bring an end to the violence in the region.

6

Rio Maria: Tragedy and Hope in the Land of Canaan

The most violent part of the Amazon is the southeast section of the state of Pará. The history of this violence began with the settlement of the region in the late 1970s. Between 1980 and 1994, the Pastoral Land Commission recorded 190 murders related to land conflicts in the diocese of Conceição do Araguaia, which is coextensive with the region. Most of the victims were peasant farmers. Several of these were union leaders. This number likely represents a low estimate, because these are only the deaths that the CPT can demonstrate to be specifically linked to land problems.

The Roots of the Violence

The south of Pará was the target of a great deal of funding from SUDAM for both mining and agricultural projects. Hence the political-economic roots of land conflicts described in chapter 1 apply more clearly to that region than to any of the other cases in this study. Originally the whole area was part of the municipal district of Conceição do Araguaia. Before the 1970s, it was sparsely populated by indigenous tribes and by a small number of settlers of European or mixed racial ancestry who survived by subsistence agriculture and extractive activity, primarily with rubber and Brazil nuts. West of the town of Conceição there were virtually no roads. The French Dominican priests who served at that time as missionaries to the area would travel on foot or horseback, taking six months to visit all the settlements in their parish. During these visits they organized Bible circles. These groups would be forerunners of base communities.

After the government announced its colonization plan for the Amazon, the south of Pará quickly became populated, as both land speculators and landless peasants rushed to the region. Roads were cut through the forest, and villages sprung up almost overnight. The spread-out municipal district of Conceição was subdivided into new towns—Santana do Araguaia, São Geraldo, Redenção, Floresta, Tucumá, Xinguara, and Rio Maria.

Rio Maria became a town in 1982. Since then, eighteen peasant farmers have been killed there over land disputes. The very process of making Rio Maria a municipal district was not without bloodshed. The most visible victim was João Canuto, a poor farmer who had helped to organize base communities, the union of rural workers, and the local branch of the Communist Party (Partido Comunista do Brasil, or PC do B). Canuto ran for mayor in the town's first election. He conducted his campaign with virtually no funds, traveling all over the countryside on a donated bicycle. Many people believe that he would have won the election, had it not been for fraud in the counting of the votes. Apparently the big ranchers feared that fraud would not be enough to defeat him a second time, so they got together to plan his death.[1] Since they killed Canuto in 1985, it is also likely that his assassination was related to his leadership of the peasant farmers in the conflict over the Canaan Ranch.

Canaan

In 1983 twenty peasant families entered Canaan, cleared some of the land, and began to cultivate it. It is not likely that they chose the area specifically because of the biblical symbolism of its name, but rather because it was not being used productively and because they were desperate for a place to grow food. After the owner of the ranch learned of their presence, he brought in hired gunmen and the Military Police to evict them. The police arrested and beat several of the farmers. A base community leader who had supported the squatters described what happened:

> The occupation began in '83. The people went in little by little. About six months later there was an eviction. They were evicted again in '84. . . . Two buses came, filled with police.
> *Were the police and the gunmen in that area at the same time?*
> They acted together—gunmen and police. They worked together. They would arrive at the same time.

This speaker, who was on the directorate of the union at that time, helped to diffuse the violence that was beginning to characterize the occupation. After two gunmen and the son of the rancher were wounded, he persuaded the squatters to seek legal means to get the land.

They thought that they did not have any resources except for armed struggle—to engage in a battle and kill a gunman. I helped them to see that they could get the land by working through the legal system.

The Pastoral Land Commission provided a lawyer to help process the land claim. Church people also collected food from other communities to sustain the farmers after they were evicted.

A young woman who participated in the occupation talked about some of the details:

The posseiros went in, and the rancher brought in gunmen to get them out. They would go back in again. They would get evicted.
How long would they wait before going back in again?
A month. There were others who would not even leave. They would hide in the forest.
And would the gunmen stay the whole time?
The gunmen, yes. When they would move off a little, the people would go in. When the gunmen would come back, the people would leave.
Did the police come, too?
They were the ones who evicted us . . . the Military Police.
Were you already married then?
I was married and six months pregnant. I lost that child.

Besides suffering violence at the hands of the police and the gunmen, the people lost the crop that they had been about to harvest. After being evicted twice, they returned a third time and stayed. By this time they had organized a base community, which strengthened their resolve. The CEB provided both group support and religious legitimation for the struggle for land. The ranch was finally expropriated by the federal government in 1986, and the land was distributed among the farmers, including João Canuto's widow.

The Struggle for Land

The Canaan conflict was only one of eleven land occupations that occurred within the municipal district of Rio Maria between 1983 and 1992. Many of these occupations resulted in the granting of land to peasant farmers, but, as yet, no one has received titles. All of the occupations have been accompanied by bloodshed, and most of the blood that was shed was that of peasant farmers. The early land occupations were not highly organized, but rather were a means of survival for peasant families. They were the result of the desperation of people who had migrated hundreds of miles only to find the promise of land to be a false one. They would enter an unused area, clear it, and plant it, often without the knowledge of the owner, who was holding the land for speculation and in some cases had never even been there. Some of these early settlements existed for over a year before the owners learned of them. It was only after the owners sent gunmen or Military Police that the squatters sought the help of the Catholic Church. As the pastor of Rio Maria, who previously was regional director for the Pastoral Land Commission, explained it:

> The people would come looking for us, because they would want to form a base community. They would want to have a priest to celebrate Mass. Or because of the conflict. Because the hired gunmen were there. Because the police were there, threatening. Because they were being evicted. And so they would look for the Pastoral Land Commission for legal defense.

Under Brazilian law, land not being used productively may be expropriated. The CPT sent lawyers to help the squatters process their claims, and also gave them advice about organizing and defending themselves. That advice usually included joining a union and starting a base community. Hence, in many cases, the base community was the product of the occupation rather than the other way around. From the mid-1980s on, the occupations were more frequently planned, but not specifically by base communities or by the union. A group of people would get together and decide to enter a particular piece of property. By this time the ranchers were more vigilant, and so the conflicts developed quickly.

Base Communities

Although the occupations were not organized by base communities as such, data from my interviews indicate that, in some cases, the organizers of occupations did have prior experience of a base community. For example, one of the union leaders stated:

> I founded the base community in Nova Vida. That was in '82. . . .
> I accompanied the occupation at Canaan as a director of the union. . . . It was in '83 that that occupation began.

Thus, the relationship between CEBs and rural activism is not as clear-cut in Rio Maria as in some other parishes. Even in cases where leaders of occupations had prior base community experience, there was not that direct sequence of CEB formation, union formation, and land occupation that I found in Arame. Neither is this to say, however, that base communities in Rio Maria have emerged only as a result of land conflicts. There has also been a diffusion effect, with CEBs giving rise to other CEBs. Three of the seven lay people whom I interviewed in that town were the founders of base communities, and one woman had started three of them.

When I arrived here, there were no communities. But I've always liked to participate in communities. . . . So I talked with [the pastor], and he gave me the information on how to start a community, and passed on some materials, and we began, holding meetings in the homes, and we reached the point of actually forming the community. And after that there were changes. And some problems after five years. There were—how can I put it?—divisions. The community separated, became divided. People withdrew a little. After that I formed other groups in nearby areas, in the same municipal district. There were three communities.

After the first community resolved its internal problems, the members asked this woman to come back and continue leading them. So she now works to keep all three CEBs going, traveling long distances on foot in her rubber thong sandals, through the dust of the summer and the mud of the rainy season, in addition to looking after her children and helping her husband with the farm work. She is also a faithful attender of parish meetings and Bible courses, even though the isolated location of her plot of land requires a trip of twelve kilometers on foot, followed by a four-hour bus ride, in order to reach the church in Rio Maria.

Support from the Bishop

One advantage that all of the base communities in the south of Pará have had is the consistent support of their bishop for human rights, agrarian reform, and lay initiatives within the church. The leader of the diocese of Conceição do Araguaia during the years of the worst land conflicts was Bishop Patrick Joseph Hanrahan, referred to in the interviews as "Dom José," an Irish missionary who died in June 1993. As of this writing, the Vatican has not yet named his replacement.

Although most of the priests and active lay people in the diocese had been initially opposed to the appointment of Dom José in 1979, because of his lack of visibility as a progressive priest and his lack of experience in a region with severe land problems, he soon won their confidence. He was apparently open to learning from the situation in which he found himself. A story told to me by one of the lay leaders in Conceição do Araguaia, and more-or-less confirmed by the bishop during a conversation in August 1992, illustrates his relationship with the military leaders who still controlled the country at the beginning of his administration. The story is about a meeting between Bishop Hanrahan and Major Curió, the military officer/congressman who was involved in GETAT. Curió had apparently wanted very much to speak with the bishop, because he had followed him to a remote rural area where there was a land occupation in progress. The officer's purpose in seeking out Dom José was apparently to try to form some alliance between church and state. The military officer told the bishop that the government's plan was to work with the Church. He was asking, however, that the Church stop "ordering the people to occupy land." The bishop replied: "See here, Major, the Church is not ordering anything. The farmers don't stop in at church before beginning an occupation. We only learn about it when the Military Police start beating in the heads of the farmers."

The telling of this story by one of the lay base community leaders suggests that the peasant farmers knew that the bishop was on their side. This was also evident in Dom José's public statements, interviews, sermons, and conversations during pastoral visits:

> To want to stay on the land, working in peace and prosperity, is a legitimate and necessary desire. The institutional Church by itself is not interested in land. It is interested in persons. It needs to preach the Good News of Jesus Christ to you; it wants to be in solidarity with your sorrows; it wants to serve. It knows that for you to live better, you need land, schools, health care.[2]

Since lay people, sisters, and priests all knew Bishop Hanrahan's position in relation to land conflicts, there developed a more-or-less uniform pastoral approach where local problems were concerned. This is not to say that all of the clergy were equally supportive of the rights of the peasant farmers, but rather that diocesan policy gave special support to those who were, as well as attracting missionaries and Brazilian priests, sisters, and lay church workers from other parts of the country who were inclined toward a social mission. The diocese also has a fully staffed office of the Pastoral Land Commission and maintains a branch of the Basic Education Movement, a grassroots project that encourages the development of political consciousness among poor people and that died out in most other parts of Brazil during the military regime.

The Party vs. the CEBs

Although the relationship between the institutional Church and base communities in Rio Maria has always been a positive one, another relationship that has become problematic in recent years is that between the base communities and the union. The original founders of the Union of Rural Workers of Rio Maria were all people with CEB experience, as was stated by an interviewee who was involved in the union from the beginning:

All the people who founded the union participated in the base communities. João Canuto, for example, gave courses to Bible circles and participated in groups in the church—of prayer, of Bible circles, of base communities. I, too, participated, for a long time. Today, I don't know if it's because of the activities that are always weighing me down, but I no longer participate.

Although this speaker was vague about the reasons for his withdrawal from church participation, this withdrawal represents a pattern among union leaders. Other interviewees suggested that the recent distancing between the union and the base communities occurred because of the influence within the union of the Communist Party. The PC do B (Communist Party of Brazil) is a Marxist-Leninist party similar to the Albanian model, more open and flexible than the old PCB (Brazilian Communist Party) but also more doctrinaire than other parties of the left, such as the Brazilian Socialist Party (PSB) and the Workers' Party (PT). One of the best-loved members of the PC do B in the south of Pará was Paulo Fonteles, a lawyer for the Pastoral Land Commission in Conceição do Araguaia, who was assassinated in 1987. It is likely because of contact with Fonteles that João Canuto and others who sought to establish a political party, when it once again became legal to do so in the early 1980s, chose the PC do B. Almost all of its founders in Rio Maria were men who had had experience of base communities, but almost all of its founders were eventually assassinated by gunmen hired by the ranchers. The present leaders of the party in Rio Maria have decreased their participation in the church. At the same time, they have remained on friendly terms with the parish priest, who has always defended the rights of rural workers. In recent years, the party seems to have moved more in line with its national organization, adopting increasingly rigid ideological positions, and thus alienating many base community leaders, who tend to prefer the more flexible, inclusive approach that they find in the PT. Since members of the PC do B dominate the union, there has been a gradual drawing apart of CEB leadership and union leadership. In 1992 several CEB people who were former members of the union directorate withdrew from active participation in the union, although remaining members. One of these explained his perception of the situation:

> The union supports the church and the church supports the union. Not the whole idea, because with that change in the union, and as we remain religious Christians, we feel a little harassed by the ideas of the party. The party has good proposals . . . but they believe that the society should change according to certain forms, and we think that you have to wait more. So the union owes a great obligation to the church here. Because if it weren't for the support of the church, the union might not get as much done as it has. And it also supports the church because of this. It owes an obligation to the church. There was a time, more or less at the end of the first directorate, that we began to see a detachment of the church from the union. Then the church asked for a meeting with the directorate, and even Dom José, the bishop, participated in the meeting. And he tried to suggest to the unionists that they should not think in such an aggressive manner. They should not think that things had to change from one hour to the next. However, some of them thought that the ideas of the church, of Dom José, didn't go far enough. So there was a split. Then there was some weakening in the union. . . . And when the violence got worse, that was when they went back and asked for support of the church. And the church saw that it was necessary, and so didn't refuse.

This parting of ways between the church and the union so far has not hampered their joint efforts toward defending the rights of peasant farmers. Land occupations are still supported by the PC do B, the union, the CPT, the base communities, the parish priest, and the sisters. During an interview, the president of the local chapter of the PC do B, while commenting that the institutional Church is not always helpful to the rural workers during land conflicts, spoke favorably of the CPT and of the priests and sisters working in the region. He was responding to my question as to whether there were any nonreligious organizations that had been helpful to the peasant farmers in the land struggle:

In this region all the class organizations, institutes, and founda-
tions that are part of this process work jointly with the Church.
Those up front—the unions of rural workers, the labor federations—receive the support of [church] organizations like FASE
and CPT. . . . I don't know of any organization of this region that
supports the struggle for agrarian reform that is not associated
with the Church, or that doesn't have links with it. . . . Here in
this region we don't have any sisters or priests who are politically
backward, who are reactionary, or who are against the people's
movement. Those whom I know of in this region here are defi-
nitely of the progressive Church, the one that is on the side of the
worker.

The positive image of the local church expressed by this party
official is probably due in no small measure to the work of the parish
priest, Father Ricardo Rezende, who came to Rio Maria in 1988 after
working for twelve years for the Pastoral Land Commission. It is common knowledge that his appointment to the parish was not welcomed
by the large ranchers. Shortly after his arrival in Rio Maria, the new
pastor was critically injured, his skull fractured, in a hit-and-run automobile collision. Newspaper reports of the collision suggested that it
was not really an accident. After three operations, Father Rezende fully
recovered, and he has continued to speak out against the violence and
injustice in the region.

Largely because of this priest's efforts and personal charisma, Rio
Maria has become the center of an international solidarity movement,
which will be described below. The movement emerged after the violence in the town intensified.

The Year of Death

In April 1990, there were four murders related to agrarian
activism. At the beginning of that month, one of the founders of the
PC do B, Brás Antônio de Oliveira, an auto mechanic and former rural
worker, was murdered, along with his shop assistant, by four men
claiming to need their services to fix a car. Later that month, three sons
of João Canuto were kidnapped, taken to a wooded area, and shot,
although one son, Orlando Canuto, managed to survive the shooting
and escape. He described the incident in an interview:

They kidnapped me with my two brothers. There were two
Military Police and two gunmen . . . together. They came to the

house saying that they were from the Federal Police. They put us in a car and took us seventy kilometers away, and there began shooting us. My brothers died on the spot, but I survived. I caught a bullet in the stomach, and I managed to run into the woods. It was night. That hampered them, and they did not find me.

Less than ten months later, the president of the union, Expedito Ribeiro de Souza, was killed, and one month after that, the new president, Carlos Cabral (João Canuto's son-in-law) was injured in an attempt on his life. There have also been several death threats against Father Ricardo, Socialist City Councillor Sebastião Vieira, and Roberto Neto da Silva, who is the local president of the PC do B.[3] Yet they persist in the land struggle. As Orlando Canuto explained:

There have been several assassination attempts against me, but I continue to resist, continue still firm. We are in the struggle because we hope that we will still succeed in winning the land, will succeed in getting agrarian reform for Brazil, because of the need of the landless worker. This is the motive that keeps me going.

Orlando's sister Luzia has also received death threats, but continues fearlessly supporting the farmers' struggle. She indicated that her fearlessness is religiously based.

I think that we all have fear. But in a just issue, in the issue of land, we struggle because of the need of the people, and because of our own need. I'm not afraid to die for a just cause. . . . I think that comes from a trust and a will to struggle that I see in the movements of the church. . . . Because of my faith in God, which I learned in the church, I have more courage to struggle. I have a lot of hope that sooner or later things will change.

Hope for Change

The fifth of the recent murders, that of the union president Expedito Ribeiro de Souza, focused international attention on Rio Maria, because European journalists had already been writing about the death threats against him. At that point, Father Rezende got together with friends and colleagues from the Pastoral Land Commission to discuss ways of mobilizing people to call national attention to the deaths in Rio Maria. These deaths were clearly not the result of random acts of violence, since the people targeted were either leaders in the land struggle or closely associated with leaders. Furthermore, the killers were acting with complete impunity. Gunmen would sometimes approach their victims in public places, and neither these gunmen nor the landowners who hired them were ever prosecuted for their crimes.

Father Rezende's group decided on two strategies. One was to organize, on March 13, 1991, a Day against Violence. In the morning of that day, families of victims of the violence gave their testimonies to government officials who had come to Rio Maria for the occasion. In the afternoon there was a large public rally that drew over 1,000 people, including progressive politicians, bishops, and performing artists, and that was reported by major national newspapers.

The second strategy, which drew on the inspiration of the Chico Mendes Comittees, was to start a nationwide network of solidarity groups. Their goal was to be the organizing of pressure, mainly through letter-writing campaigns, to compel the Brazilian government to enforce the law. Within a few months, Rio Maria Committees had been organized not only in several cities in the north and south of Brazil but also in Germany, France, Britain, and the United States.

Rio Maria stands out in the south of Pará because of its strong message of hope. Although there are many regions of Brazil in which the Pastoral Land Commission has worked hard to publicize human-rights violations, sharing information with such organizations as Amnesty International and America's Watch, the Rio Maria movement may be unique in having focused worldwide attention on one small corner of the Amazon region. Because of this narrow focus, it has been possible to observe tangible results of the movement. The first was the provision of Federal Police protection for four people who, because of their leadership in the land movement, have been the victims of death threats and of actual attempts on their lives. Even more important, however, has been the pushing into action of a sluggish legal system. On April 28, 1994, José Ubiratan Matos Ubirijara, a former member of the Military Police, was convicted of the murder of José and Paulo Canuto and of the attempted murder of Orlando Canuto. He was sentenced to fifty years in prison. This was only the second time that anyone was convicted for the killing of rural workers in the Amazon, the first being the conviction of Darly and Darcy Alves for the assassination of Chico Mendes. On June 23 of the same year, Paulo Cesar Pereira was tried for the attempted assassination of Carlos Cabral. Although found guilty by the jury, he received a suspended sentence of two years with probation. The lighter sentence was likely the result of the location of the trial. The first trial was held in Belém, the capital city of Pará. The second was held in Rio Maria itself, where the presence in the courtroom of a large number of local landowners likely intimidated the judge and jury. This demonstrates the importance of a change of venue for any murder trial associated with land problems in Rio Maria.

The letter-writing campaigns have resulted in changes of venue for some of the cases, including the trials for the murders of the Canuto brothers and of Expedito Ribeiro de Souza. The latter case is also significant because not only the gunman but also the rancher suspected of ordering the death and his manager, who contracted the gunman, have been charged. The date for this trial was set just as this book was going to press.

The central committee in Rio Maria is one organization in which base community members and the Communist leaders of the union continue to work together, despite their ideological differences. Those who attend the meetings of the committee include, among others, the president of the PC do B, the city councilor from the Socialist Party, officers of the union, an attorney from the Pastoral Land Commission, and people active in base communities, as well as the Catholic pastor and the sisters who work in the parish.

Conclusion

The Rio Maria movement is not a solution to all of the problems that plague the peasant farmers of southeastern Pará. There is still violence in neighboring towns. There are still thousands of families who are without land, and those who do have land face the same problems as farmers throughout the Amazon region: low prices for crops, lack of resources to use modern farming methods, and the absence of roads, schools, and health care. What the Rio Maria Committees have done, however, is provide a model of how to stop the murders of rural organizers, so that they may continue their work to bring about agrarian reform and begin to address all the other problems faced by rural poor people. The conspicuous presence of church people in the origin of this movement also contributes to a sociological model of the function of religion in social change.

7

BYE-BYE BRAZIL:
ALONG THE TRANSAMAZONIC HIGHWAY

"The Amazon Rain Forest—haven't you ever heard of it?" the Gypsy Lord asks the young Indian chief. There is irony in this piece of dialogue from Carlos Diegues's 1980 film *Bye-Bye Brasil*, which dramatizes the changes going on in people's lives as a result of the rapid modernization of the country. The Gypsy Lord is the leader of a rag-tag road show that is criss-crossing the north of Brazil in an increasingly desperate search for audiences who have enough money to pay for admission but have not yet been seduced by television. His question is particularly poignant because the young chief has just asked him for a ride to the city of Altamira on his flat-bed truck for the small number of remaining members of his village, whose way of life has been destroyed in the process of the white man's demolition of the forest. Moments earlier, the scenery in the film was shifting from lush greenery to the blackened skeletons of burned trees.

The Colonization Project

Along the eastern stretch of the Transamazonic Highway (extending from Marabá westward to Altamira in the state of Pará), where this scene in the film takes place, it would be difficult to find any large expanses of rain forest. This was the area the federal government targeted in the 1970s for agricultural development and the resettlement of impoverished farmers from the northeast. The first ten kilometers on each side of the road were to be set aside for the farmers, with plots of one hundred hectares for each family. The rest was to be divided into tracts of five hundred hectares for cattle ranches. The majority of farmers who initially settled along the Transamazonic did not come on their own initiative. They were granted plots of land under the government's colonization project. One of the church people who works in this region described the process of colonization:

The people were brought in by airplane, and were told not even to bring pots and pans, or anything, because they would receive a house, three hectares already cleared, and a cow. There would be sewing machines. So the people came. When they got off the plane in Altamira, there were no pots and pans. The women and children were taken to a big camp area, and the men were taken off to be surveyors. Some of the women didn't see their husbands again for four or five months. Then the men were told that they could pick up their piece of land. It was all forest. There was no house. There were no three hectares. There was nothing. They had to clear it themselves. Then they brought their families and built them a little hut.

After arriving at their new homes, the families had to face attacks of malaria and rains so heavy that they had to sleep with their hammocks hung high, while the water rushed beneath them across the dirt floors of their huts. After the rainy season was over, the farmers began their planting. However, the government agents had provided them with the wrong kind of rice, and so the first crop failed.

The people got started in terrible misery. Then IMATER—the technicians sent from the government—told the people that the land was very poor, that it wouldn't sustain good produce, and that they should throw down grass seed.

The purpose of the grass was to graze cattle. Since most of the farmers could not afford to buy even one cow, planting grass meant preparing to sell their land to ranchers. Because of the failure of the first rice crop, the farmers were deeply in debt. Since they had little prior experience with banks, they were fearful of the consequences of being unable to pay these debts. In their fear, many of them did sell the land that they had been granted. Ranchers were waiting to buy it, and the desperate farmers accepted the low prices they offered.

Innovations in the Local Church

Meanwhile, changes were occurring in the institutional church in the Prelacy of Xingu, based in Altamira. Bishop Erwin Krautler, an Austrian missionary who was appointed to the prelacy in 1980, was taking a critical look at the pastoral orientation of the area under his authority and shifting it toward the preferential option for the poor.[1] He encouraged the priests to change their approach from desobriga—which meant racing all over the countryside to administer the sacraments, visiting

each village only once or twice a year—to the organizing of base communities. A priest from Altamira, Father Lucas, began organizing CEBs along the eastern stretch of the Transamazonic. Although, in a prelacy with only twelve priests, it was not possible for him to spend a great deal of time in any one area, he did manage to start seven communities.

Meanwhile, also in 1980, Michel LeMoal, a French missionary who had worked for three years in the Diocese of Conceição do Araguaia and was known locally as "Miguel," came to Altamira. Besides organizing a diocesan office of the Pastoral Land Commission, Miguel, who was a former priest, also helped orient the clergy to more effective methods of working with poor people, which would be helpful to them in organizing base communities. The present coordinator of the CPT in Altamira described Miguel's work:

> The Prelacy of Xingu was very closed at that time. It did not have any opening for the organization of the people. The Church was resolving to place a priority on social questions, but it did not know how. So Miguel began to work with some of the priests. . . . He taught them the method for listening to the people, and, soon after, the people began to wake up.

With the help of Miguel, people from the base communities began organizing a union. The CPT coordinator described the chronology of the establishment of the base communities and the Union of Rural Workers of Altamira:

> First the CEBs were organized. With time there was a change in the pastoral line of the Church. This change opened the space for the creation of the union. The union was born from a discussion in all the CEBs.

It is clear from this statement that the creation of the union was a direct consequence of the work of base communities. Unlike many of the municipal districts in Maranhão and in some other parts of Pará, there was no preexisting pelego union that had to be won over through elections. Since the union was started by CEB members, it has always been strong in its support of the farmers in their struggle for land.

More CEBs

The base communities along the eastern stretch of the Transamazonic got a special boost in 1981. That year, Dorothy Stang, a

Sister of Notre Dame de Namur from the United States, who had been working for fifteen years in Maranhão and Pará, approached Bishop Krautler about working in his prelacy. She wanted to start a new program of pastoral work in a region that was both spiritually and materially needy.

> I had known about Altamira for a long time, because I was living near Marabá, and it was the next area up [the Transamazonic]. I knew that there were very few pastoral agents there. And it was an area occupied by people that were destitute. So I spoke to the bishop, and the bishop said, "I'll accept your offer on one condition: that you live with the people."

This happened to be exactly what Sister Dorothy had in mind. So she went to a rural area in the municipal district of José Porfírio, about seventy kilometers east of Altamira. At first she lived with one of the families in their small, flimsy shack without electricity or running water, and began getting to know the residents of the area, visiting existing base communities and helping to start new ones. After a year-and-a-half, the people of the base communities built Centro Nazaré (Nazareth Center), a complex of simple buildings that include a small mud-and-wattle house (still without electricity and running water) for Sister Dorothy and the two young Brazilian lay women who work with her, a chapel, a meeting room, and a training center for school teachers. But even more important than this physical environment is the high level of community organization it evidences. After Sister Dorothy's arrival, the number of base communities increased from seven to twenty-seven. Within a few years, the people in these CEBs felt the need to start an organization that would address the material needs of peasant farmers, thus enabling them to survive in the region and to resist the temptation to sell their land.

Staying on the Land

In 1986, base community members formed the Associação Pioneira Agrícola Transaleste (the Pioneer Farming Association of the Eastern Transamazonic). A chief concern of the association has been finding ways for poor farmers not only to gain land but also to stay on it. As in other parts of northern Brazil, the farmers who gain land remain poor because of low prices for crops and lack of access to markets, technical assistance, roads, schools, and health care. The base communities and the association have worked on all these areas. They have

pressured the government to provide schools, and there are now twenty-seven in the area. There is a teacher-training program at Centro Nazaré that was sponsored by the government and that has produced more than thirty graduates. The government also agreed to hire a person with paramedical training to staff a health center. Primitive roads have been cut into the areas where people have their plots of land. Members of the association organized a cooperative rice field in order to raise money to buy a machine for hulling rice. With the help of contributions from Catholic parishes in the United States, they purchased a large truck for transporting their crops.

One problem that the members of the association have not yet solved is that of low prices for their rice crop. The farmers are too poor to hang on to their rice until the time of the year when the prices are high. They have begun talking about ways to start a cooperative that would buy the rice from its members at the usual low price, store it until the time of year when the price reaches its peak, then sell it and share the profits. The main obstacle at this point is raising the initial funds to pay the members for the first crop.

In an area that is very distant from the nearest union office, which is located in Altamira, the association has also filled the role (filled by unions of rural workers in most of the other municipal districts in this study) of supporting the peasant farmers in land conflicts. The fact that the eastern Transamazonic was an area of colonization administered by the federal land reform institute (INCRA) did not prevent land robbing by big ranchers. As in other parts of Pará, ranchers who received land from the federal government fenced in areas that were much larger than what they were granted. Not only did the government not do anything to prevent this from happening, but people who organize the farmers suspect that the taking over of their land by ranchers was part of the government's plan. As one person stated in an interview:

> We found out eight years ago that on this stretch, from Marabá to Altamira, the government had a hidden project to make it a part of the Serras de Carajás. This area was to turn into huge cattle-raising land, and they would use the railway system to the port of São Luís.

This speaker believes that the government never intended to grant land permanently to the peasant farmers, but brought them to this area, first of all, to dissipate the pressure for agrarian reform in their area of origin (the northeast) and, second, to clear the land so that it could be taken over by ranchers. This explanation seems supported by the recommendation made to farmers by government technicians that they give up on trying to farm the land and plant grass instead. What government people did not take into consideration was that the farmers might become mobilized to resist displacement and that, furthermore, the ranks of the original settlers would be swelled by those who had not been part of the colonization program. President Médici's slogan, "Land without people for people without land," stimulated a flow of migration by thousands of desperate people who did not wait for a more formal invitation. These people began to push beyond the ten-kilometer limit designated for small farms on each side of the Transamazonic Highway and to clear and plant land that INCRA had intended for cattle raising. These settlers entered the areas that were not being used productively, without calling attention to themselves, trying to get in and cultivate the land, so that they could establish a claim to it before the absentee owner learned of their presence. A leader in the community association explained the process:

And so they enter, little by little, in order to become posseiros. Then the rancher comes in, and we go looking for justice.

Since many of the would-be ranchers had not actually used this land, the peasant farmers were able to make a claim to it. However, these people, acting out of desperation, were not organized and did not know how to process the claims. This was where the association was able to help them, as was explained by another one of the interviewees:

The group that's in the struggle, that's in the woods, doesn't have a [base] community that's already organized. All they have is a need. The organized group would go where there was the need, and help those people to get organized. And what would happen was that a new base community would be born.

The farmers who participated in base communities and found ways to stay on the land came into conflict with ranchers, some of whom had legal titles and some of whom did not, and many of whom had been absentee owners up to this time. The ranchers called in the state Military Police to evict the farmers. Those farmers who were organized into base communities resisted and complained to INCRA. As a result, there were cases in which the Federal Police came to defend the farmers. The ranchers responded with further violence. In one conflict, hired gunmen opened fire on unarmed people. Although no one was killed, several farmers were injured. One of the CEB leaders told about the incident:

Soon after we began this work with the base communities, we got quite a shock. I was shot. I caught a bullet here [showed his hand]. . . . A gang of one hundred gunmen came. They shot ten people.

Death threats have also been used by the ranchers in their efforts to intimidate the militant farmers. Although the association has tried to keep its elected leadership out of the public spotlight so that they will not be killed, ranchers have continued threatening church people and those farmers whom they suspect to be leaders.

In the region surrounding Centro Nazaré there have been twelve major land conflicts since 1983. Nine of these have resulted in the expropriation of land for peasant farmers. Three are still unresolved. Through the work of the association, which fights land battles by legal means, establishing claims through INCRA, 1,138 families have gained land.

Movement for Survival on the Transamazonic

The farmers' association in José Porfírio was instrumental in organizing a larger effort, the *Movimento pela Sobrevivência na Transamazônica* (Movement for Survival on the Transamazonic), intended to mobilize farmers beyond their municipal district. In 1992, this movement staged a large demonstration in order to gain recognition from the government. The regional coordinator of the CPT explained the movement's goals:

Two thousand people were camped in Altamira for eight days, from May 31 until June 7 of this year. The objective was to bring the government here, to this region, to negotiate with the movement on the proposals for this development. The movement elaborated alternative proposals for the development of the region— education, health, agricultural politics, and a series of other things. And they staged the encampment so that the government would come to negotiate here.

This demonstration, which was supported by the unions, by the church, and even by some of the local mayors, helped launch the Movement for Survival on the Transamazonic. The statement of objectives of this movement, found in its organizing document,[2] reveal a combination of the goals of democratic participation, economic development, personal betterment, and concern for the ecosystem. The stated objectives are:

1. To guarantee the participation of the people in the overall development of the Amazon, creating conditions to reduce their constant
   relocation to other regions.
2. To launch a process of discussion about society as a whole, having
   in view a new project of development in the reclaiming of the colonization of the Transamazonic without causing environmental
   harm, while promoting the development of the human person and
   guaranteeing social, economic, and cultural betterment to the people who are suffering most.
3. To gather together all the social sectors and the people in general,
   unifying their struggles, so that, organized, they may guarantee
   their survival on the Transamazonic, improve their lives, produce,
   and preserve [the environment].

The document then goes on to give a brief history of the problems in the region, stating that the hidden purpose of the colonization
project was not really "Land without people for people without land"
but rather to use the peasant farmers as a pool of cheap labor for the
clearing of the land, in addition to diffusing the pressure for agrarian
reform in other regions. Twenty years after the beginning of the project,
this area has been "transformed into a mixture of progress and aban-
donment."[3] The federal government has withdrawn its support of colonization, leaving more than a million people uncertain about the
future. The document advocates that the people take control of the situation, in order to be able to continue living in the region, where, with
proper use of the natural resources, it is possible to achieve a decent
standard of living without destroying the natural environment. It then
goes on to outline projects to be undertaken by the new organization:
agriculture and environment, land use, health, education, urbanization,
roads, energy, and agricultural loans.

One of the organizers of the movement explained the process of its
formation:

We have this project going now because the government is trying to
starve out the Transamazonic. . . . We started it two years ago
because all government projects had been cut. The initiative came
from our association and from the unions. We would have meetings
of three or four unions all together—big pastoral events where the
diocese would bring all of us together. This year we had representatives that sent a small group to go all over Brazil and make people
aware that the Transamazonic is being killed. All of this huge colonization program is death-ridden. The government now feels that it

is enough developed, that there are enough people here, that they can bring in big agricultural business. And they want to starve us out. Right now we have a team that's in Brasília, that's working with the president and with government ministers. And we're working on health, education, and projects to get land documents.

It may be too early to predict what will be the long-term effect of this new movement. Nevertheless, it is clear that the peasant farmers along the Transamazonic Highway have become organized and do not intend to remain helpless victims of government policy. It is also clear that base communities have had a strong role in the organizing of the movement. If the people involved in it succeed in their goals, they will have effectively derailed the plan, initiated under the military regime, to develop the region by means of a model that disregards human needs, human rights, and ecological balance. They will have replaced an elitist model of modernization, focused on quick profits, with a plan for the modernization of social relations, focused on democratic participation.

Conclusion

This case stands in sharp contrast to the interior of the island of São Luís. In both cases, a North American sister was instrumental in organizing base communities (in fact, the two sisters are of the same congregation). In both cases, the federal government had its master plan for development—"the Big Projects," as they are known in Brazil. In one case, the communities mobilized to design their own plan for survival of their families and of the ecosystem. In the other, the villages were virtually all destroyed, and the one remaining village may be dying a slower death, along with the natural environment. A key difference between the two cases appears to be the clergy. The priests in the Prelacy of Xingu have been receiving consistent signals from their bishop that he is on the side of the poor and that he supports their work with base communities. In São Luís, the work of the sisters and of the lay leaders was undercut by the pastor whom the archbishop appointed. These two cases combined show the importance of both the institutional Church and the base communities in social change.

REFLECTIONS ON THE CASE STUDIES

The cases presented in this section of the book were chosen to show a variety of ways in which base communities have interacted with a conflictive rural context. They were selected not by any sampling technique but rather for the way that their unique characteristics contributed to the understanding of the relationship between religion and mobilization. This process of selection has led to an uneven distribution of cases among the three states—three in Maranhão, two in Pará, and one in Tocantins. The Tocantins case, however, actually includes three parishes. They were treated together because they are all located in the Bico do Papagaio region and because the pastoral action among the parishes there is unified. This geographic clustering occurred because the total number of fifteen parishes were selected according to two criteria: presence of CEBs and presence of land conflicts. Because the Bico do Papagaio, in the north of Tocantins, has a history of rural violence, three of the parishes happened to be there.

A similar clustering of three parishes occurred in the south of Pará, which, according to annual reports of the CPT, has even more violence than the north of Tocantins. In that situation, however, all three were not included in the case study, because Rio Maria displayed its own set of unique characteristics in relation to both local and international mobilization.

The six cases show a mixture of failure and success in the struggle of poor people against prevailing definitions of modernization and progress in the Amazon, as formulated by the Brazilian government and by national and foreign economic interests. They also show that in those places where there has been some measure of success, there has also been consistent support by sectors of the Catholic Church, particularly through the base communities and the Pastoral Land Commission. Part III will provide an analysis of the various elements that enter into the process by which religion may serve as a means of empowering peasant farmers.

PART III

ANALYSIS

8

HELP AND HINDRANCE: THE INSTITUTIONAL CHURCH

It is sometimes difficult to figure out precisely what the Brazilian Catholic Church is doing in relation to people of the poorer classes. On the one hand, there is the image of liberation theology, which places the weight of the Bible behind its critique of the existing world order, leading some North Americans to believe that Brazilian Catholicism is revolutionary. The news that we receive of the statements and actions of such religious leaders as Dom Hélder Câmara, former Archbishop of Olinda and Recife, and Cardinal Arns, Archbishop of São Paulo, would make it appear that the Church is firmly on the side of the oppressed. Then we learn of the resignation from the Franciscan order of liberation theologian Leonardo Boff, who is much loved by base community people,[1] after years of patiently enduring repeated silencing; the conflict between priests in Recife and Dom Hélder's more traditionalistic successor; the apparent withdrawal of the Church's support from base communities in São Paulo, whose strength and numbers had been attracting the attention of North American social scientists throughout the 1980s. Such mixed signals lead one to ask exactly what is going on.

Church Policy: Changes and Reversals

These seemingly contradictory images are rooted in the internal processes of the religious institution, processes that produce changes and reversals in ecclesial policy. It is important to keep in mind that a main concern of bishops is the organizational strength of the Church, a concern that, in some social contexts, will lead all but the most conservative members of the episcopate to open up the institution to new ideas and practices. This could result in a shift in the religious division of labor (as defined by Maduro), with increased decision-making power for the laity of the subordinated classes. In other contexts, this same concern will lead to a reaffirmation of orthodoxy.[2] It is also important to recognize individual variations among the bishops themselves and to note that a new policy in one diocese which draws worldwide attention may not necessarily be representative of dioceses throughout the nation.

Thus, inconsistencies in pastoral approaches in Brazil have been a result of variations among bishops and priests in terms of their implementation of new ecclesial policy, as well as the Church's subsequent withdrawal from the policy itself. As seen in Arame, for example, those inconsistencies resulted in the introduction of a new pastoral approach, followed by attempts to reverse it, followed by conflicts between clergy and lay people. Yet, even in a single diocese, there may be different experiences, as seen in the parishes of São Cristóvão (in São Luís) and Santa Rita. In order to understand how a specific church policy—the preferential option for the poor—was introduced, inconsistently applied, and partially withdrawn, it is useful to look at the process of its emergence.

Option for the Poor: Historical Development

Four events are significant in understanding the development of the Brazilian Church's option for the poor and the application of that policy to the issue of agrarian reform: (1) the founding of a national episcopal conference in 1952, (2) the adoption of unified pastoral planning in 1963, (3) the participation by Brazilian bishops in the Medellín Conference in 1968, and (4) the founding of the Pastoral Land Commission in 1975. The establishment of the National Conference of the Brazilian Bishops (*Conferência Nacional dos Bispos do Brasil*, or CNBB) was important because it provided a voice to articulate the position of the episcopate as a whole on a variety of ecclesial and social issues, as well as a vehicle for coordinating pastoral action. Since the Brazilian Church began its encouragement of lay leadership and action toward social reform shortly after the founding of the CNBB, this body became a means of consolidating these changes. Its leadership has been sometimes progressive, frequently moderate, but never ultraconservative. As a result, the documents that all of the bishops sign usually set a tone for the Church that is more innovative than the positions some of these bishops would take on their own. This has enabled priests, sisters, and lay people to engage in social and pastoral activity of which their local bishop might not be supportive, drawing their legitimation from stated policies of the CNBB.

The founding of the CNBB made possible, eleven years later, the formulation of pastoral plans that would affect the Brazilian Church as a whole, beginning with the Emergency Plan (*Plano de Emergência*), adopted in 1963, and the Unified Pastoral Plan (*Plano de Pastoral de Conjunto*), adopted in 1966. These documents were written at the urging of Pope John XXIII, who was concerned about the weakness of the Church in Latin America.[3] Their purpose was the revitalization of the Church in the face of modernization. The pastoral plans emphasized innovation within the Church and human social development, bringing both of these priorities together in the encouragement of base ecclesial communities.

This new institutional approach was reinforced at the Second General Conference of the Latin American Bishops (CELAM II) held in Medellín, Colombia, in 1968.[4] The purpose of this meeting, which began as the idea of Dom Hélder Câmara and the Chilean Bishop Manuel Larraín, was to apply the religious renewal that came out of the Second Vatican Council to the Church in Latin America. The documents which resulted from this meeting helped to institutionalize the preferential option for the poor for the Roman Catholic Church throughout the continent.

Finally, the founding of the Pastoral Land Commission provided an agency through which the Church would take a strong position on the side of agrarian reform and the rights of peasant farmers. The origin and functions of the CPT will be described later in this chapter.

Having sketched the key developments that led to the Church's advocacy of social and ecclesial change, let us look at the processes that created the societal context for this new position. Throughout the history of Brazil, beginning in colonial times, the Church was mostly on the side of the landowning elite. Since the landowners had control over the lives and the loyalties of the peasants, the clergy allied themselves with these wealthy people, assuming that spiritual and material benefits would thus trickle down to the poor. The peasants appeared to be loyal to Catholicism, although their belief system was not informed by much religious instruction and was mixed with a variety of folk customs. The relationship of the clergy to these people was mostly limited to the celebration of Mass in rural villages about once a year, usually on the feast day of the village's patron saint. The priests dealt with the poverty they saw on those visits by encouraging the elite to do works of charity. They did not do anything to discourage the peasants from thinking that their poverty and their obedience to the landlords was the will of God. After four-and-a-half centuries, however, the Church appeared to make a complete about-face, as it redefined the poor as important actors in both Church and society and encouraged them to take action to transform oppressive social structures.

The societal context in which this change occurred was one in which the bishops perceived the Church as having lost its influence over the beliefs and behavior of the majority of Brazilian Catholics,[5] an influence that had been rooted in the rural social structure. This new context was created by the industrialization that began in Brazil in the 1930s and accelerated during the 1950s, resulting in mass migrations of peasants to urban areas. These migrations broke the hold the landowners had held over the peasants, and led the latter to see that the world they had known was by no means absolute. At the same time, there were changes occurring in the countryside that would affect the thinking of those who remained on the land. The whole system of agriculture was becoming modernized. It was changing from the old semifeudal estate model to that of capitalist enterprise. Peasants were being evicted from land that their families had farmed for generations and replaced by underpaid wage workers who had no access to plots of land for their own use. This threatened not only the economic security of the peasantry but also their traditional worldview. Since their religiosity was part of the old order, their ties to the Church were weakened.

Thus, the world was changing both for the peasants who remained on the land and for those who migrated to the urban areas. As a result, they became open to new ideas, both religious and political. People who had been nominally Catholic began joining Pentecostal Protestant sects. Others were attracted to socialist-led peasant leagues, which promised to protect their right to stay on the land. The bishops became concerned about this apparent decrease in adherence to Catholicism. In this context, the preferential option for the poor, as it was articulated during the 1960s, may be understood as a survival mechanism. The new emphasis on addressing social problems may be seen as an attempt to undercut the efforts of socialist movements, while the creation of small, grassroots groups for worship and Bible study likely followed the example of the Protestant sects.

Although this analysis presents changes in ecclesial policy as a contingency, as a response to a crisis, it is important to note that the Church's new approach did not remain at this level. It became institutionalized through the pastoral plans and through the documents of the Medellín Conference. The process of the establishment of the preferential option for the poor as an official policy would solidify it, even after the social conditions had changed. Thus, although some aspects of this policy could be understood initially as a conservative response to socialism, the same policy would serve a different function under the military regime that took power in 1964. Since the bishops now had an official position on the side of the oppressed, the Church would become a source of criticism of the economic policies and human rights abuses of the regime as well as a space for protest and activism for change. During the years of the most severe repression (1968 to 1978), the Church was virtually the only such space.

Sources of Inconsistencies

Nevertheless, as demonstrated by the case studies, there were inconsistencies. Although all the bishops may have signed the documents generated by the CNBB, they did not embrace the Church's new policy with equal enthusiasm. Neither did all the priests. Religious sisters formed a separate category because they were of two very different types: those who performed conventional roles, such as teaching in private schools, and those who opted for a more active pastoral ministry. By virtue of becoming involved in the latter, sisters were already being innovative. Hence, sisters in pastoral roles have generally tended to support the option for the poor.

Inconsistencies among the priests and bishops created the problems seen in the cases of Arame and of the parish of São Cristóvão in São Luís. These inconsistencies have become further intensified in recent years because of changes in the Vatican, which also functions with a priority of preserving the Church's influence, specifically, the influence of the pope and the bishops. When the emphasis on lay initiative threatened to diminish the power of the hierarchy, the Vatican reasserted the traditional religious division of labor. The practical consequence for Brazil of this revival of orthodoxy in ecclesial policy has been the replacing of progressive bishops who die or retire with others who follow more traditional approaches. One of the most dramatic cases is that of the archdiocese of Olinda and Recife, where Dom Hélder Câmara, upon his retirement, was succeeded by Dom José Cardoso Sobrinho. The whole pastoral policy of the archdiocese has changed, resulting in conflicts with lay people, sisters, and priests, the closing of a seminary in which training included close contact with the poor, and the loss of a uniform direction for the Church in that region. One priest who has been working in a poor parish in that diocese for many years told me that he now focuses on the *pastoral do quintal* (pastoral approach of the back yard). For him this means that he is still working along the same lines as he always has, but quietly, in his own limited area, not drawing attention to his community activities. He said that he missed the sense that he used to have that his work was part of a larger diocesan effort.

A slightly different situation, although with serious consequences for CEBs, is the one in São Paulo, where the archdiocese of the progressive Cardinal Arns was recently subdivided, and the newly created dioceses placed under the control of bishops who are not supportive of base communities. During the 1980s, the cardinal had taken a great deal of initiative to stimulate the growth of CEBs, even selling his palatial residence in order to generate funds to build community centers in which they could meet. After the subdivision, he was cut off from many of the communities he had helped to create. Hewitt's research in São Paulo suggests that the grassroots church in that metropolitan area has become weaker because CEB members are demoralized by the loss of the support they have come to expect from the clergy.[6]

These recent developments in Brazilian Catholicism reflect the reaction which emerged within the Latin American Church against the consequences of the Medellín documents. That reaction became visible as early as the 1970s, when conservatives among the episcopate began the preparations for the Third General Conference of the Latin American Bishops (CELAM III), to be held in Puebla, Mexico. Liberation theologians who had been influential as consultants at Medellín were being excluded. However, they still went to Puebla, setting up their base of operations near the official meeting so that progressive bishops could consult them before drawing up the documents. As a result, the Puebla conference, which took place in 1979, not only reaffirmed the preferential option for the poor articulated at Medellín but went beyond it, taking a much stronger position on human rights.

During the following decade, however, the Vatican policy of replacing progressive bishops with those who emphasize more traditional concepts of holiness created a decisive shift in power within CELAM. As a result, the conservatives finally exerted their influence over the Fourth General Conference, held in Santo Domingo in 1992. The Santo Domingo documents repeat the language of Medellín and Puebla, referring to human rights, the preferential option for the poor, and the importance of transforming unjust social structures, but in subtle ways undermine the consequences of the previous conferences.[7] Base communities are barely discussed. They receive about one-half of a page in an eighty-page document. In two other places there is passing mention of them in connection with "ecclesial movements." Generally, ecclesial movements are understood in Latin America to refer to conservative middle-class organizations of European origin, such as Focolare or Opus Dei. To classify base communities with these movements is to suggest a very different direction from that which CEBs have taken in the past. Although the Santo Domingo documents do acknowledge the importance of certain features that may be considered characteristic of base communities—that is, lay leadership in areas with a shortage of clergy and the role of the laity in the transformation of social structures—there is a constant emphasis on the teaching authority of the bishops (the magisterium) and on the importance of following specifically Catholic social teachings. There is also repeated reference to holiness in a manner which suggests an individualistic, otherworldly religiosity, rather than the communitarian, this-worldly spirituality of the base communities.

The change in the composition of the Latin American episcopate between Medellín and Santo Domingo, along with the differences among priests and bishops that have always existed, explains the inconsistencies in pastoral policy that are evident in the Brazilian Catholic Church. There is one progressive position, however, on which the bishops have been consistent. This position, which appears in the Santo Domingo documents and is given a discussion of two full pages, is the advocacy of agrarian reform. The situation of land tenure and utilization is presented as "one of the most pressing claims on human development,"[8] and there is an encouragement of solidarity with "those organizations of small farmers and indigenous people who are struggling through just and legitimate channels to hold onto or reacquire their lands."[9]

Consistency with regard to agrarian reform is also characteristic of the Brazilian episcopate. It is the one issue on which all of the bishops are united, at least in terms of verbal commitment, despite the diversity of their views on other pastoral and social issues. This consistency is reflected in the policies of a national Church-linked organization: the Pastoral Land Commission.

The CPT

The Pastoral Land Commission (Comissão Pastoral da Terra, or CPT) was begun by a group of Brazilian bishops in 1975. Father Ricardo Rezende, who is a former regional coordinator of the organization, describes its origins:

> The CPT was founded after CIMI [*Conselho Indígena Missionário*— Missionary Indigenous Council], which was founded to deal with the problems of indigenous people. After that, bishops involved in CIMI, like Dom Pedro Casaldáliga and Dom Tomás Balduino, became concerned about the problems of the peasant. That was during the military dictatorship. It was a time of a lot of difficulties, a lot of conflict. And at that moment there arose the idea of creating an organization oriented toward the peasant, to give support and solidarity to the rural workers.[10]

The CPT grew out of a meeting of bishops organized by Dom Moacyr Grecchi in the city of Goiânia in 1975. This meeting may be seen as representing the Catholic Church's response to the problems generated by the government's new policies in relation to rural areas. Its stated purpose was "to sketch the basic lines for practical and pastoral attitudes in the face of the existing and latent conflicts between cattle companies and *posseiros*, as well as of the internal migrations resulting from those conflicts."[11] The CPT's specific pastoral mission was to be to help the local clergy to get to know the reality of the lives of their people. In order to do this, it would systematically gather data on rural problems. This is an activity of the CPT that has continued to the present time.

Since this founding meeting occurred during the military regime, the place where it was held was kept under surveillance by the police, who visibly surrounded the building. Nevertheless, their presence did not deter the bishops from creating an organization that would have an impact lasting far longer than the dictatorship.

Although the founders of the CPT were Catholic bishops, as have been all of its national presidents, it is not officially an agency of the National Conference of the Brazilian Bishops. As Father Rezende explains:

> The CPT is an ecumenical organization, with a pastoral relationship with the CNBB. Members of the Lutheran Church also participate. . . . The vice-presidency has been occupied by a Lutheran minister. . . . The link with the CNBB is pastoral, not legal. The CNBB does not choose the president of the CPT.

Officers of the CPT are elected by its assembly, which is composed of laity and clergy, and the president appoints the national secretary. So far, all of the national secretaries have been Catholic priests, although this is not an official requirement.

The organization is subdivided into nineteen regions, with regional offices usually located in state capitals. In addition, many dioceses maintain local offices as well. Ten of the fifteen parishes in this study were located in dioceses with CPT offices.

The sources of financial support for the CPT provide another example of its relative autonomy from the CNBB. It is funded by grants from Roman Catholic philanthropic organizations located in Europe, primarily in Germany and the Netherlands. Thus, although the CPT maintains friendly relations with the CNBB, its financial accountability is outside of Brazil. This could potentially allow staff members of the organization to function independently of the authority of the bishops. In any case, the relationship of the CNBB to the CPT appears to be a supportive one. As stated above, agrarian reform is one issue on which all the bishops have been united. This unity adds further strength to the work of the CPT.

As mentioned above, the CPT began with its main purpose as documentation, and this task has remained central to its work. Its regional offices gather data on all forms of conflict related to land. This includes occupations, evictions (legal and illegal), destruction of the crops of peasant farmers, burning of houses, assassinations, attempted assassinations, verbal death threats, violence against indigenous people, and labor violations, including numerous cases of slavery. The annual reports contain detailed information on these categories of conflict, including the names of people killed or threatened with death and the names of those believed to have perpetrated the crimes. Cases are listed by state and municipal district. Sources of information include eyewitness accounts, newspaper articles, and reports from churches and other organizations. As a result of these reports, the CPT has come to be recognized, even by persons with no connection to the Catholic Church, as the most reliable source of data on rural problems in Brazil.

In addition to documentation, the CPT is actively involved in defending the rights of the rural poor and in trying to bring about agrarian reform. The staff members in its regional and diocesan offices spend time visiting rural areas. They advise peasant farmers on starting unions of rural workers or on working within existing unions, and they give support to opposition groups within nonmilitant unions. The organization provides attorneys to help people through the process for gaining legal title to their land, to help farmers in resisting expulsion from land, to come to the aid of those who have been imprisoned or tortured, and to offer legal advice to the families of those who have been victimized by violence.

More recently, the CPT has been developing programs to offer peasant farmers the technical assistance of agronomists, who help them stay on the land by advising them on how to make it more productive. These agronomists provide information about farming methods that are protective of the environment, as well as about the choice of crops that are good for the soil and that bring a good return on the market.

There is also a religious component to the work of the CPT, which includes the annual land pilgrimages (*romarias da terra*). These events, which are organized by regional offices, use the symbols of traditional folk religion to strengthen people's sense of legitimacy of the struggle for land. Between 1,000 and 30,000 people have participated in each of these gatherings, which combine the centuries-old custom of pilgrimage, which has always been meaningful to the Brazilian peasant, with the contemporary theme of agrarian reform.

Another religious activity of the CPT is the encouragement of base communities. Some of my interviews with CEB members indicated that their communities began on the suggestion of CPT staff members. The creation of the CEBs results in a redirection of the religiosity that is already characteristic of many rural people, helping them to make their faith more biblical and communitarian. Thus, there develops a mutual support between the CEBs and the land struggle—with the spirituality developed in the base community giving people support in the struggle, while the struggle itself reinforces the solidarity within the base community.

There are certain policies that orient the work of the CPT. First of all, there is the advocacy of nonviolence in the struggle for land. CPT staff members explicitly discourage the use of weapons, and that attitude has been picked up by people active in base communities. Second, the CPT refrains from actually organizing land occupations, but rather provides support to occupations organized by peasant farmers themselves. That support may come in the form of material aid (for example, collecting food for people in an occupation), as well as legal assistance (providing an attorney to help process land claims). This nondirective approach closely relates to a third point: The CPT does not seek to become a social movement in the sense of directing the peasant farmers to follow specific tactics. An agronomist who works for the CPT explained its role in relation to land occupations:

It only enters after an occupation exists and when the problems begin, such as violence. And then the CPT acts . . . to try to help the people to organize themselves internally, to arrange for meetings of people from several areas, to exchange experiences, to find ways for the people to stay on the land, to conquer that land, to stimulate the creation of small groups for coordination within an area, to stimulate participation in a union.

This work is based on the belief that the organization of a peasant movement must come from the peasant farmers themselves. The CPT is there to facilitate, to advise, and to offer whatever legal and religious resources it is able to provide. It would be contrary to its policy, however, to impose prepackaged solutions. This has resulted in some mutual criticism between people involved in the CPT and members of the Movement of the Landless (*Movimento dos Sem Terra*). The latter organization, begun by people connected with the church in the south of Brazil but now autonomous, has formulated a specific policy of organizing land occupations, and some of its members have been accused of advocating violence. In any case, this movement has not taken hold in the north. Most of the peasant farmers whom I interviewed had never heard of it. The only exceptions were in one municipal district, where one of the base community leaders had been a national secretary for the Movement of the Landless, and in another, where the daughter of a base community leader was among seven members of the movement who had been arrested in a distant city and charged with inciting guerrilla activity (the charges were never proven, and the seven people were eventually released).

In addition to providing written documentation and direct support to peasant farmers, the CPT also serves a public role in relation, for example, to the courts and the mass media. A staff member explained these functions:

> The CPT acts with great power in the work of denunciation. . . . Sometimes we have to confront a judge with a denunciation. There is also the link with the press, with international human rights organizations, and the government. Often we accompany farmers as far as Brasília, in order to give reports to the federal agencies.

The impact of the CPT on the lives of poor people in the Amazon region is evident from the interview data. In the initial interviews with peasant farmers, I had not asked specifically about their opinion of the CPT. There was a question, however, that asked whether there were any non-Church organizations in the region that were giving the farmers support in their struggle for land. In all but one municipal district (the one in which a CEB leader was involved in the Movement of the Landless), people replied that there were not. However, interviewees in six parishes spontaneously volunteered the information that the CPT had been very helpful. In subsequent interviews, I did specifically ask people whether the CPT had been helpful to them and in what ways. In almost all cases, people replied positively, saying that the CPT had given advice and orientation to enable peasant farmers to stay on the land, had sent agronomists and lawyers, had provided people with assistance in preparing needed documents, and had helped organize the union. In the words of the peasant farmers themselves:

> The CPT was the first organization that gave support and that informed the people that the land did not have a title. And after we won the union, they continued to give support.

The CPT helps a lot because, at the hour of necessity of the people, the CPT sends lawyers, for example, when [the police] arrested a farmer illegally. They also help in the building of the union and in several of the projects of the farmers' association. They have agronomists who help the farmers.

The CPT is a great force that helps us a lot, because all of us of this region are people without schooling. Sometimes we need to write a report, or we need to write a denunciation, and they show us how. They help us and they teach us. They help with the work of the union assembly, to write reports, to organize demonstrations. And if there is violence against the workers, they provide a lawyer to help us take it to court.

The CPT is everything for us. When we organized the association, they gave encouragement. They gave information. They encourage us in everything.

These interviews with CEB members, as well as with activists not specifically connected with the Catholic Church, present an image of the CPT that is consistent with the organization's official position, as seen through its documents and in my interviews with CPT staff members. It appears to be the single agency that is doing the most to help rural poor people gain and hold on to land and to organize efforts toward agrarian reform. Its ties to the Catholic Church both strengthen its legitimacy from the point of view of peasant farmers and help to keep bishops and other church people on the side of agrarian reform. Thus, the CPT provides an institutional means though which religion is contributing to democratic social change.

Conclusion

The analysis in this chapter shows the contradictory directions within the Roman Catholic Church that explain the inconsistencies in pastoral policy seen in some of the case studies. The concern of the episcopate will generally be focused on means to enable the Church to exert influence over the society, through the political behavior of the lay people. To do this, ways must be found to keep the laity within the Church. Sometimes this is done by giving the laity increased decision-making power, which we may interpret as a temporary shift in the religious division of labor. At other times, however, the bishops demand a return to orthodoxy. The support of even the conservative bishops for land reform suggests that the bishops are aware that they cannot push the laity too far on issues of survival.

9

BASE COMMUNITIES: LINK BETWEEN RELIGION AND AGRARIAN ACTIVISM

In Brazil, base ecclesial communities are a primary link between religion and social change. As the manifestation of the Roman Catholic Church among poor populations, they are comprised mainly of people who have a stake in transforming the existing social structure. In rural areas, most members of CEBs are peasant farmers, often those without land of their own. Hence, the rural base community represents the Church at the everyday level of agrarian inequality and conflict. Also, since base communities are practical organizations, insofar as their members discuss the application of their religious beliefs to solving problems in their social milieu, these members are likely to be active participants in efforts toward agrarian reform.

Origins of the Base Communities

Social change was not the initial, explicit purpose of those clergy who came up with the idea of base communities. They were a pastoral innovation, a means of revitalizing the Church, despite a shortage of priests, in the face of aggressive proselytizing by Pentecostal Protestants. They became vehicles of social change for three reasons: (1) They developed at a time when the Church was beginning to pay attention to social problems, partly as a result of the Catholic Action movement that was influential in Brazil in the 1950s and early 1960s,[1] partly as a defensive reaction to the growing strength of socialist groups; (2) CEBs emphasized lay initiative, and, since the majority of the lay people in Brazil are poor, this would open up a space for the poor to develop and express their viewpoints; (3) the model of group dynamics used in the CEBs was the conscientization method developed in the Basic Education Movement, a church-related organization which emphasized a critical analysis of the social reality.[2] After 1964 that critical analysis took on added importance. When the generals took over the government, all other groups working for social change were suppressed. Base communities, which appeared to be innocuous Bible study groups, were allowed to continue, thus becoming the only space for expressing dissent during the most repressive years of the military regime.

Although the unit that is presently known as the base community gradually evolved from pastoral experiments in various dioceses, there is evidence that the earliest of these occurred in Maranhão.[3] At first they were not called base communities but rural chapels. As early as 1952, Dom José Delgado, who was at that time the archbishop of São Luís, was seeking a way to help priests manage their very large, spread-out rural parishes. His solution to this problem was parish decentralization. He subdivided the parishes into chapels which would be administered by lay people. His auxiliary bishop, Dom Antônio Fragoso (who later became bishop of Crateus), organized training programs for the lay leaders, and afterwards maintained close contact with them.

The Question of Episcopal Support

In 1963, both bishops were transferred to other dioceses, and Dom José Delgado was replaced by Dom João José da Mota, who was not supportive of lay leadership and who remained in São Luís for twenty years. The seeds of the CEBs had been planted, however, and they would continue to flourish. Priests and sisters had become accustomed to encouraging lay leadership, and hundreds of lay people had already gone through Dom Antônio's training programs. Furthermore, not all of these people would find themselves in a diocese controlled by a conservative bishop. Over the next two decades, new dioceses would be created in Maranhão, and some of these would be headed by bishops who did encourage CEBs. As will be shown below, a statewide network of base commuities would link people from different dioceses, helping to sustain CEB membership in dioceses with unsupportive bishops.

Considering the recent experience of São Paulo, however, where the base communities have been weakened by the subdivision of the archdiocese into several smaller dioceses, some of which are headed by bishops not supportive of CEBs, we must still ask why communities in Maranhão continued to flourish when episcopal support was not always there. There are at least four relevant factors that distinguish the two cases. First of all, there is the fact that the vast majority of CEBs in Maranhão are rural, while those in São Paulo are on the urban periphery. Because of the vast geographic distances between rural

CEBs, the lay leaders are able to develop greater autonomy from the clergy than those in urban areas. Urban parishes tend to be much more compact. In São Paulo, the CEBs are so close together that several groups may share one community center, and that center is likely to be a short drive from the parish house. Thus, a priest can participate in CEB meetings frequently. If he withdraws his support, it will be felt immediately.[4] In rural areas, however, a priest may visit a CEB once a month or even only once every six months, depending on the condition of unpaved roads during the rainy season. This means that when a change in diocesan policy reaches the parish level, it may take some time before all CEB members become aware of it, and, in areas where the visits of the priest are infrequent, they may even be able to ignore it.

A second difference between Maranhão and São Paulo relates to the diversity among the bishops. Since the subdivision of the archdiocese of São Luís occurred gradually, as a natural development that resulted from migrations and population increases throughout the state, there was no one type of bishop assigned to each new diocese. A few of the bishops were supportive of base communities. Others did not actively promote CEBs, but neither did they prevent sisters, priests, and lay people from organizing them. This environment in which CEBs were free to develop had an impact even in those dioceses with bishops who were opposed to innovations in the Church. As peasant farmers continued to migrate in the traditional fashion characteristic of people in Maranhão—moving either because the land became exhausted or because grileiros pushed them out—those with CEB experience in their previous dioceses would sometimes organize CEBs in their new locations. Both these lay people and the progressive sisters and priests who found themselves with an unsupportive bishop would get support from their counterparts in other dioceses. One of the vehicles for this support was the statewide gathering, a practice which began in Maranhão in 1970, five years before the national gatherings of base communities began to be organized.[5] These statewide meetings were held twice a year from 1972 through 1981, and have been held annually since that time, allowing for frequent contact among lay people, sisters, and priests from all twelve dioceses.

The third factor that distinguishes Maranhão from São Paulo is the social climate of popular movements. With the easing of political repression after 1978, poor people's movements flourished in São Paulo. Once CEB members became involved in these movements, they had less time to devote to their base communities, even though the CEBs had been the training ground that prepared people for activism. In Maranhão, on the other hand, nonreligious social movements have not taken hold on a large scale, and, consequently, CEBs have remained the chief vehicle for activism. Because much of this activism is related to land issues, people need the base communities for their survival. Many of the strongest CEBs in Maranhão (with strength defined in terms of number of members, frequency of meetings, lay initiative in religious matters, and involvement in social activism) are located in areas with a recent history of land conflicts.

The fourth factor relates to the timing of the development of base communities in the two regions. As mentioned earlier, the predecessors to CEBs in Maranhão, the rural chapels, were begun in the 1950s. By 1965, the first groups calling themselves base ecclesial communities were already in existence.[6] This was a time when there was strong support for this type of innovation, integrating lay initiative in religious matters with activism on social issues, both from the National Conference of the Brazilian Bishops and from the Vatican. The greatest period of growth of CEBs in São Paulo, however, was in the 1970s and early 1980s. At this point, the conservative forces in the Latin American Catholic Church were beginning to mobilize in reaction against the consequences of the Medellín conference, and these forces were strengthened by the shift in Vatican policy toward renewed orthodoxy that became evident after the arrival of Pope John Paul II in 1978. By this time, the strength and relative autonomy of CEBs in Maranhão were well established.

The Role of the Pastoral Agent[7]

Since the religious literature on CEBs sometimes gives the impression that they spontaneously arise from the lay poor people themselves, it is important to look at the role played by middle-class pastoral agents (sisters, priests, and lay church workers) in their development. The interviews both with members of base communities and with pastoral agents included questions about how the CEBs in the parish had begun, whether sisters and priests were supportive of them, and whether there were differences in pastoral styles among the sisters and priests. Since interviewees in each parish were from any number of different CEBs, there were varied responses to the question of how the CEBs were begun. In all but one of the parishes, however, the responses showed the importance of pastoral agents in the origins of the communities.

The base community began with the people meeting in the houses of neighbors. It began with the help of Sister Francisca.

There was an accompaniment by a priest—almost nine years with Father José. He gave a lot of encouragement, and it was through him that we discovered what a base community was. He helped us very much to continue.

It was with the support of Father Osvaldo, because it was at that time that we were beginning to get to know him. And he gives us complete support, including with things we don't know, because we are a new community.

Table 9.1 shows the distribution of responses to the question of who started the base communities.

TABLE 9.1

Who Started the CEBs?

CEBs begun by:	Number of Parishes			Total (3 states)
	Maranhão	Pará	Tocantins	
Priest(s) only	1	0	1	2
Sister(s) only	0	1	0	1
Lay missionary only	0	0	1	1
Farmers themselves only	0	0	1	1
Priest(s) and sister(s)	1	0	0	1
Priest(s), sister(s), and lay missionary	0	0	2	2
Priest(s) and farmers	2	2	0	4
Priest(s), sister(s), and farmers	1	2	0	3
TOTALS	5	5	5	15

There were only two parishes in which everyone replied that the CEBs had all been started by priests, one in which they said that all had been started by sisters, and one in which the credit was given to a lay missionary. In three more parishes, the responses indicated a variety of pastoral agents—priests and sisters, or priests, sisters, and a lay missionary. Hence, in seven out of the fifteen parishes, the persons responsible for starting CEBs were middle-class pastoral agents. There was only one parish in which all the respondents said that the CEBs had been started by the peasant farmers themselves. In the remaining seven, the responses indicated a combination of farmers and pastoral agents. Even in the one parish where the peasant farmers themselves had organized the communities, as well as in cases of individual CEBs within the other parishes where lay people had taken the initiative, interviewees indicated that they later sought the guidance of a priest. Following are explanations by two of the farmers as to how they started base communities:

> When I first came here, I saw so many people—boys, girls, married people—who were not yet baptized. I looked at these people, in such an isolated place. I felt the necessity, the necessity of the people. And I went to Colinas and got Father Martinho. He celebrated the first Mass here. He did fifty-eight baptisms that day, including children and older people. Then he gave us help here for about a year.

> I was invited to take a Bible course in Conceição do Araguaia with Father Pedro and Sister Aurora. After that course, I came here and I felt that there had to be a base community. I began to work, to raise up the community. And in Xinguara, when I created the community there, it was Father Chico who helped us.

In all cases where at least some of the interviewees indicated that CEBs had been begun by lay people, these lay people had migrated from other parishes where they had had experience of a base community, usually one organized by a sister or a priest. Thus, it would appear that the pastoral agents are key actors in the development of base communities. Although other researchers have claimed that encouragement from bishops is a necessary condition for the flourishing of CEBS,[8] this has not been the case for all of the parishes in this study. The presence of strong and numerous base communities in dioceses in which bishops are either opposed to lay initiative or refrain from actively encouraging it—and these two possibilities represent the majority of dioceses in this study—suggest that other factors are involved. The interviews I conducted reveal that those factors are the pastoral agents, who support each other through interdiocesan networks, and a social context in which there are agrarian conflicts and a virtual absence of nonreligious activist groups supporting people engaged in those conflicts.[9]

Although most of the pastoral agents function in an indirect manner in relation to CEBs, there is admittedly some directness in their initial contact with potential CEB members. Several sisters and priests stated in interviews that that contact began in the context of traditional circuit visits to the isolated sections of the parish, at which times people expected the priests to celebrate Mass and to perform baptisms and weddings. The priests and sisters used this opportunity to suggest to the lay people a new way of relating to the Church, one in which they themselves would take responsibility for the religious life of their community, as leaders of Sunday worship in the absence of a priest and as instructors for people preparing for marriage or for the baptism of their children. People were invited to attend Bible courses and leadership training courses. The sisters, priests, and lay pastoral agents who teach such courses encourage a socially critical interpretation of the Bible. Generally they lead people to this interpretation not by lectures but by raising questions and facilitating discussions.

In response to the question of whether sisters and priests are supportive of base communities, all of the lay interviewees in parishes where there were sisters replied that they were supportive. This was also the case with most of the priests, although there were six parishes where people gave mixed responses. In five of these, respondents qualified their answer, saying that some priests were more supportive than others.

Yes, but not this priest here. It seems like he only gives support to the rich. Not to the poor.

In the south I knew priests who did not give support. Conservatives. They defended big property. But here, for example, all give support.

The priests—not all. There are many who give support. The bishop is very good. He always gives support. There are priests who give support, but they do not participate in an area of conflict. Perhaps they are afraid. They try to remain more neutral. Then there are other priests who are giving real support. For that they are threatened with death.

In the sixth parish, people said that the previous priest had been supportive, but the present one was not.

Differences among Pastoral Agents

The questions about pastoral agents also turned up some differences between sisters and priests in relation to pastoral approaches, although it is important to emphasize that these differences do not show up in all cases.[10] Some of the lay people said:

The sister is more together with the people. She has a special affection.

The nuns have a much better method. They converse more, on specific subjects. . . . It's their manner of organization, of orientation.

An important factor accounting for the differences between sisters and priests that do appear is institutional role. The actual day-by-day work of organizing and supporting the base communities is carried out mainly by women religious. Sisters who work at the grassroots level are almost always directly involved in some aspect of CEB work—for example, community organizing, youth groups, women's groups, child health work, political education, and leadership training. The work of the priests, however, is restricted by their sacramental and administrative functions. Several of the sisters talked about this difference. For example, one said:

The majority of the people are very traditional in terms of faith. They demand very traditional things—baptism, marriage, Mass from time to time, feast days—and for that the priest always has to be present. A priest who assumes a parish doesn't have a choice. He has to appear in the villages, in the communities, on those occasions. . . . But the sister, who is not part of the hierarchy, often can freely choose the number of villages she will visit and the pastoral sectors in which she will work. So she is freer to work in chosen areas and thus can go deeper.

A lay woman also attributed the difference between priests and nuns to the sacramental function of the priest:

The priest celebrates the Mass, the sisters don't. They are different from the priests because they *visit* the communities. They take whole days to visit the communities.

The time and energy of the CEB-oriented clergy is largely taken up with traveling to communities to say Mass—sometimes as many as eight communities in one week. This work is particularly burdensome for those priests whose parishes are spread out over a large rural area with poor roads. Travel by some combination of jeep, boat, bicycle, motorcycle, horseback, and foot is not uncommon. The published diary of a priest in one of the parishes of the Amazon region contains repeated references to the hectic pace of ritual duties in a large rural parish:

We went to the Santa Luzia community where, besides the Mass, there were twenty-two baptisms. We left there exhausted.[11]

Although there are clergy who manage to be effective, even charismatic, community organizers in spite of their work load, it is clear that women religious have an advantage in this task. Because they are free of ritual functions, they have more time and energy to devote to organizing the base communities. There are some pastors who recognize this and leave the organizing work entirely to women religious. There are others who do all of the work related to the base communities because they do not have sisters in their parish. There are yet others who share the work with sisters but acknowledge that women do a better job of it. This was indicated in interviews with priests:

Those who work at the level of the community, those who accompany it, and those who give the most to this work are the women.

They work better than a priest in the community.
In what sense?
Animating the people. Getting to know the people. Preparing the people to live their faith. . . . If this community had ten priests, maybe these priests could do the work that those three sisters are doing.

Within the context of his sacramental role, the priest still has opportunities to influence the ideological development of CEBs. Many of the priests whom I observed and interviewed were clearly oriented toward liberation theology. The way they conducted Mass, the selection of hymns, and the topics of sermons demonstrated (1) the encouragement of lay input and (2) an emphasis on themes of social justice.

Sisters can also encourage lay input and emphasize social justice. There is another area, however, in which priests make a unique contribution to the development of base communities. That area is institutional support and legitimation. Some priests use their institutional legitimation to give support to the side of the peasant farmers, while others use it to dominate sisters and lay people. The priest has authority over the women religious and the lay workers in his parish, and he has the option to decide whether to wield that authority or to develop an egalitarian model. Furthermore, lay people recognize the priest's authority. Sisters have told me that they would have little influence with the majority of the laity if they ever appeared to be in opposition to the pastor. On the other hand, lay people will support both sisters and priests against the bishop, and have indicated this in interviews. Some of the situations described in this book demonstrate that (1) the priest has more influence than the bishop in the generating of base communities, especially in rural areas, and (2) if there is opposition from the parish priest, women religious encounter great difficulty in organizing the communities. This greater influence of the priest was clearly seen in the case studies in São Luís and Arame. When the bishop wanted to undercut the lay initiative in the base communities, he had to appoint a new pastor to the parish. Of course, the bishop does have the authority to remove a priest of whose approach he does not approve, but there are limitations to this strategy. In one of the dioceses in this study, the bishop had to stop expelling progressive priests and sisters because he was aggravating an already serious personnel shortage.

There may also be some difference in pastoral style between sisters and priests because of gender expectations. Among the lay people who stated that they saw differences between priests and sisters, many attributed this to the fact that the sisters are women. In addition, since the majority of base community members are women, it may be that they relate more easily to someone of their own sex. They stated, for example, that sisters get closer to the people, that they are like mothers to the people, and that they are easy to talk with.

> The sister—I don't know if it's because she's a woman—but we find it easier to relate to her and to talk about problems. With the priest we feel more of a distance. For me, the sister is almost like a mother.

> When a sister is in the midst of the people, we don't find differences between her and the people. The priest is different. . . . I find the priest more closed and the woman more open.

On the other hand, it is important not to exaggerate gender differences among pastoral agents. Many of the progressive priests are working hard to develop more interactive, less authoritarian ways of interacting with lay people, and are also making an effort to treat sisters as equals. The success of the efforts of some of these priests is evidenced in the fact that about half of the lay interviewees said that they saw no differences between sisters and priests. Hence, it is likely that the ability of the sisters to get closer to the people is related less to gender-typed behavior than to institutional role—which allows the sisters freedom from the ritual functions that are central to the role of the priest.

Sociopolitical Consequences of Base Communities

Once rural base communities are established, the pastoral agents visit them monthly or less often, depending on the difficulty of travel conditions in a particular area, leaving the weekly operation and the main responsibility for the CEB to the lay leaders. If a CEB runs into difficulty, for example, because of internal conflict, a pastoral agent is likely to visit the community and try to help its members resolve the problem, ideally by encouraging them to talk about it, rather than to impose a solution.

The fact of lay leadership of the CEBs is important in relation to their sociopolitical role. Because they are lay led, it may be said that, while they represent a direct influence of religion on the social environment, they do not represent a direct institutional influence. In other words, the sociopolitical consequences of CEBs do not indicate a merger of church and state. This point is particularly salient in light of the increasing religious pluralism that characterizes contemporary Brazilian society. The domination of the political scene by a single religion would have a detrimental effect on the potential for democracy. On the other hand, the political influence of CEBs, as lay groups, is a democratizing one, particularly in rural areas.

As will be shown in chapter 10, the mobilization of peasant farmers has led to their gaining land. My interviews with the farmers, as well as with those rural leaders who have no formal ties with the Church, indicate that CEBs are contributing to these victories. To demonstrate the specific role of CEBs in this process it is necessary to show that (1) discussions in the communities help rural poor people to become aware of their rights in relation to land and give them courage to persevere in the struggle, and (2) CEB members seek out organizations and people, such as lawyers, who can help them to achieve those rights.

Evidence for the first point—that discussions in CEBs help people to become aware of their rights and give them courage—can be drawn from responses to the questions in the interviews as to the importance of the base community in the subject's life and the importance of faith in relation to the struggle. In relation to one or both of these questions, 84 percent of the peasant farmers interviewed (34 men and 27 women) drew a clear connection between the faith developed in the base communities and the struggle for land, saying, for example, that participation in the base communities helped them to become aware of their rights or gave them courage.

Only by means of the CEBs do we discover our rights, as workers, in relation to agrarian reform.

I have faced this struggle in the union movement because of the Word of God, because I've studied about the struggles for land in the Old Testament, for example, in Canaan. Because of this I began to study the federal constitution . . . where many rights of the rural workers are guaranteed.

The base community helped me because it has given me the strength to keep going. . . . I feel that God always protects me, helps me. I have never stopped being at the service of God. When gunmen came to my house—it happened several times, because I was marked to die—the Bible was always on my table. . . . And for this reason I would never want to live in a place where I could not organize a base community.

The interviews also give evidence of the second point—that CEB members seek out organizations and people who can help them to achieve their legal rights. In all but two parishes,[12] interviewees reported getting help from the Pastoral Land Commission, and in four cases they referred to specific lawyers sent by that organization. In three parishes where land occupations occurred without prior organization, people later sought help from the Pastoral Land Commission and from the Union of Rural Workers.

Getting help from people or organizations and linking faith to activism are two characteristics of CEB members that demonstrate connections between base communities and rural mobilization. The characteristic style of faith developed within the CEBs provides an illustration of how belief, according to Maduro's theory, may have an influence on the larger society, along with the other components of religion—that is, practice and organizational structures. This change in belief is derived from religious practice—that is, the study of the Bible in relation to a critical analysis of people's experience of an oppressive social system. The organizational structure of the base community provides people with a source of support for these new beliefs and practices. Chapter 10 will take this analysis a step further by providing evidence that CEB participation actually leads people into commitments to practical action—specifically, joining rural unions and participating in land occupations.

10

CEBs, Rural Unions, and the Struggle for Land

The previous chapter examined the links between base communities and agrarian activism through the statements of belief and experiences of CEB members themselves. This chapter will continue the analysis by reporting interviewees' estimates of rates of participation of CEB members in rural unions and in land occupations or in resistance to eviction from land. These two criteria—union membership and actual action—will thus be used to reinforce the evidence of the direct connection between religion and rural mobilization. In addition, indications of the actual impact that CEBs are having on the rural social structure will be presented in the form of information about their success in gaining land as well as about violence and death threats against the peasant farmers and their parish priests coming from large landowners.

The STRs

Rural Unions in Brazil are called "STR"s—*Sindicatos de Trabalhadores Rurais*. The literal English translation, "Unions of Rural Workers," may be a bit misleading. In English the word "workers" generally refers to people who earn a wage, in contrast, for example, to a tenant farmer, who might be considered self-employed. However, in Brazilian Portuguese, the word "worker" has a broader meaning, that of working *class* or popular class—in other words, poor people. In the rural context, those classified as workers might include not only wage laborers, such as cowhands or sugar cane cutters, but also tenant farmers, squatters on public land, small-property owners, or people who survive mainly by extractive activity, such as rubber tappers. Thus the term *trabalhador rural* (rural worker) is often used interchangeably with *lavrador* (peasant farmer). The only apparent distinction between the terms is that *trabalhador rural* implies a certain consciousness of class, and hence is likely to be used more often by people who are members of militant rural unions.

Militant unions (in contrast to pelego unions, which, as explained in chapter 3, are controlled by people favorable to large landowners) are those which provide local support to rural working-class people in all aspects of the land struggle—for example, land occupations, evictions, cases of forced labor, legal problems, harassment by government agents, and victimization by violence. In many cases, there is a relationship of mutual support between the unions and the Pastoral Land Commission. CPT agents frequently encourage peasant farmers to form or join unions, so that they will have an organization assisting them at the local level. Help from a union is likely to be more immediate than that from the CPT because every municipal district may have a union, and its directorate is composed of people who are scattered throughout the rural area, thus providing the peasant farmer with a close connection. The president of an STR receives a small salary, which enables him or her to be available full time at the union headquarters in town. The unions cannot, however, carry on the defense of rural workers on their own, because their economic resources are limited. The CPT, on the other hand, has some resources to provide the assistance of attorneys and agronomists. It also has contacts with international organizations that can call attention to particularly severe problems, such as the murder of an activist or the violent eviction of farmers from their land.

Unions, Corporatism, and the Church

To understand the origins of the distinction between militant and nonmilitant unions, we need to look at their rather convoluted history. During the 1930s, a time when labor unions in other parts of the world were being organized by workers with socialist leanings, Brazilian unions were part of a strategy for maintaining government control over all sectors of society and preventing any form of dissent. In 1930, military intervention installed the presidency of Getúlio Vargas, a populist leader who ran Brazil for fifteen years, first as president, then as dictator, and, six years after the restoration of democracy, as the democratically elected president.[1] Vargas's model was corporatist—that is, establishing interest groups allegedly to represent the various sectors in Brazilian society but organizing them vertically, with government control, rather than horizontally, according to social class.[2] Unions were established and regulated by the government. Thus, every occupation in Brazil became unionized without the workers gaining any real economic or political power. This strategy effectively turned unions into paternalistic structures, doling out social assistance (such as limited medical and retirement benefits) and preventing them from becoming militant class-based organizations, at least for the duration of the dictatorship. Since there were no signs of mobilization in the countryside in the 1930s, Vargas did not arrange for the organization of rural unions. However, as will be shown below, the corporatist structure would be in place to be applied to organizations of peasant farmers thirty years later.

This corporatist model has provided the legal basis and the structure by which many unions in Brazil operate to the present day. With the end of Vargas's Estado Novo regime in 1945, however, some space opened up for alternative organizations. In the rural areas, the first to emerge were peasant leagues started by members of the Communist Party in the 1940s, although the strongest leagues would be those organized by the Socialist lawyer Francisco Julião in the 1950s and early 1960s.[3] Because these organizations were not officially established as unions, they were initially free of direct government control. Between 1955 and 1960, their membership increased to an estimated 100,000 people.[4] They became particularly strong during the presidency of Juscelino Kubitschek (1956-1961). This president, who sought to move Brazil into the modern era by accelerating industrialization, building roads, and planning the new national capital of Brasília, was supported more by urban business leaders than by the rural oligarchy. The urban elite favored moderate agrarian reform because they perceived it as a way to create a rural middle class that would be potential consumers of industrial products.[5] So in the political climate of the Kubitschek administration, the peasant leagues flourished.

Meanwhile, their rapid growth raised antisocialist fears among the Roman Catholic clergy, who sought to establish their own rural unions as alternatives to the peasant leagues, thus keeping the peasants under the wing of the Church. This motive was explained by a bishop:

> Then there were the peasant leagues, whose leader was said to be "red," Marxist, Communist. . . . This was not the only reason the Church was concerned about strengthening the rural unions. However, Pope Pius IX did say that the Church had lost the [industrial] working class and must not also lose the rural class.[6]

This bishop had been involved, as a young priest, in a church program in the Archdiocese of Natal, in the northeast region of Brazil, called the Rural Assistance Service (*Serviço de Assistência Rural*, or SAR). SAR combined religious ministry with social work, in the effort to deal with problems of poverty and social disorganization that were plaguing the region around Natal in the 1940s and 1950s. By the late 1960s, people in SAR were becoming concerned about the Communist threat that they perceived in the peasant leagues. That was the point when they began organizing rural unions.

SAR's initial strategy was to organize the unions in the parts of the Natal archdiocese that were adjacent to the state of Paraíba, where Julião's leagues were especially strong.[7] In Pernambuco, where the peasant leagues had originated, a similar effort (*Serviço de Orientação Rural de Pernambuco*, or SORPE) was begun by a priest who had been in contact with people in Natal. These unions organized by church people were far less militant than the peasant leagues. Rather than advocating agrarian reform, they sought protection for the rights of peasants and sugar cane workers under the existing system of land tenure. Eventually, both Julião's leagues and the Church's unions would come under government regulation.

Paradoxically, it was a president with a leftist image, João Goulart, who would establish corporatist control over the peasant movement. Goulart, whose administration lasted from 1961 to 1964, was actually a populist in the Vargas tradition. It is likely that he courted the left in an attempt to control it, although this flirtation gave him enough of a "Communist" image among his enemies to enable them to justify the military coup that ended his administration in 1964. In March 1963, Goulart enacted the Rural Labor Statute, which extended federal legislation to rural workers, establishing norms for the organization and recognition of their unions.[8] Goulart's plan was that in order for peasant organizations to be legally recognized, they would have to be established as unions, and whatever group (peasant leagues, Catholic Church, or Communist Party) had the largest number of unions in a particular state would get to control the state federation.[9] Thus, the peasant leagues and the Catholic Church entered into intense competition. However, when the military later took over the government, the new regime outlawed the peasant leagues and solidified corporatist control over the rural unions. This control remained in effect until the political opening of 1978 once again allowed for more autonomy within the workers' movement.

Base Communities and Militant Unions

The Church-linked unions that emerged in the 1980s turned out to be considerably more militant than those of the early 1960s. There are two likely reasons for this. First, the experience of the repression between 1968 and 1978 pushed the Brazilian Catholic Church to the left. Social programs previously encouraged by the clergy to undercut socialist movements were themselves transformed into leftist initiatives as the Church became the only space for dissent. The second reason for the difference between previous and present unions is in the sources within the Church of union organization. In their earlier incarnation, rural unions were mainly the creation of the clergy. The newer unions, on the other hand, have been started by lay members of base communities who are also peasant farmers (and membership is not restricted to people active in the Catholic Church). Thus, the lay leadership nurtured in the CEBs stimulated more activism from people at the bottom of the social structure. For these landless peasants, agrarian reform would become the central issue, and, as a result, the unions they created after the end of the military regime would be as militant as the peasant leagues had previously been.

Vestiges of corporatism still remain in the syndical structure, which accounts for the existence of both militant and nonmilitant workers' organizations. Rural unions must be part of state and national federations, and there can be only one union representing each occupational category in any municipal district. Because of the rapid settlement of Legal Amazônia, however, there have been many new municipal districts established in the past twenty years. In those places, base community members have frequently been the first people to organize rural unions, and these unions have been aggressive in helping peasant farmers to become aware of their legal rights, to gain land, and to develop a belief in the need for more structural change by means of agrarian reform. This was clearly the case in Arame, in Rio Maria, and in the three parishes studied in the Bico do Papagaio. In other places, however, activists have had to contend with pelego unions. Thus, in some municipal districts, particularly in Maranhão, where there are older settlements, as well as in a few places in Pará and Tocantins, a major task for activists from the CEBs has been to win elections within the pelego unions, so that they may gain control of their directorates and shift their focus toward mobilization of the rural population. Prior to achieving this goal, they form militant opposition groups within these unions. This was the case, for example, in Santa Rita until 1986.

Table 10.1 shows the different patterns of the emergence of STRs in the fifteen parishes studied. In six of the municipal districts, the union was founded by members of CEBs.[10] In six other cases, a union that had been manipulated by the landowners was taken over by base community members. This is a consistent pattern that emerged from the interviews with people whose unions were previously pelego.

TABLE 10.1

Patterns of Emergence of Rural Unions

Type of Pattern	Pará	Maranhão	Tocantins	Totals
Founded by CEB members	2	1	3	6
Taken over by CEB members	2	2	2	6
Not yet taken over	1	2	0	3
TOTALS	5	5	5	15

One of the CEB members who was also a union officer described the process by which a union is taken over:

> In '82 we began to take over the union. It began at the grassroots, with the ACR,[11] in the church. . . . We lost the first election, in '82. After, in '84, we formed a slate. Then we won the directorate, but the president remained pelego. In '88 we won the presidency.

In the three remaining cases, the union has not yet been won over. In only two of these cases is the problem the usual type of pelego union. These two unions have within them opposition groups organized by people from CEBs. The third case is a peculiar one in which the union leadership appears to have elements both of the Communist Party (PC do B) and of organized crime. The main activity of the union officers is the processing of requests from elderly people for government retirement benefits. Potential retirees need to document the fact that they have been engaged in the line of work from which they seek to retire. The government recognizes the union as a source of the documentation that these people are, indeed, rural workers, but does not require that these workers have been members of the union. This particular union, however, does require the elderly people to pay membership dues in order to obtain the documentation they need in order to qualify for the retirement benefits. Base community members have criticized this union for (1) taking advantage of impoverished old people for financial gain and (2) failing to devote time to organizing the workers for dealing effectively with land problems. In this municipal district, very few of the base community members are active in the union. A few CEB leaders have been elected to the board of directors, but not in sufficient numbers to change the union's orientation or to challenge its present leadership.

Table 10.2 shows the present predominance of CEB people in union leadership and in general membership.

TABLE 10.2

CEB Members' Participation in Rural Unions

Composition of Union	Pará	Maranhão	Tocantins	Totals
Majority of leaders are from CEBs	3	3	5	11
PC do B dominates leadership	2	0	0	2
Pelego union with CEB opposition	0	2	0	2
Totals for leadership	5	5	5	15
Majority of members are from CEBs	3	3	5	11

In eleven of the unions, the majority of the leadership is composed of people from base communities. In the remaining unions, two are dominated by the Communist Party and two are pelego, with a militant CEB-led opposition. The eleven unions with the predominance of CEB people in their membership are not exactly the same ones as the eleven with a majority of leaders from the CEBs. One of the unions that is dominated by the PC do B still has a majority of base community people in its membership, because it was founded by CEB members and the distancing from the PC do B leadership is a recent phenomenon. On the other hand, one of the formerly pelego unions which now has a majority of base community people in its leadership has a membership in which less than half are CEB people. In this union, however, the majority of *active* members are from CEBs.

All of the militant unions support occupations of land by peasant farmers. Let us now look at the participation of base community members in those actions.

Land Occupations

In addition to joining or starting unions, there is evidence that CEB members participate in land occupations. The interviews revealed that there are three types of occupations: organized takeovers, spontaneous entrance, and resistance to eviction. These three types will be described below. Table 10.3 illustrates the number of parishes in each of the three states studied according to type of land occupation. Organized takeovers occurred mostly in Maranhão, spontaneous entrance in Pará, and resistance to eviction in both Maranhão and Tocantins. The total number of land occupations for Maranhão (seven) exceeds the number of parishes studied in that state (five) because interviews in two of the parishes indicated that there had been more than one type of occupation.

TABLE 10.3

Number of Parishes with Each Type of Land Occupation

	Pará	Maranhão	Tocantins	Totals
Organized takeovers	0	4	1	5
Spontaneous entrance	4	0	1	5
Resistance to eviction	1	3	3	7
TOTALS	5	7	5	17

Organized takeovers—that is, those for which people got together in a group and decided to occupy an area of land—occurred in five of the parishes. In three of the cases in Maranhão, the decision to occupy land emerged from discussions in base communities. One of the organizers of an occupation, who was also a base community leader, described the process:

> Thanks be to God, with the power of the base communities, the people began the land conquests. There have been large numbers of workers who became conscious and participated in the struggle. . . . We have this consciousness because of the work of Father José.

In a fourth case, also in Maranhão, some of the occupants were CEB members, although strategies for the occupations were not discussed within their communities. In the fifth, which was in Tocantins, the CEBs were organized after the occupations were already in progress.

Spontaneous entrance refers to occupations which happened without much advance planning or any intention to make a public statement but simply out of people's desperation to have a place where they could grow food. These occurred in five parishes (four in Pará and one across the Araguaia River in a nearby area of Tocantins). In many of these situations, landless farmers would secretly enter, clear, and plant an area without the immediate knowledge of the owner, who, in most of these cases, was not using the land. This situation was described in an interview with a priest who has worked for many years in this region, both in a parish and in the CPT:

> In the south of Pará the occupations are not normally begun by means of a reflection, whether religious, unionist, or political. Normally what brings on an occupation is the law of need, the law of necessity. People came from all over Brazil, wanting to survive . . . in desperation, in hunger, needing land. And at the same time there were huge expanses of uninhabited land, not worked, without fences. . . . Because of their need, the men began to occupy areas. And at the beginning these areas were occupied for four, five, six years without anyone even noticing, because land had been bought from an airplane. Suddenly, one day the ranchers were saying "The land is mine." . . . Then the period of terror began.

In each of the five parishes where there were spontaneous occupations, there were some farmers involved in the occupations who had already had experience of a base community, which was likely why they went to the church for help after the occupation was in progress. However, the occupation could not be said to have been organized specifically by base communities, since it was not really organized at all.

The most common form of occupation found in this study was resistance by peasant farmers to eviction from land that they were already occupying. This was the principal pattern in seven of the parishes—three in the state of Maranhão, three in the north of Tocantins (the Bico do Papagaio region), and the one on the Transamazonic Highway in Pará. Maranhão is an area of older settlement than the other two states studied. Therefore, the peasant farmers had been on the land for many years by the time that grileiros came and tried to take it away from them. The parishes in the Bico do Papagaio were settled mainly by peasant farmers from Maranhão and Piauí who had begun arriving in the 1960s and early 1970s, shortly before the grileiros came. In the seventh case, the settlement along the Transamazonic, the situation was similar to these six cases in Maranhão and Tocantins because conflicts with ranchers emerged after the farmers had already been settled through the government's colonization program. In any case, in all seven of the parishes in which the main form of activism was resistance to eviction, the great majority of people participating in this resistance, as well as the leaders, were members of base communities. Thus, it could be said that the CEBs organized the resistance.

A woman who is a member of a base community described the process of discussion that gradually led people to action:

> The sisters would raise questions. . . . "Well, folks, what are we going to talk about today? What is the subject?" Our work was to study the Bible. And I said, "The subject today will be how to enter into the struggle for the land." Because there was a lot of time that we had already been studying that. . . . We could not go on like this for a whole lifetime, only meeting, studying, and discussing this part of the law, and never taking action. That day we saw that we had to take action in the struggle for the land.

Table 10.4 shows the participation of CEB members in land occupations.

TABLE 10.4

CEB Members' Participation in Land Occupations

Composition of Occupation	Pará	Maranhão	Tocantins	Totals
All participants were from CEBs	1	3	3	7
Most participants were from CEBs	0	2	0	2
Few or no participants were from CEBs	0	0	1	1
Occupation not organized	4	0	1	5
Total number of parishes	5	5	5	15

In all but one of the parishes in which the land occupations were organized, the action was carried out by members of base communities. In seven cases, interviewees stated that all were CEB members, and in two cases they said that most of the participants were. The pattern of CEB membership in the land occupations is similar to the pattern of CEB membership in the leadership of those actions.

As mentioned earlier, in the five parishes where occupations were spontaneous, some of the farmers had had previous experience of CEBs. In those situations, new CEBs were organized after the initial phase of the occupation, and served as a means of keeping the activists cohesive.

In the one parish where there was no base community involvement prior to the organized occupations, the parish priest did organize CEBs after the occupations were in progress. However, he was transferred out of the parish before the communities had existed long enough to grow strong without his help. In an area of that parish which I visited, and where the land occupation had been successful, the base community still exists, but with only a small number of families who participate regularly. Large numbers of the original settlers, discouraged by the lack of infrastructure and poor prices for crops, have sold their land at low prices. The people who bought the land do not participate in the CEBs.

The Question of Religion

The predominance of base community members in unions and in land occupations raises the question of whether these unions are actually clerical organizations. It could be argued that these are revivals of the Church-controlled unions of the early 1960s and that their updated message of land reform masks their domination by priests.

In the interviews, however, union members made it clear that, although the unions and the community associations are encouraged by the priests, sisters, and CPT agents, they are autonomous organizations, open to people of all faiths or no faith. Given the growing strength of Protestant sects in Brazil, one may ask why the membership of the unions does not reflect more religious pluralism. The answer appears to be in the policies of the Pentecostal congregations themselves. One interviewee, when asked whether there are members of the local community association who are not CEB members, replied:

The association is open. There is no discrimination by race or religion. But what happens is that the Protestants distance themselves. We give space for them, but they don't associate with us.

A religious sister indicated that the problem might be the attitudes of the ministers:

They [the lay Protestants] don't come. When some of them did start to, their pastors made them aware that 'earthly people' and 'people of God' can't work together. They told their people that they had to get out of our groups. That we smoke, we drink, we dance, and therefore we are 'earthly people.'

Several union leaders said that they had tried to recruit Protestant members but that the ministers opposed their joining. The ministers' recommendation for dealing with poverty was to pray about it. One Pentecostal woman in Maranhão was severely berated by her minister because she organized people to resist eviction.

> He came here telling me to give my house to the rancher. I did not accept that. And he called me all kinds of names. He called me irresponsible, incomprehensible, dumb, stupid.
> *Because he did not want you to participate in the land struggle?*
> He did not want that. No. In no way.... So he became angry. But I still go to church. I think it's very important.... And I will not let go of this struggle either, because I need the land.

Another Pentecostal was heard arguing with his pastor on this issue. This interaction was described by one of the union leaders:

> I heard a minister talking to a member. He said that the member was very much in error, because he was of the Assembly of God and was involved in a [land] invasion. So the Protestant said to his minister, "Brother, look what there is here [in the Bible]. See how God ordered Moses to take his people out of the land of the Pharaoh to go to the land of milk and honey."

Judging by the small number of Protestants in the unions, it would appear that most of the Pentecostals do not argue with their ministers on this issue. One of the union leaders said he knew persons who told him that they could no longer participate in the union because their ministers had prohibited them from doing so.

This provides an interesting contrast with regard to the consequences of religious belief.[12] Members of both Pentecostal churches and base communities meet in small groups to study the Bible, and they believe in the power of the Holy Spirit in their lives. However, while the faith of CEB members strengthens their resolve to struggle for land, the faith of Pentecostals directs their attention to spiritual salvation. Thus, in effect, by encouraging passivity on the part of their adherents, the Pentecostal churches are helping to support the existing situation.[13]

In terms of the option of an individual for Pentecostalism over the base communities, one can understand the appeal of the former. The Pentecostal churches offer a spirituality that consoles the poor in their afflictions and distracts them from their everyday hardships. The base communities, on the other hand, do not promise people relief from worldly problems; rather, they encourage them to think about confronting the established order. In northern Brazil, this confrontation often entails a risk to one's life.

Violence in the Land Struggle

Death threats against peasant farmers, particularly those suspected of being leaders of land occupations, and against church people have occurred in all of the parishes included in this study. In ten of the parishes, people associated with CEBs have been killed, including one priest. In another, several people were shot at and wounded. Interviews with peasant farmers contain descriptions of these experiences:

> Just five months ago they killed a worker. The guy who shot him works for a rancher who persecutes all kinds of organizations—the Church, the union. . . . Someone said that I'm on the list of those who could be killed at any moment.

> I have often been threatened with death, I have been arrested, I have been tortured, I have been through everything. But I never lost faith in God and I never let go of my struggle. I had to spend three months away from home in '87 . . . because of a death threat.

> When the people entered the land, the ranchers sent hired gunmen to throw them out. . . . They knocked down the shacks. . . . First came the gunmen. After that the police came, too.
> *Were any people killed or wounded?*
> Eight people were wounded.

This violence continues up to the present time. Table 10.5 summarizes data on rural violence from the Pastoral Land Commission for the three states during the time period since the beginning of this study.[14]

TABLE 10.5

Violence Against Peasant Farmers and Church People

Type of Violence	Pará	Maranhão	Tocantins	Totals
Murders	60	25	8	93
Attempted murders	27	20	6	53
Death threats	164	75	49	288
TOTALS	251	120	63	434

(Derived from annual reports of the Pastoral Land Commission)

Among the people killed during this time were thirteen union leaders.[15] Among those who suffered attempts on their lives were eight union leaders, one priest, and one staff member of the Pastoral Land Commission. Those receiving death threats included thirty-two union leaders, eighteen priests, three lay staff members of the Pastoral Land Commission, one religious sister, and one bishop.[16] Two of the priests threatened were also staff members of the CPT. The remaining victims represented in table 10.5 were mostly peasant farmers. Despite all this violence against them, base community members have generally advocated avoiding the use of weapons, although there have been some cases in which the peasant farmers did take up arms, such as in the killing of the one gunman in Arame. The annual reports from the CPT indicate that most of the violence has originated with the ranchers, their gunmen, and the police.

Gaining Land

In the midst of the tragedy of numerous deaths, there have been successes in the gaining of land. In all fifteen parishes, the great majority of the occupations have resulted in the granting of land by the government to poor farmers, although in most cases people are still waiting to receive the titles. The amount of land granted has ranged from fifty to two hundred acres, except for one parish, where a large number of people received only ten acres. Given the primitive farming methods available to the average peasant, who cannot even afford to buy fertilizers, this is not enough land to sustain a family for more than a few years.

The peasant farmers are able to gain land because, under certain circumstances, the law is in their favor. However, the difficulty for people with little formal education or financial resources is their lack of knowledge about the law and their lack of the means to have it enforced. This is where the CPT is helpful, in providing information to the farmers and providing lawyers to help them process their land claims. There are three common criteria by which the farmers have been demonstrating their right to the land: length of occupancy, proof of falsification of the title held by an alleged owner (or the complete absence of a title), and lack of productivity on the part of some landowners who do have legal titles. Many cases include two or three of these criteria.

The first criterion results from a longstanding Brazilian law that a squatter who farms a piece of land for a year and a day has the right to remain on it, unless the land is sold by the state to a specific owner. In the seven parishes where the principal form of activism has been resistance to eviction, the peasant farmers were covered by this law, because they had been occupying the land for more than one year. In some parts of Maranhão, their families had been there for several generations.

The issue of false titles or no titles arises both in areas of long settlement, where the grileiro will arrive in a place after the farmers have been working the land for many years, and in areas of newer settlement, where the false owners will try to prevent landless people from settling. In the latter case, the farmers can still gain land if they manage to occupy it and stay for a year while trying to prove that the grileiro's claim is false. In situations in which the false owner is not using the land productively but rather holding it for speculation, the farmers are likely to be able to validate their own claim because they are actually cultivating the land.

The criterion of productivity can even cause the legal owners of land to lose their titles. Because the government's motive in granting land in the Amazon was to develop the region, there is a provision for the expropriation of land that is not being sufficiently utilized to qualify as an agrarian enterprise. Since there are many ranchers who have never occupied the land that was granted to them, peasant farmers who do occupy and cultivate the land are able to make a claim to it.

Conclusion

It should be clear, from the participation of CEB members in unions and in land occupations, from the degree of violence against them, and from the results of these occupations, that base communities have been having an impact on the structure of agrarian relations of production in Maranhão, Pará, and Tocantins. Thus, it may be said that they have been functioning as a prophetic movement. Another aspect of rural life that has been challenged by CEB members is sexual inequality. This is important in relation to the land struggle because of the contribution to that struggle made by women who are freeing themselves from traditional gender expectations. The impact of CEB participation on women will be the focus of the next chapter.

11

DAUGHTERS OF JUDITH:
WOMEN IN THE LAND STRUGGLE

A topic that kept coming up in my research, even when I was not specifically looking for it, was the change in women as a result of participation in CEBs. The night I arrived in Arame for the first time, people were already telling me that I had to visit the Women's Center on top of the hill. Within a couple of days I learned about the first land occupation in which women participated and how they had gone to one of the priests to ask for a Bible course beginning with the Book of Judith. The theme of the oppression of women kept appearing in the large gatherings of CEBs that I attended, both on the regional and national levels. The issue of sexual equality also came up in informal conversations. In 1990, the year that I began this research, the theme for the Brazilian bishops' annual Campaign for Fraternity (which CEBs use for reflection and discussion during the Lenten season) was "Woman and Man: Image of God." Several people pointed that out to me over the next three years.

Given the prevalence of women's issues in the CEBs, it is not surprising that they have been appearing in the literature on Brazilian base communities.[1] So far, however, studies seem to have been limited to urban women, particularly on the periphery of São Paulo. Thus, they may not be generalizable to all base communities in Brazil, since the majority of them are still located in rural areas.[2] Also, these studies have focused mainly on women's attitudes and behavior, without examining the impact that the CEB experience may have on men's attitudes and behavior toward women. In this chapter I intend to balance the research by examining the views of both female and male members of base communities in the rural north.

Three underlying questions guided the section of the interviews related to women:

1. What evidence is there of the development of feminist consciousness among women in rural base communities and of a change in attitude toward women among men in these communities?

2. What are the specific characteristics of this new feminism, in terms of both belief and action?
3. What are the mechanisms by which this feminism is developing?

Before presenting the interview data, I would like to discuss some general lines of difference and similarity between my findings and those of researchers who have studied the experiences of women in the urban south.

Related Studies

Two social scientists who have done research on women in base communities in São Paulo are Sonia Alvarez and Carol Drogus.[3] Alvarez challenges the notion that the CEBs are empowering women. She points to sexism in the Roman Catholic Church, evidenced in papal and other documents, and shows, through her field research, how some priests try to control the women's groups and withdraw their support if they start talking about sexuality and abortion. Drogus, on the other hand, while recognizing the sexism inherent in the Church's pastoral practices and teaching, including the present viewpoint of the Vatican, points out that the CEBs have "perhaps unintentionally, proved a great force for mobilizing women."[4] She explains that this happened because the communities encouraged the development of lay leadership without specific reference to gender. Since the majority of people who participate in religious activities are women, they became the primary beneficiaries of this new lay orientation. As will be shown later, these observations are applicable to women in rural CEBs as well.

Both Drogus and Alvarez accuse the Church of confining women to their role as mothers, but Drogus also notes that the women themselves find their identification as mothers to be meaningful. Her research shows that CEB women are more easily mobilized for community activism if they perceive the issues to be related to children—for example, day care and public health issues. Although traditional Church teaching does encourage the commitment of women to motherhood, it is important to emphasize that this commitment originates with the women themselves, and is then reinforced by the Church. This point can be missed by middle-class feminists, who, in their activism around issues of contraception and abortion, sometimes seem to present children as obstacles to the liberation of women. Working-class women, on the other hand, are more likely to place an explicit value on their identity as mothers. In Brazil, when CEB women seek empowerment, they do so without rejecting that maternal identity. This may be less a result of religious ideology than of the absence, for working-class women, of sufficient educational and career options to compete with the satisfaction that they may derive from caring for their children. Their experience may thus lead women to accept the Church's teaching on motherhood without question. I will return to this issue when discussing the interview data.

Both Alvarez and Drogus describe characteristics of CEB women in the city of São Paulo that do not apply to rural communities in the north. For example, Alvarez notes both the strong presence of middle-class feminist organizers and the restrictive influence of the priest over the base communities. I have not encountered middle-class feminist organizers in the rural north. As for the priests, they cannot exercise a stranglehold over the women's groups in rural areas, because the parishes are very spread out and the frequency of visits of the priest varies from once a month to twice a year.

Drogus notes the reluctance of many CEB women in São Paulo to define themselves in class terms and to participate in politics. She reports that some women are critical of the views of those who are involved in political parties. Again, I have not observed these characteristics in the rural north. In many cases, the membership of local chapters of leftist political parties is comprised entirely of CEB members. Several of the women whom I met in the course of my research, including some of my interviewees, were candidates for local political office, and none of the other women expressed disapproval of them. In fact, the most activist women were often praised by the other CEB members, both male and female.

One other area in which I which I disagree with both Drogus and Alvarez is their apparent rejection of class analysis in relation to feminism. They are both critical of liberation theology for its emphasis on social-class oppression. This tendency to downplay class inequality seems to be characteristic of middle-class liberal feminism, but is not consistent with the experience of CEB women. Since they have never been middle-class,[5] they are likely to perceive economic and sexual oppression as being linked. As these women become empowered, they do not usually identify their struggle as separate from that of men of their own class, but rather choose to struggle alongside the men. Perhaps in accusing liberation theology of being sexist, Drogus and Alvarez are really accusing it of being Marxist. Rather than going into an abstract debate over the relative merits of Marxist feminism vs. liberal feminism, however, I prefer simply to point out that the viewpoint of women in base communities may be affected more by their own class experience than by the imposition of an economic analysis on them by the clergy. Although it is certainly plausible that priests attempt to impose their views, the same accusation could be made of middle-class feminists if they deny the relevance of class inequality in the everyday experience of CEB women.

The Lives of Rural Women

In order to describe the changes that are taking place in the lives of women who participate in base communities, it is useful to explain first what the lives of those who don't participate are like. In general, peasant women in northern Brazil live under great restrictions. They do not travel even into town without their husbands' permission, and spend most of their time in or near their homes. Decisions are made by the husbands. The women have full responsibility for the care of the children, of which there are usually many. Cooking is a constant chore, because the rice and beans that are the staple foods require long preparation time, and kitchen equipment is primitive. In addition, in Maranhão and the north of Tocantins, women supplement the family income by harvesting the nuts of the babaçu palm tree, which are sold for their oil. The work is exhausting, since, before cutting the nuts into small pieces, they must first break open the hard shells. The women do this by sitting on the ground with an axe or large knife, using their feet or legs to hold the handle steady. They then place the babaçu nut on the blade of the axe and strike it with a heavy stick.

In order for women to become free of their restrictive role, three factors are required: (1) reasons to leave the house; (2) belief of a woman in her right to do so; (3) change of attitude in the husband or willingness of the woman to risk conflict with him. In the last case, a support group can be helpful.

The Interviews

The sample of interview subjects for this part of the study is slightly smaller than that for the study as a whole, because at first I was asking questions about changes in women's lives only of female members of base communities. When it became evident, however, that other people also had a great deal to say about the topic, I began including these questions in all the interviews. Thus, the final count of interviewees who have responses about women was as follows: thirty-two female members of CEBs, thirty-three male members of CEBs, one lay female pastoral agent, one lay male pastoral agent, eight sisters, and ten priests. In each parish, I had asked my contact person to include women among the interviewees, but had not specifically asked for those in leadership positions or with a feminist consciousness. As a result, I had the opportunity to interview women with different characteristics. In addition to the majority of female subjects, who were articulate, assertive, and involved in church and community action, there were four who seemed passive, uninformed, and lacking in experience of activities outside of their immediate environment.

The interviews included questions about the participation of women in the base communities, the union, and land-related activism; changes in the attitudes and behavior of women; changes in the attitudes and behavior of men toward women. During the third stage of the project, when it had become clear that there were real changes in the attitudes and behavior of both women and men, I included questions to probe possible sources of those changes.[6]

Feminist Consciousness: Changes in the Women

For the purpose of this analysis, I am defining a feminist consciousness in women as a belief in equal rights with men and a willingness to participate in activities away from the home, such as courses in the Bible or in leadership training, annual meetings of CEB representatives, union activities, land occupations, or political demonstrations.

Almost all lay interviewees, both women and men, reported changes in the attitudes and behavior of women. There were six women, however, who did not report change. One of these had always been very active, even before participating in the base communities. Four were women with young children who either did not have the support of their husbands to participate in activities outside of their immediate area or, in one case, chose not to accept the husband's offer to look after the children so that she could participate. She seemed to lack confidence that a man would know how to take care of them. The sixth was an older woman, a leader in her community and an articulate interview subject, who suddenly became silent when I raised the question of changes in the lives of the women. I tried various ways to prompt her, with little success. She did say that there were changes in her own life, but would not elaborate. Finally she said that the women should get united, to work together, but that they were very weak and nervous. She compared the women in her CEB unfavorably with those in a neighboring village, where there was a very active mothers' group.

Twenty-seven women did report changes in the lives of women who participate in base communities. In response to a prompt asking whether participation in the community changed their relationship with the family, several of the women gave strong, immediate responses, sometimes laughing:

> Ave Maria! It changed a lot! As soon as the women got to know their own rights, everything changed.

> Yes, it's different. Because when women become leaders in the community, leaders of the union, the husband gets another level of consciousness. She can go wherever she wants to. With my husband, for example, I'm off to one place and he's off to another. Sometimes he gets in when I'm leaving. Other times I get in when he's leaving. We understand what we're doing. I think. He thinks. We talk to each other.

> Women who participate in the community have a greater vision of their rights. Women who do not participate consider themselves to be totally in their husbands' custody.

> [She smiled] Yes, it changed it! [She laughed] A lot. Virgin Mary! It changed a lot! I think that before my family and I slept in a perpetual sleep. We didn't know anything of the reality. But today I'm not the same person. Neither is my husband.

The changes which the interviewees reported were not restricted to an awareness of women's rights. They also indicated a new orientation to their participation in the church and to their activism in the community.

> Participating [in the base community] gives us knowledge of things that are happening. We are participating in the lives of neighbors and of the community in general.

> There already are women who are participating in the union, serving on the directorate.

All of the men I interviewed reported changes in the lives of women who participate in base communities, and several seemed eager to inform me of those changes. For example, one of the men said:

> When the women start participating in the base community, they begin to develop. They discover the rights that they have, that they can also participate in the struggle.

Some of the men expressed particular appreciation of the activism of women in the land struggle:

> When we are in the struggle we feel the presence of the women at our side, and we become stronger. They have seen that they are important, and that the women are not there only to cook. They are important to the struggle for liberation.

> Here the women were the most courageous, because in the struggle for the land we ran away. All the men ran and the women stayed.

> The resistance of the woman is stronger than that of the man. The woman has more strength and more courage. In an area of conflict, the first thing that happens is that the husband runs away from the house. And the woman stays at home. She faces the gunmen. She faces the police.

The pattern of the women facing the police, the gunmen, or the landowners also emerged in interviews with women:

> We are always up front, conversing with the police, conversing with the land owner. Our husbands hide and we face them.

In the cases of spontaneous entrance into the land, the most common practice was for men only to enter the area and clear it for planting. The pattern of men running away and women staying behind appeared more often in those places where there was resistance to eviction. There were two reasons for this pattern, in addition to the courage of the women, which several interviewees acknowledged: (1) Since the women felt tied to the home and responsible for the children, running away was not a viable option; (2) both women and men believed that, if gunmen or police were going to use violence, it would be only against the men.

> A lot of women faced gunmen, faced everything, faced the rancher, whoever appeared here. They faced them. The men could not stay because [the gunmen] wanted to get the men.

Some of the interviewees admitted, however, that there were situations in which people had guessed wrong about the police not being violent with women.

During the conflict, my wife told me to go hide with the other men, while she stayed, cooking for everybody. The police came and tried to find out where the men were. When she wouldn't tell them, they overturned all the cooking pots.

During the time of the land struggle, the men could not live at home. . . . And the women stayed home and tolerated the beatings when the police came.

They also torture women, wanting them to inform. . . . They abuse them. The police beat them. They set the houses on fire.

These testimonies to the courage of the women emerged spontaneously in several of the interviews, in response to the question of whether women had participated in land occupations or in resistance to eviction.

In addition to the lay people, all of the sisters and most of the priests interviewed agreed that there had been changes in women as a result of participation in base communities. There were three priests, however, who claimed to have no knowledge of the subject. Two were new to their parishes and to Brazil. The third was native to the region where he was working, but the abruptness of his reply suggested that he did not wish to discuss the matter.

Two of the priests were particularly interesting in their attitudes. One of them volunteered information about the women in his parish before I even had the opportunity to introduce that topic. In the course of talking about the various activities of the CEBs, he mentioned the mothers' clubs and spontaneously made the following statement:

The greatest force today in the base communities is the women. Women are struggling, getting organized. And they are beginning to discover their own identity as women.

Since this priest seemed especially articulate on the subject of women, I tried various ways to get him to admit to his own role in helping to generate their feminist consciousness. He finally told me that his training had in no way prepared him for any such thing. He was from northern Italy, where he had been educated in a conservative seminary in which nothing about women was ever taught. He claimed that it was the process of the development of critical social consciousness within the base communities that had led the women to learn to perceive themselves in a new way, and that he then learned from them.

The second priest, a native Brazilian, had this to say in an interview:

> To the extent that women participate in meetings and gatherings they begin to discover, by means of the base community, their citizenship and their rights. And they begin to question *machista*[7] relations. Sometimes that creates conflict, because the rural man is very *machista*, very authoritarian. Women stay in the kitchen. They suffer a lot.

I later revisited this priest's parish and had the opportunity to observe his interaction with a young married couple who were visiting from the countryside. After lunch the priest began washing the dishes and invited the young man to help. As they were working, I overheard him advising the man to do this at home.

Feminist Consciousness: Changes in the Men

There are more women than men who participate in base communities. This fact provides the opportunity to contrast the experience of women whose husbands are community members with those whose husbands are not. One of the women explained the difference:

> There are women who have a lot of difficulty because the husband does not let them participate in the group. Men who are not part of the church, who do not know the movement of the base communities, do not accept that. But the men who are of the base community do not prohibit their wives from participating.

In response to the question of whether CEB participation brings about a change in a woman's life, all of the women volunteered information in relation to conflict, saying either that they did or did not have conflicts with their husbands. Table 11.1 summarizes their responses.

TABLE 11.1

Women's Descriptions of Husbands' Responses to CEB Participation

Caused conflict with her husband	9
No conflict—related other women's conflicts	10
No conflict—husband was already CEB member	10
No conflict but no change	3
TOTAL	32

Nine of the women said that they had had conflicts with their husbands when they first began participating in base communities, but most of these were resolved.

> When I began to participate my husband was against it. When I participated in a demonstration at the Land Reform Ministry, it was secretly. I left the house saying that I was going to another place, because twice he went there and grabbed me. . . . My faith helped me a lot with this. . . . He spent several weeks without talking to me. Today, thanks be to God, he has changed completely.

> At the beginning of our struggle my husband did not even want me to go out of the house. I had to stay home. He did not want to stay with the children.
> *So later there was a change?*
> It was a big change. He recognized that I had to do those things.

> At first he was angry with the union, but later he saw that we had some victories. And after everything was over he completely agreed. He agreed that I should be a candidate [for town council], and he agrees when I have to travel. And he stays with the children day and night.

Ten women said that they had not had problems with their husbands, but then told about others who had had conflicts. Some of these were not able to persuade their husbands to change their attitudes, and so could not participate in the community.

> There are some who have come here to the women's center crying, because their husbands said that they did not have the right to go to meetings.

> When a friend of mine joined the women's association, her husband said that it was connected with the Workers' Party, that it was Communist, that he didn't want to let her participate in any way. But the members go slowly with their husbands, talking to them like this: It is not Communist. It is a society. [They talk about] the work that we do. And they go and explain. There are a lot of women who have already won their husbands over, and now they, too, are involved [in the base community].

Ten others indicated that they had never had problems because their husbands were participating in the base communities and/or in the unions from the beginning of their own participation. The remaining three did not admit to perceiving any conflicts, but neither was there any visible change in their lives.

It is likely that these numbers do not reveal the true extent of non-CEB men's resistance to changes in their wives, because my interviews were only with present members of base communities. It would have been more difficult to locate the women who could not participate because of the opposition of their husbands. It is significant, however, that ten of the women who had had no conflicts with their own husbands reported the experiences of women who did have such conflicts. The activist women seem very much aware of the fact that many other women remain confined to their homes.

The male CEB members spoke favorably of the rights of women. Some of them contrasted their attitudes to what they had been in the past, indicating their present beliefs that men should help at home and that women should participate in activities outside the home:

This is new. It was the base community that taught it. A few years back there was *machismo*, but it appears that that has ended in the base community. The man is feeling responsible for helping the woman in the house.

We used to think that the role of the woman was only to take care of the house. Today we know that it isn't like that. . . . The woman is a human person . . . who has rights. Today we have that consciousness.

The most conspicuous change in the behavior of men who participate in base communities is their willingness to take care of children while their wives go into town, or even to a distant city, to take part in a Bible course, leadership training course, or CEB gathering. The question of who takes care of the children was not part of my main interview outline, but rather was a prompt used when people did not respond immediately to the query of whether there had been changes in the lives of women as a result of the base communities. After several people had replied that the husband would take care of the children, I began asking the question even of people who responded more quickly to the question of changes in women's lives. The total number of people asked was thirty. Table 11.2 shows the responses.

Among the sixteen women to whom I addressed this question, ten immediately replied that the husband would stay home with the children. Two mentioned the husband among the list of possibilities

TABLE 11.2

Care of the Children

Response	CEB Women	CEB Men	Total
First response was "husband"	10	6	16
Husband included among others	2	5	7
Husband included after direct question	3	3	6
A husband would not do it	1	0	1
TOTAL	16	14	30

of persons who could stay, along with a neighbor, older daughter, or other relative. Three did not immediately mention husbands, but, when asked directly if there were husbands who would stay with the children, replied in the affirmative. One older woman said that she did not know of any men who would do that. Among the fourteen men who were asked who would stay with the children, six immediately answered "the husband," five mentioned the husband among the possibilities, and three replied in the affirmative to the direct question of whether the husband would stay with the children.

Both men and women made it clear that a man who participated in a base community was far more likely than any other man to be willing to take care of his children while his wife went away to a course or meeting. I asked several interviewees whether this practice of men taking care of children had emerged only after participation in the base community. All but one replied in the affirmative.

> Yes. Only after. The husband didn't use to do that. No way! . . . I would say, "I have to go to Esperantinópolis. Can you look after the children?" And he would say "No."

One man did tell me that he had previously taken care of his children, and so had his father. He then specified that his father would watch the children while his mother went to wash the clothes. When I asked whether the practice of men taking care of the children while their wives went out of town for a Bible or leadership training course was a new pattern, he conceded that it was.

Although rural CEB women expect their husbands to share in the care of the children, this does not imply a rejection of their role as mothers. Motherhood remains of central importance in their lives.

Motherhood

There are three main characteristics of the version of women's liberation defined by the rural base community women: (1) a belief in the rights of women as equal to those of men; (2) the integration of this belief with the struggle for land—that is, these women do not struggle exclusively for women's rights but for the right of both men and women to land; (3) a high value placed on fertility.

The first two characteristics are evident from the interviews already quoted. The third is the one that is least understood by middle-class urban feminists. It is often attributed to the fact that these women are Roman Catholic and therefore under the domination of the male clergy with their traditional attitudes in opposition to reproductive choice. In fact, rural Brazilian Catholics tend to have little knowledge of the moral theology of the official Church. For example, CEB members do not seem to pass judgment on those among them who, after being abandoned by their spouses, or separating from a difficult marriage, cohabitate with someone else. Also, it is not uncommon for CEB women to have tubal ligations when they attain the number of children they want, in disregard of the institutional Church's ban on contraception. Although family size is likely to be larger than what middle-class urban feminists would consider desirable, this may be attributed to the fact that these women are rural people, not simply that they are Catholic. Since children who do farm work are able to produce more than they consume, they are assets to their parents.

This high valuation of fertility was evident in the women's bloc of the national base community gathering that I attended. A banner dedicated to a woman who was killed during a land occupation portrayed her with a child in her arms. Another banner symbolically depicted a woman as pregnant with the spirit of the community. One of the symbols passed around during a ritual was a bowl of seed, understood not as a male element but as a symbol of the fruitfulness of the earth. Women in rural CEBs do not perceive children as obstacles to their empowerment; rather, they identify themselves as mothers and integrate their concern for the welfare of their children into their belief in the struggle for a better world.

Furthermore, orientation to family and children is not restricted to women. In the interviews, I found rural CEB men to be as likely as the women to speak in terms of their children. For example, one man, in describing the motivation behind an organized land occupation, said:

Our community made a decision for our children . . . because we were dying of hunger.

Another man who had survived a land struggle, despite several attempts on his life, said:

I am grateful to God. I am grateful for a piece of land, where I can survive with my children.

The devotion of both men and women in rural areas to their families has likely made it easier to persuade male members of CEBs to share in the care of their children, thus freeing up the women for greater community involvement. My favorite example of this is a woman who was a candidate for local political office. After our interview, she climbed up on the back of a truck headed into town to participate in a campaign rally, leaving her seven children—six by birth, including an infant, and one foster child—in the care of her husband.

These findings contradict the position of Alvarez and reinforce that of Drogus regarding the question of real change in the lives of base community women. Alvarez has missed the evidence of change because of her insistence on a narrow definition of feminism centered on explicit demands for contraception and abortion. Given the longstanding belief of the Roman Catholic Church that human life begins at conception, it would be unrealistic to expect it to take an official position favoring abortion. Furthermore, if the subject of abortion comes up among the women in a base community, it is more likely to happen in an urban CEB, since the experience of people living in an agricultural setting leads to a high valuation of fertility.

Sources of the Changes

When it had become evident that there were changes in both women's and men's attitudes, I added interview questions to probe possible sources of those changes. It was clear to me that all of the religious sisters whom I had interviewed so far, as well as the majority of the priests, gave at least verbal support to equality between the sexes. Furthermore, the sisters, in the example of their own pastoral work, provide models of women in a nontraditional role. They lead religious rituals in the absence of a priest or in cooperation with a priest, organize base communities, and give courses on the Bible and in leadership training—functions that are very different from the traditional roles of women religious as private school teachers, nurses, and parish housekeepers.

The regional base community gathering that I attended also promoted, through rituals, songs, and discussions, the idea of the liberation of women, as did the nationwide gathering. At the regional gathering, an entire day of the four-day meeting was dedicated to the theme "Woman Oppressed, Liberated, and Liberating." The day began with a Mass at which, in addition to hymns supporting this theme, there was a penitential rite, Scripture reading, and discussion of the reading—all related to women and inequality. The most powerful symbolism appeared at the Offertory. A young black woman stood before the altar, facing the assembly, with twelve pieces of rope loosely tied to her arms, legs, neck, and waist. A representative of each of the twelve dioceses present removed one piece of rope while offering a prayer related to the liberation of women. The prayers were oriented to change, both to making changes within the participants themselves and to challenging existing social structures.

This observation, combined with the attitudes of the sisters and most of the priests, led me to consider the possibility that the new feminism in the base communities was being imposed on CEB members by middle-class pastoral agents. A statement made by one of the sisters I interviewed could be interpreted as giving evidence to this possibility. She was responding to the question of whether participation in the base communities changes the lives of women. After describing how that happened, including the changes in the attitudes of men, she added:

> And we make mighty sure in the Bible course that we bring in the value of the woman.

At the same time, I was aware of the possibility that the change in people's consciousness could be a result of processes within the CEBs themselves—that is, the combination of Scripture study, particularly passages on justice, with critical reflection on participants' everyday reality. Since the majority of CEB members are women, this reflection could lead them to question the sexual inequality in their daily lives.

What I learned from the interviews with lay people was that, although the attitudes of the sisters and priests, along with the themes discussed at courses and meetings, encouraged both women and men to rethink their assumptions about the roles of women, the main influence seemed to come from the experience of the local base community. People indicated that their attitudes had begun to change *before* they attended courses or regional meetings. One woman explained it this way:

> [The women] learn more things within the community. They arrive in the community for a meeting. They organize those groups more. And the woman has this important representation.

A man said:

> [The women] wake up by means of the community. If they stay
> only at home . . . they don't have access. So they participate in a
> meeting, in an assembly. They will see that the rest of the women
> have instruction, have strength.

The experience within the base community combined more than
one factor that would lead to changes in the attitudes of both men and
women: (1) the process of discussion and reflection within community
meetings that leads people to take a critical look at the problems in
their lives; (2) the development of leadership roles within the community, which could be held by women as well as men, and the experience
by both men and women that a woman could be an effective leader
(some interviewees admitted that at first there was opposition to
women leaders by the men in their community); (3) the legitimation of
travel away from home provided by church meetings.

Conclusion

The base communities have thus provided the three factors mentioned earlier as necessary for women to break out of their confinement
to the home. Courses and gatherings have supplied them with reasons
for leaving the house, sometimes for as much as a week at a time. The
process within the CEBs has developed the women's beliefs in their
right to have a life outside the home. The CEB itself, as a group of people who share beliefs, has provided a source of support for new ideas
and behaviors in both women and men.

PART IV

CONCLUSION

12

BEYOND THE AMAZON:
RELIGION AND SOCIAL CHANGE

Although studies related to the Amazon are of current interest, the implications of this research go beyond the cases I have described and analyzed. The findings about the relationship between religion, grassroots mobilization, and agrarian reform may provide a basis for studies in other parts of the world.

Land and Mobilization

Land remains a central issue in the global economy, even with the world becoming mechanized and commercialized. As the dominant countries increase their demands for agricultural and mineral products, and the leaders of heavily indebted Third World countries look for ways to bring in new investments, peasant farmers keep losing their land. It is taken over by individuals and companies that introduce modern techniques to produce crops for export or that build a railroad or an aluminum refinery. Thus, not only are rural families deprived of their homes and livelihood, but the decrease in crops for local consumption also results in an increase in hunger among other sectors of the population.

In those places where peasants resist this trend toward making them landless, they are frequently assisted by nongovernmental organizations (NGOs) that are seeking to democratize social processes through grassroots mobilization. These organizations promote social change through advocacy and education, while challenging official government policy.[1] Some of the NGOs that have emerged in the north of Brazil include the Movement for Survival on the Transamazonic, the Rio Maria Committee, and the Father Josimo Human Rights Commission. A larger NGO that has branches in that region is the Pastoral Land Commission.

Religious groups can be effective NGOs, both because of their international contacts and because of their legitimacy with local people.

The Pastoral Land Commission is a particularly good example in this regard. The interviews in this study demonstrate the high esteem in which this organization is held by peasant farmers and local organizers. At the same time, the CPT's national reputation and international contacts strengthen its impact on government policy. In addition to publishing annual reports in the conventional print medium, the CPT participates in the Alternex computer network.[2] This enables it to exchange information about justice, human rights, and environmental protection, or violations of these, with representatives of other NGOs throughout the Americas, Europe, and Australia, using electronic mail and electronic bulletin boards.

The example of the CPT also shows how religious organizations can make a distinctive contribution in working at the grassroots level because they are able to provide otherwise powerless people with organizational structures for channeling their activism as well as belief systems that enable them to break out of their traditional fatalism. The notion of the will of God is reinterpreted. Rather than being used to convince peasants that they should accept all the decisions of more powerful people, God's will comes to be seen as a mandate to work for justice. Faith, instead of helping people to bear their suffering, gives them courage to face the dangers inherent in the struggle for change. This recalls the image of the rural leader who was not afraid when the gunmen came, because his Bible was on the table.

In Brazil there are connections between NGOs and base communities. Many organizations provide consultation and advising (*assessoria*) to grassroots groups. In addition, CEBs themselves may help to organize an NGO, as was the case with the Movement for Survival on the Transamazonic. CEBs also provide a vital connection between larger, national organizations and people at the grassroots level. It would be interesting to study NGO activity in other countries of the southern hemisphere, including those countries both with and without base communities, in order to examine the various types of groups that organize people who would otherwise be powerless.

Theoretical Implications

There is also theoretical generalizability in the findings of this research, in the form of a contribution to the literature on religion and social change. The interview data support certain elements of the theory of Otto Maduro, as will be shown below. At the same time, these data also challenge fundamental assumptions that observers of Latin America often draw from the two theories that are brought together within Maduro's conceptual framework—that is, those of Marx and Weber. The most obvious challenge is to Marx. Although there is much in my analysis of rural mobilization that is indebted to Marxian sociology—specifically, social-class analysis, the influence of political-economic factors on the production of ideas, and the conflictive nature of the process of change—there are two aspects of Marx's conceptual framework that find contradiction in the Amazon. The first is his belief that the peasantry would not be likely to become mobilized for change. The second is his assumption that religion is not only the opiate of the people but also a mere epiphenomenon that would not take an active role in social transformation.[3] The prospect that peasants organized into religious groups would develop a change-oriented belief system, along with collective action to alter the position of their class, would have probably seemed absurd to Marx.

Max Weber came closer to the truth in demonstrating the transformative power of religion, although he attributed that power mainly to Protestantism. A culture influenced by Roman Catholicism would, within Weber's framework, be too traditionalistic to contribute to economic change. The peasantry would be especially subject to a traditionalistic mentality. Weber, like Marx, did not attribute to rural poor people a strong role in social-historical processes. Nevertheless, he did allow for the possibility that the peasantry could become a carrier of a new belief system. This would be likely to happen if the peasants were threatened with enslavement or proletarianization. Both of these have occurred in northern Brazil. The Pastoral Land Commission has documented numerous cases of actual slave labor in the Amazon region. Labor contractors hired by ranchers lure landless peasants to an isolated area, hundreds of miles from home, with the promise of good pay for clearing land. Once there, they are forced to work without pay, frequently beaten, and shot if they try to escape. Proletarianization is sometimes a more gradual process, with peasant farmers supplementing their livelihood by doing seasonal wage work or looking for jobs in the cities between the harvests. It can also be abrupt, however, such as when peasants are evicted from their land and thus forced to look for wage work.

Beyond the application or contradiction of specific aspects of the theories of Marx or Weber, my research lends support to Maduro's synthesis of their theories. Maduro's conceptual framework suggests that a shift of power in the Church could allow more input into decision making from lay people of the poorer classes, and that this shift could be related, at least in part, to the development of a prophetic movement, such as is seen in the base communities. It should be clear from the information presented in this book that the lay leadership developed in the CEBs is exerting a transformative power on the political-economic system. There is one area, however, in which Maduro's theory falls short, and that is in explaining inconsistencies in pastoral policy. When Maduro developed his conceptual framework in the context of the Latin American Catholic Church of the 1970s, he may have been a bit too optimistic. At that time, the Church did appear to be changing and shifting some power downward. Today, however, Latin American Catholics and observers of their church have a different perception— that is, one involving a hierarchy that is pulling back from the preferential option for the poor. For example, in the case studies in Arame and São Luís, the relationship between religion and mobilization that was strong at the time that the parishes were founded was disrupted by the alternation between priests who were favorable toward base communities and those who were not. This change in the lower clergy was paralleled by a change in bishops.

One sociologist whose work is instructive for understanding these inconsistencies is Jean-Guy Vaillancourt, who presents a Gramscian analysis of Vatican policies.[4] He shows that, in different ways, each pope has sought to influence society through the political behavior of Catholics. For Vaillancourt, Catholic social teaching represents an effort to keep the faithful away from leftist tendencies rather than to promote real structural change. When people take the social teachings too far, the Vatican will try to restore orthodoxy. Vaillancourt's analysis may be interpreted to mean that some popes will open the windows to renewal, in order to hold restless lay people within the Church. However, when the laity and some of the clergy start sounding like the very leftists from whom the Church was trying to save them, other popes will close the windows and bolt the shutters as well. The same dynamic may be observed in the policies of the Latin American Bishops' Conference (CELAM), which underwent visible changes, with the approval of the Vatican, between the meetings in Medellín and Santo Domingo.

This state of affairs has produced the kind of paradox that sociologists love to study: specifically, how measures that begin as a means of stopping change may sometimes produce the opposite effect. Vaillancourt's suggestion that some ecclesial innovations were intended to turn Catholics away from Communism is completely applicable to the Church in Brazil. Anti-Communism was a feature of ecclesial policy throughout the 1950s and early 1960s, even inspiring initial relief on the part of the bishops at the news of the military coup in 1964. Nevertheless, the rural mobilization that the clergy encouraged as a means of undercutting the socialist peasant leagues eventually provided a model for unions that turned out to be far more militant than those the Church originally advocated. These unions, still encouraged by the Church through the Pastoral Land Commission and through many parish priests and sisters, tend to develop socialist ideologies and frequently overlap in membership with the Workers' Party, the Socialist Party, and, in some areas, the Communist Party. So it is not surprising that the bishops and the Vatican are now advocating a more "spiritual" interpretation of Roman Catholic belief.

Crisis and Future Prospects

Where does all this leave the Brazilian Catholic Church today? Clearly it is in a state of crisis, as is the Latin American Catholic Church in general. The Santo Domingo conference was an obvious attempt to reverse the direction begun at Medellín, in its de-emphasis of base communities and in its individualization of the believer's relationship with God. Furthermore, the authority of the bishops was emphasized as the only source for the interpretation of the preferential option for the poor and as the standard to which lay leaders must conform. In dioceses with bishops who are not supportive of CEBs, the demands of the Santo Domingo documents could spell death for the communities.

But can Medellín really be reversed? On the one hand, the support of the hierarchy for progressive tendencies can certainly be withdrawn. On the other hand, one may question whether that support is the only factor maintaining the preferential option for the poor. Medellín had a strong impact because many people—including active Catholic lay people, sisters, priests, and a few bishops—were ready for it. They were living on a continent filled with human suffering, and CELAM provided a new theodicy—that is, a religious explanation—for that suffering.[5] That new theodicy explained poverty and oppression in terms of structural evil and an excess of riches in the hands of a few. Thus, sin came to be perceived as social, in terms of one's participation in the advantages deriving from unjust, unequal societal structures and in terms of one's indifference about the need to change those structures. With this interpretation of sin, salvation also had to be defined collectively; that is to say, one could not be a good Christian without engaging in the struggle to change an oppressive society.

Once that message has caught on among the rural poor, it is unlikely that they and the pastoral agents who work with and for them will be willing to pretend that they have never heard it. Members of rural base communities are refusing to let the Church change its mind. During my field research, when I would ask people what they thought about recent actions of the Vatican, they would sometimes reply that there might be difficult times ahead but that the base communities would continue because they are the work of the Holy Spirit. Since, according to Roman Catholic belief, the Holy Spirit maintains the life of the Church, these respondents were essentially saying that CEBs are intended by God to be an important part of that Church.[6]

Beyond this ecclesial issue, there is also, in the minds of base community members, the issue of survival. While the bishops may be concerned about institutional survival, the poor worry about physical survival. Peasant farmers need land. They know that without it, they and their children will starve. Migration to the urban areas is a poor solution because of chronically high unemployment. There are not enough jobs in the cities to employ all the people who are presently in the countryside. For those who wish to remain on the land, CEBs provide moral and organizational support. People who have learned how to struggle for their rights to land through the base communities are not going to accept any message from the hierarchy that the Church must return to purely spiritual concerns, with "holiness" emphasized at the expense of liberation. Perhaps the bishops know this. This may be why even the conservatives among them have remained united with the others in favor of agrarian reform.

Thus, it is likely that, for the foreseeable future, rural base communities will continue to meet, pray, read the Bible, and struggle. The long-range consequences of their struggle will depend on a combination of peasant demands and government response. It is possible that people will cease making demands once they have gained land. It is also possible that piecemeal responses on the part of the government, such as limited colonization programs, could pacify sufficient numbers of rural activists in order to derail any effective movement for change. Of course, for this to happen, the government-sponsored colonization programs would have to be successful, and their record so far has not been good. Frustrated expectations, if anything, are likely to increase the demands of landless farmers.

Church people, including both base community members and pastoral agents, have the potential for continuing to play a role in stimulating those demands. They may encourage peasant farmers to think beyond the acquisition of a plot of land, keeping them mindful of the structural changes that will need to be made in order to protect their rights in the long range. In addition, the Church, through the Pastoral Land Commission and the National Conference of the Brazilian Bishops, may exert institutional pressure on the government to bring about promised reforms. The bishops' favorable view of the Pastoral

Land Commission, combined with that organization's funding sources independent of the local church, make it likely that the CPT will be able to continue its work for some time to come. Finally, the verbal support given by government officials to agrarian reform provides Church activists with a wedge on this issue, particularly in relation to a legal structure through which peasants may make claims for land.

The acquisition of a plot of land, however, does not put an end to the problems of Brazilian peasant farmers. There continues to be violence against the farmers, union leaders, and church people. This impedes progress toward agrarian reform, by tying up the CPT and the unions in protests against the violence. In addition, the lack of roads, schools, health care, access to markets, good prices for crops, credit, and technical assistance keeps thousands of families in poverty. On the other hand, the experience of the farmers' association organized by CEB members along the eastern stretch of the Transamazonic Highway shows that community mobilization can be effective in obtaining roads, schools, and health care. Furthermore, the providing of the technical assistance of agronomists hired by the CPT suggests what might be done on a larger scale, if, for example, the government were to provide the needed resources through the ministry of agriculture. These are likely future directions for the activism of base communities in the Amazon.

Implications for Further Research

But what about CEBs in cities? Are these findings generalizable to them? Perhaps only partially. Recent studies of base communities and other religious groups in urban areas—particularly those done by John Burdick in Duque de Caxias and by Cecilia Mariz in Rio and Recife—indicate that many people of the poorer classes prefer Pentecostal or Afro-Brazilian religions. In addition, W. E. Hewitt's research in São Paulo has led him to predict a bleak future for base communities because of changes in church policy. Before offering suggestions of how the present study may point to directions for research on urban CEBs, it is important to mention differences between the two contexts. The most salient differences are the plurality of possibilities for survival and the plurality of options for activism that exist in cities. Urban areas provide a range of possibilities for survival, although they are not all equally desirable. The more fortunate members of the working class get the better-paid factory jobs. Others seek work in the service sector, domestic help, or odd jobs. In the rural north, on the other hand, there are very few wage positions, particularly in regions with cattle ranches, which are not labor-intensive enterprises. Beyond temporary work in clearing land or building a mine or a dam, or gold prospecting, which is unpredictable and characterized by a high degree of violence, the main hope for survival is access to land. For many people, their participation in a base community is tied to their activism in gaining land. In terms of the activism itself, there are different ranges of options in the city and countryside. In metropolitan areas there are many organizations and political parties that are not specifically church related. Activists do not have to turn to CEBs for a source of mobilization. However, my interviews show that, in the rural north, the activist groups are almost always linked to the Church.

This is not to say that there are no possibilities for the generalizability of these findings to urban CEBs. We may look at the factors that have made many rural base communities strong and investigate whether these same factors are present in any urban communities. The experience of CEBs in the rural north can be instructive by suggesting possibilities for the study of the urban communities, examining, for example, the following:

1. The origins of the communities: Innovations that came mainly "from the top down," as in São Paulo, Recife, and Duque de Caxias, can be more easily impeded by intervention from the top than those innovations that developed from multiple sources, including lay initiative, as in Maranhão. Furthermore, as Burdick's study shows, the enthusiasm of liberationist priests for "the new way of being Church" encouraged by a progressive bishop may result in a distancing from the Church of lay people who are not yet ready for those changes.

2. Their degree of lay autonomy: Communities that depend on the frequent presence of a priest or other pastoral agent are more vulnerable to a change in ecclesial policy than are those communities that have developed a strong lay leadership and a sense among the laity that they, not the hierarchy, are the Church.

3. Their importance in relation to poor people's empowerment: If the base communities are only a small part of the popular mobilization in their region, they will not have the same vitality as communities that are the main force for such mobilization. Although, as mentioned above, a plurality of options is a characteristic of urban life, CEBs may remain strong if they, as CEBs and not simply as individual members, constitute the leadership in local movements. This was clear in the north, where the few non-Church activists whom I located recognized that the leadership in the land movement came from the Church.

4. Poor people's perceptions of the possibilities of structural change
    affecting their immediate environment: Peasant farmers who are
    members of CEBs believe that they can gain land through their
    activism. However, people who do not believe that mobilization
    will lead to positive changes in their lives will be more likely to
    seek the religious comfort found in Protestant sects and Afro-
    Brazilian spiritualism.

Further research may indeed demonstrate that base communities
will not remain viable in the cities, but it would be a serious error to
generalize this finding automatically to the countryside. Because of the
urban bias of many of the recent studies, some observers have concluded that the importance of CEBs is declining in Brazil as a whole.[7]
This conclusion does not ring true when I examinine my findings gathered in the rural north and recall my observations there. The urban
focus of the recent studies may be understandable in light of the fact
that the majority of Brazilians now reside in metropolitan areas. On the
other hand, millions of people still do live in the countryside, and two-
thirds of all base communities are rural.[8] Furthermore, the rapid urbanization of Brazil has rural causes. It is a consequence not so much of the
expansion of economic opportunities resulting from industrialization as
of the expulsion of peasant farmers from the land. Therefore, what goes
on in the rural areas is important for the whole society. The action of
CEBs in relation to peasant mobilization may thus have more impact on
the future of Brazil than the action of CEBs in the cities. This would
suggest that researchers who study the progressive Catholic Church in
Latin America may need to pay closer attention to what is going on in
rural areas.

APPENDIX:
GAINING ACCESS AND GATHERING DATA

There is likely to be a problem of access whenever one does research with groups of people whose activities are resulting in threats to their lives. Outsiders are likely to be viewed with suspicion. The best way to gain entry into such a situation is through individuals who are trusted by the local people. At the same time, this method of access may generate a concern that these contact persons will seek to influence the direction of the research by their choice of what the researcher will have the opportunity to observe or whom she will interview. Although measures can and should be taken to minimize this bias, as will be discussed later, the potential for it is, to some extent, inevitable, since without the cooperation of contact persons, the researcher would have no access at all to interviewees in politically sensitive situations.

When I decided to do a study of base communities in the north of Brazil, I was fortunate to have had previous acquaintance with a congregation of religious sisters who had been working since the mid-1960s with the rural poor in several states of the north and northeast regions. With their help, I gained immediate access to parishes in the states of Maranhão and Pará, and the persons I met in those locations gave me further contacts in Tocantins. In each area people identified me as a friend of Sister or Father So-and-so, and gave me a warm reception.

The initial choice of Maranhão was related to the location of my first contacts. When I began to plan this study, however, I made subsequent choices of sites in Maranhão, Pará, and Tocantins on the basis of visible connections between base communities and activism, using methods that will be described below.

I went to Brazil for two months in 1990, two months in 1991, and five months in 1992. The 1990 study was preliminary in relation to the subject of base communities and land conflicts, and was conducted at the same time as my research on the roles of pastoral agents. Because my gathering of information related to the land problem was not fully organized at that point, I did not include the locations visited in 1990 in the present study, except for three which I subsequently revisited.

During the 1990 study, I began asking interviewees about places in Maranhão and neighboring states where there were or had been land conflicts. I then began obtaining the annual reports of the Pastoral Land Commission (CPT) in order to use them to discover which areas had a high number of conflicts. Although a Church organization, the CPT is widely recognized by non-Church people as the most reliable source of data on rural violence in Brazil. I studied the CPT reports published in 1990, 1991, and 1992 to discover the locations that had one or more of the following: land occupations, evictions, and violence against persons, particularly those associated with the Church. Maranhão, Pará, and Tocantins were among the states that revealed various combinations of these occurrences, with Maranhão and Pará frequently at the top of the national list for the numbers of murders related to land conflicts.

Through the literature on rural mobilization, I discovered that parts of these three states were considered to be in one of the frontier areas—that is, regions in which specific government policies had encouraged the migration of thousands of peasant farmers without providing for land titles. Since this combination of mass migration and false promises is likely to cause the kinds of disruptions in people's lives and worldviews that could produce a potential for activism, I decided that a region that included a frontier area would be a particularly good laboratory for my study.

I selected fifteen parishes, five in each of the three states. There were three reasons for the use of the parish as a unit of study:

1. Base communities in Brazil are virtually always subunits of a parish.
2. In northern Brazil, a parish is often coextensive with a town or small city. I was able to find the names of municipal districts with land problems through the published reports of the CPT, then look up the address of the local parish in a church directory.
3. A parish is administered by a specific person, usually a priest, occasionally a sister, with whom I could likely gain contact through personal references.

The decisions regarding research sites were based on a combination of a study of documents published by the CPT and recommendations by individuals familiar with land conflicts. In selecting the parishes, it was neither desirable nor possible to apply random-sampling techniques, for the following reasons:

1. I was interested in places with the strongest evidence of rural mobilization, and so was aiming to visit as many as possible of the

parishes that showed this strongest evidence, rather than a sample of all of the municipal districts mentioned in the CPT reports.

2. Because of the difficulty of long-distance travel in the Amazon, with bad roads and unreliable bus connections, I maximized the time available for the research by choosing places that were no more than twenty-four hours bus travel from either the nearest airport or my previous and next destinations. As a result, there was some geographic clustering of parishes.

3. I could not draw a sample directly from the written reports, because they do not provide the exact type of information that I would have needed in order to do so. Specifically, they do not indicate whether land occupations or violence against farmers in particular areas are related to base communities. To go to such an area on the basis only of the information that there had been an occupation and/or violence there, without first locating a contact person who could introduce me to potential interviewees and verify that there were, indeed, base communities in the area could have resulted in a great waste of time.

This still leaves the question of whether it was desirable to make contact through the Church rather than through some other organization that might lead me to militant farmers who had not been organized by religious groups. I did, in fact, attempt to do the latter. I went to the headquarters of the Workers' Party (PT) in São Luís, interviewed members of two nonreligious organizations in Imperatriz (CENTRU and the Movement of the Landless), and in other locations made contact with members of the Union of Rural Workers, of the Socialist Party (PSB), or of the Communist Party (PC do B). People in all of these organizations told me that the Catholic Church was the single organization doing the most to help organize the rural workers. At the PT headquarters in São Luís, I was told that virtually all of their members were active Catholics and that any information they could give me would likely be identical to what I would learn from Church agencies. Since some of the interviewees in the preliminary study had been critical of the Movement of the Landless, I thought this movement would be a good source of a different viewpoint. However, when I interviewed the regional coordinator of this movement, she told me that most of their organizers, herself included, had come out of Catholic grassroots groups (base communities and youth groups). The founder of CEN-TRU told me that he had been raised Protestant and was no longer affiliated with any religion but that most of his staff were persons who had come out of the grassroots Catholic Church and maintained their religious ties. All of the most militant rural unions that I found had been either started or won over by persons active in base communities. Finally, those members of political parties who were not practicing Catholics still stated that certain elements of the Church were doing the most for change in the rural milieu. I concluded from this that, even if I had been doing a study of rural problems without specific reference to religion, the most efficient source of contacts would still have been the progressive sector of the Catholic Church.

Nevertheless, the issue of bias in selection needs to be addressed. Since my contacts were church people, is it possible that I got to go only to those places that they wanted me to see? This may have been a factor in the preliminary stage of the research in 1990, when my knowledge of the geography and social context of the three states was limited. For the main part of the project, however, which was conducted in 1991 and 1992, I selected the sites then asked those people whom I already knew to advise me whom to contact at each one.

Selection of interviewees, on the other hand, was more subject to uncontrollable factors. I would tell my local contact person whom I wished to interview: six to eight people, including CEB members, union leaders (who were usually CEB members), and the parish priest and/or sister, with, wherever possible, an equal number of women and men. Although it would not have been feasible to ascertain the subjective criteria by which each contact person selected one individual rather than another, my request in terms of categories was generally met. In eight of the fifteen parishes it was met exactly, including in two places where the priest did not seem to be on entirely friendly terms with the union leaders. In most of the other places, the only discrepancy was in the sex ratio (usually more men, but occasionally more women). In one parish, however, I did suspect that a priest was not being fully cooperative. For example, he would not help me with transportation and made disparaging remarks about some of the people I wanted to interview. In the effort to get around his interference, I made additional contacts through lay people, and later interviewed a sister who had previously worked in that parish.

In some places, despite people's apparent good intentions, there were complicating factors that were beyond anyone's control. Transportation was a serious problem, especially in Tocantins. There were two parishes in which I could not get to all the interview subjects whom contact people had recommended because transportation arrangements failed. Sometimes people were difficult to find or were away from home altogether during the period when I was there. In the absence of telephones in those areas, it was usually not possible to make or confirm appointments. Beyond the transportation problems, three interviews were discarded because the person did not have the information needed, did not answer the questions clearly, or did not seem to understand the questions. The final tally of usable interviews came to 107, with a mean and median of 7 per parish. (The organizers of CENTRU and of the Movement of the Landless were not counted into this mean and median because they were not geographically located within one of the parishes studied.) The breakdown was as follows:

40   CEB men
32   CEB women
13   priests
 9   sisters
 5   lay church workers
 8   lay persons who were not directly involved with CEBs.

Of the last category, four were rural union leaders, one was a non-Catholic attorney employed by a human rights committee sponsored by the Church, one was a member of an Assembly of God congregation who had been severely criticized by her pastor because of her activism on land issues, and two were the organizers of the non-Church-affiliated movements. I had deliberately arranged interviews with four of these people because of their apparent lack of formal religious ties, in order to obtain the point of view of those who might be less likely than other interviewees to be concerned about the Catholic Church's public image.

The interviews were taperecorded. I personally transcribed them in Portuguese, largely word for word, then translated them into English. Although I had a list of topics, my preferred technique was to ask a few leading questions and encourage the interviewee to talk freely. In many cases people would cover a topic before I got to the question. When they did not do so, I used the following list of questions (which were specific to CEB members and modified for other interviewees):

1.   How long have you lived in this region?
2.   Where did you come from?
3.   When did the base communities begin here?
4.   How did they begin?
5.   What are the land problems here?
6.   Have people been killed?
7.   Have people been threatened with death?
8.   When did the union begin in this area?

9. How did it begin?
10. Approximately what percentage of the union members are also members of base communities?
11. Approximately what percentage of the union leadership are also members of base communities?
12. Have there been land occupations or resistance to eviction in this area?
13. Were those who participated in these struggles members of base communities?
14. Were the leaders of these struggles members of base communities?
15. What is the importance of the base community in your life?
16. Can you think of specific situations in which your personal faith helped you in the land struggle?
17. Are there differences between women who participate in the base communities and those who don't?
18. Do husbands accept those changes in the women?
19. Are husbands who are CEB members more likely to accept the changes?
20. If a woman goes to a course or meeting away from home, who takes care of the children?
21. Are there women in the union/community association?
22. Are there women in the leadership of the union/community association?
23. Did women participate in land occupations or in resistance to eviction?
24. Have you been to courses or meetings away from home?
25. Did they talk about women's issues there?
26. Do the priests and/or sisters of this parish support the struggle for land?
27. Does the bishop of this diocese support the struggle for land?
28. Has the Pastoral Land Commission been helpful in this region?
29. Are there any organizations supporting the workers that are not connected with the Church?
30. Is there anything I have not asked that you believe is important to talk about?

I asked priests, sisters, and lay pastoral agents almost all of these same questions, except for 15, 16, 24, 25, and 26. In the interviews with persons not associated with base communities, the questions were specific to the organizations they represented and to their opinion of the role of the Catholic Church in the land struggles.

There was a certain amount of evolution in the questions over the course of the study. This happened for a variety of reasons. One was that some information that was spontaneously given in the earlier interviews (such as the fact that people saw the Pastoral Land Commission as especially helpful to them) seemed important enough to solicit through a direct question. Also, as it became evident that women who participated in the land struggles seemed to be breaking out of the traditional restricted position of rural women, I began probing more into this apparent change. One of the questions related to this topic was modified as a result of the preliminary responses. I had been asking people whether participation in the land struggle had changed the position of women in the family. It soon became evident, however, that the key factor in this change was participation in the base community and that the women's social activism flowed from that. So I changed the question to focus on CEB participation. Another reason for changes in the interview was that some questions that were used to prompt a nontalkative interviewee turned out to produce such good results that I made them into standard questions. One of these followed the query of whether men were supportive of the changes in women's behavior as a result of CEB participation. The prompt was to ask who took care of the children if a woman went out of the village for a course or a meeting. Some other questions were dropped because they did not seem meaningful to the interviewees and produced vague or contradictory responses. For example, at first I was asking everyone whether the present climate at the Vatican was interfering with what they were doing. It soon became evident that many rural workers had no idea of the pope's point of view with regard to land struggles. So I continued asking that question only in interviews with sisters, priests, and those lay people who were active as leaders, adding it on to the question about the local bishop.

The 107 interviews were my main source of data. In addition, to obtain further information on land conflicts, I did documentary research at the regional office of the Pastoral Land Commission in Belém, going over the data from all of the annual reports of that organization from 1980 through 1991. (After returning home in December 1992, I obtained the reports for 1992 and 1993 as soon as they became available.) I also read reports and newspaper clippings available at the Pastoral Land Commission in São Luís and in some of the parishes. Finally, I used published sources, as well as interviews, for the historical information included in some of the chapters. My preference is always for accounts of direct experience—hence the primary reliance on interviews. Although individuals sometimes had lapses of memory in relation to actual dates or specific facts, I compensated for this by asking the same questions of more than one person and checking information against written documentation wherever available.

I had originally intended to include participant observation as part of this research. As it happened, however, it was not possible to carry it out systematically in all fifteen locations. Ideally, I would have participated in meetings of base communities in all the parishes. The geographic spread of each parish made this impossible. Rural base communities are often located very far from the parish church. Because they are lay-led the priest does not always know the day and time when they meet. When the priest goes to visit the community, with frequencies varying from once a month to twice a year (depending on the size of the parish and the condition of roads), what occurs is the celebration of Mass, not a base community meeting. So when I went with a priest, the Mass was what I got to observe. After attempting participant observation of community meetings during the preliminary stage of the study, I decided to focus on the interviews instead. I did, however, manage to attend a few community meetings as well as liturgical celebrations, regional CEB gatherings in Maranhão in 1990 and 1992, and the large nationwide CEB gathering held in Santa Maria in the state of Rio Grande do Sul in 1992, and took notes. Although this aspect of the research was not sufficiently consistent to qualify as what I consider to be systematic participant observation, the experience of attending these meetings, liturgies, and gatherings did deepen my understanding of the CEB experience and its relationship to the social milieu.

NOTES

Introduction. Religion and Rural Conflict

1. See, for example, John Burdick, *Looking for God in Brazil: The Progressive Catholic Church in Urban Brazil's Religious Arena* (Berkeley: University of California Press, 1993); Carol A. Drogus, "Popular Movements and the Limits of Political Mobilization at the Grassroots in Brazil," in *Conflict and Competition: The Latin American Church in a Changing Environment*, ed. Edward L. Cleary and Hannah Stewart-Gambino (Boulder, CO: Lynne Rienner, 1992), 63-86; W. E. Hewitt, *Base Christian Communities and Social Change in Brazil* (Lincoln, NE: University of Nebraska Press, 1991); Scott Mainwaring, *The Catholic Church and Politics in Brazil, 1916-1985* (Stanford, CA: Stanford University Press, 1986); Cecilia Mariz, *Coping with Poverty: Pentecostals and Christian Base Communities in Brazil* (Philadelphia: Temple University Press, 1994).

2. The classic statement of this position may be found in Gustavo Gutierrez, *A Theology of Liberation* (Maryknoll, NY: Orbis, 1973). A more recent statement of the connection between the Bible and activism toward social change is in Roy H. May Jr., *The Poor of the Land: A Christian Case for Land Reform* (Maryknoll, NY: Orbis, 1991).

3. See, for example, Michael Novak, "Subverting the Churches," *Forbes*, January 22, 1990, 94; Novak, "Why Latin America Is Poor," *Forbes*, April 17, 1989, 76. Although Andrew Greeley makes reference to his viewpoint on Latin American religious activists in some of his sociological work—with one particularly bizarre comment in relation to Sandinistas in *American Catholics since the Council: An Unauthorized Report* (Chicago: Thomas More Press, 1985), 221—his most strident expression of it is in his novel *Virgin and Martyr* (New York: Warner, 1986).

4. The political biases to which I am referring are related to people's desire to see change emerging from the bottom of the society or controlled by those at the top. These points of view may color one's perception of whether the source of change in the Church is the laity of the poorer classes or the hierarchy.

5. Alejandro Cussianovich, *Religious Life and the Poor: Liberation Theology Perspectives* (Maryknoll, NY: Orbis, 1979); João B. Libânio, "Igreja, povo que se liberta: III Encontro Intereclesial de Comunidades de Base," *Síntese* 5 (1979): 93-110.

6. Thomas C. Bruneau, "Base Christian Communities in Latin America: Their Nature and Significance," in *Churches and Politics in Latin America*, ed. Daniel H. Levine (Beverly Hills, CA: Sage, 1980), 225-37; W. E. Hewitt, "Strategies for Social Change Employed by Brazilian CEBs in the Archdiocese of São Paulo," *Journal for the Scientific Study of Religion* 25, no. 1 (1986): 16-30. This position has also been expressed by Daniel H. Levine and Scott Mainwaring in "Religion and Popular Protest in Latin America: Contrasting Experiences," in *Power and Popular Protest: Latin American Social Movements*, ed. Susan Eckstein (Berkeley: University of California Press, 1989), 203-40.

7. Madeleine Adriance, "Agents of Change: Priests, Sisters and Lay Workers in the Grassroots Catholic Church in Brazil," *Journal for the Scientific Study of Religion* 30 (1991): 292-305; see also Adriance, *Opting for the Poor: Brazilian Catholicism in Transition* (Kansas City, MO: Sheed and Ward, 1986).

8. Rogério Valle and Marcelo Pitta, *Comunidades eclesiais católicas: resultados estatísticos no Brasil* (Petrópolis: Vozes, 1994). The estimate of 75,000 is derived as follows: The researchers sent questionnaires to all parishes in Brazil and received responses from 40 percent of them. These responses enabled them to count 46,045 groups defined as "Catholic ecclesial communities." This led to an estimate, based on the 40 percent response rate, of approximately 100,000 such groups for the country as a whole. In order to determine which of these could properly be termed "base communities," they used data derived from the questionnaires, specifically fixed-choice questions about the existence of a community council, Bible reflection groups, and lay leaders who prepare people for the sacraments. Three out of four of the groups surveyed met these criteria, hence the figure of 75,000 base communities from an estimated total of 100,000 church groups.

9. Paulo Freire, *Pedagogy of the Oppressed* (New York: Seabury, 1970). This method was developed in the Church's Basic Education Movement, which was staffed largely by people with experience in the Catholic Action movement, and is closely related to that movement's method of "see-judge-act." See Adriance, *Opting for the Poor*, 46-52; 112-13, for a description of the connections between Catholic Action, the Basic Education Movement and the base communities.

10. In Valle and Pitta's study, 19,483 church groups were involved in activities that were termed "socioeconomic" or "political" (Valle and Pitta, *Comunidades eclesiais católicas*, 56). This comes out to 56 percent of the groups which they classified as base communities.

11. Arame is pronounced "ah-RAH-mee." This town is the subject of the first of the case studies in Part II.

12. Adriance, "Agents of Change."

13. The details of the methodology are described in the Appendix.

14. Portions of this section and of the subsequent one have been adapted from my article, "Base Communities and Rural Mobilization in Northern Brazil," *Sociology of Religion* 55, no. 2 (Summer 1994): 163-78, © Association for the Sociology of Religion, 1994.

15. See Otto Maduro, *Religion and Social Conflicts* (Maryknoll, NY: Orbis, 1982).

16. See Karl Marx and Friedrich Engels, *On Religion* (New York: Schocken Books, 1964); Max Weber, *The Protestant Ethic and the Spirit of Capitalism* (New York: Scribner, 1958); Max Weber, *The Sociology of Religion* (Boston: Beacon Press, 1964).

17. Maduro, *Religion and Social Conflicts*, 107.

18. See, for example, José de Souza Martins, *Os camponeses e a política no Brasil* (Petrópolis: Vozes, 1990); Gerrit Huizer, *The Revolutionary Potential of Peasants in Latin America* (Lexington, MA: D. C. Heath, 1972); Zander Navarro, "Democracia, cidadania e representação: os movimentos sociais rurais no estado do Rio Grande do Sul, Brasil, 1978-1990" (paper presented at the International Congress of Latin Americanists, Tulane University, New Orleans, LA, July 7-11, 1991); Jeffrey M. Paige, *Agrarian Revolution: Social Movements and Export Agriculture in the Underdeveloped World* (New York: Free Press, 1975); Pedro A. Ribeiro de Oliveira *Religião e dominação de classe: gênese, estrutura e função do catolicismo roman-isado no Brasil* (Petrópolis: Vozes, 1985); James C. Scott, *The Moral Economy of the Peasant* (New Haven, CT: Yale University Press, 1976); Scott, *Weapons of the Weak: Everyday Forms of Peasant Resistance* (New Haven, CT: Yale University Press, 1985).

19. A sociological analysis of millenarian movements may be found in Ribeiro de Oliveira, *Religião e dominacião de classe*, 241-63.

20. Authors who mention these specific forms of organization include Paige (*Agrarian Revolution*, 345) and Huizer (*Revolutionary Potential of Peasants*, 19).

21. These authors include José de Souza Martins, *Caminhada no chão da noite: emancipação política e libertação nos movimentos sociais do campo* (São Paulo: Hucitec, 1989); Joe Foweraker, *The Struggle for Land: A Political Economy of the Pioneer in Brazil from 1930 to the Present Day* (Cambridge: Cambridge University Press, 1981); Merilee Grindle, *State and Countryside: Development Policy and Agrarian Politics in Latin America* (Baltimore: Johns Hopkins University Press, 1986); Navarro, "Democracia, cidadania e representação"; Richard Pace, "Social Conflict and Political Activism in the Brazilian Amazon: A Case Study of Gurupá," *American Ethnologist* 19, no. 4 (1992): 710-32; Marianne Schmink and Charles H. Wood, *Contested Frontiers in Amazonia* (New York: Columbia University Press, 1992).

22. I am defining this range with Thomas Bruneau (*The Political Transformation of the Brazilian Catholic Church* [New York: Cambridge University

Press, 1974]) as religiously neutral and politically on the right, with a North American developmentalist view, and José de Souza Martins (*Os camponeses e a política no Brasil*) as religiously committed and politically on the left, with a critical Latin American view.

23. Maduro, *Religion and Social Conflicts*.

24. See Robert McAfee Brown, *Gustavo Gutierrez: An Introduction* (Maryknoll, NY: Orbis, 1990); and Harvey Cox, *The Silencing of Leonardo Boff: The Vatican and the Future of World Christianity* (Oak Park, IL: Meyer Stone, 1988). An update on Boff's situation may be found in Mev Puleo, *The Struggle Is One: Voices and Visions of Liberation* (Albany, NY: State University of New York Press, 1994).

25. See, for example, Burdick (*Looking for God in Brazil*) and Mariz (*Coping with Poverty*). Burdick points out that a generous estimate of CEB members would indicate that they comprise only about 5 percent of the population of Brazil, while some studies would place the percentage of Pentecostals to be about double that.

26. Weber, *Sociology of Religion*, 50.

27. May, *Poor of the Land*, 53-55.

Chapter 1. The Military Regime and Agrarian Policy

1. Information for this chapter came from my interviews, supplemented by the following sources: Sue Branford and Oriel Glock, *The Last Frontier: Fighting over Land in the Amazon* (London: Zed Books, 1985); José de Souza Martins, *Os Camponeses e a Política no Brasil* (Petrópolis, Brazil: Vozes, 1990); M. Regina C. de Toledo Sader, "Espaço e luta no Bico do Papagaio" (Ph.D. diss., University of São Paulo, 1986); Armando Dias Mendes, "Major Projects and Human Life in Amazonia," in *Change in the Amazon Basin, Volume I: Man's Impact on Forests and Rivers*, ed. John Hemming (Manchester, U.K.: Manchester University Press, 1985), 44-57; Foweraker, *Struggle for Land*; Octavio Ianni, *Ditadura e agricultura* (Rio de Janeiro: Civilização Brasileira, 1979); Johan M. G. Kleinpenning and Sjoukje Volbeda, "Recent Changes in Population Size and Distribution in the Amazon Region of Brazil," in *Change in the Amazon Basin, Volume II: The Frontier After a Decade of Colonisation*, ed. John Hemming (Manchester, UK: Manchester University Press, 1985), 6-36; Radames Rios, "Multinationals Given Free Reign in Brazilian Amazon," *Latinamerica Press*, December 2, 1982; Schmink and Wood, *Contested Frontiers in Amazonia*.

2. Branford and Glock, *Last Frontier*, 23; de Toledo Sader, *Espaço e luta no Bico do Papagaio*, 35.

3. Volkswagen quickly sold this ranch after a Catholic Church organization, the Pastoral Land Commission, discovered the use of forced labor on

that property. Most of the work of clearing the land for pasture is done by sub-contract, and when conditions of forced labor are exposed, the companies, like Volkswagen, often deny knowledge of the practice. (This information is from a conversation with Father Ricardo Rezende, a former regional coordinator for the Pastoral Land Commission.)

4. Branford and Glock, *Last Frontier*, 43-44.

5. According to Branford and Glock (*Last Frontier*, 44), SUDAM approved 358 cattle projects from 1966 to the end of 1978, the rebates for which came to an equivalent of about half a billion British pounds, which at the time was equivalent to more than one billion U.S. dollars.

6. Branford and Glock, *Last Frontier*, 49, 67.

7. Branford and Glock, *Last Frontier*, 75; Schmink and Wood, *Contested Frontiers in Amazonia*, 77-78.

8. Branford and Glock, *Last Frontier*, 83.

9. Foweraker, *Struggle for Land*, 159.

10. Local populations did not necessarily receive benefits from this infrastructure. For example, I have noticed that rural people living in the vicinity of the big mining and industrial projects often do not have electricity, although high-voltage wires pass near their villages. Furthermore, the flooding that resulted from the building of the Tucuruí Dam in Pará made thousands of peasant farmers homeless, with little or no compensation for the loss of their land.

11. In its social and economic characteristics, Maranhão is a mixture of the northeast and the north. Some land is titled, but most is public. It has long been occupied by both indigenous people and peasant farmers. In terms of the quality of land, it is superior to both regions. The red clay soil of Maranhão is deeper and richer than what is found in many parts of the Amazon, and, at the same time, the area is not as arid as much of the northeast.

12. Between 1960 and 1970, an estimated 170,000 people moved to the region along the Belém-Brasília (Branford and Glock, *Last Frontier*, 20). This road connected the newly built national capital, Brasília, with the city located at the mouth of the Amazon River, and, along with the construction of the capital, reflected a goal, held by presidential administrations even before the military coup, to develop the interior of the country. Other roads constructed after the coup included Perimetral Norte, Cuiabá, Caracaraí, and the Transamazonic Highway.

13. Foweraker, *Struggle for Land*, 100.

14. Branford and Glock, *Last Frontier*, 65; Schmink and Wood, *Contested Frontiers in Amazonia*, 76-77.

15. Farm produce prices are fixed by the Commission for Financing and Production, with the intention of providing a stable food supply. There are minimum prices that are supposed to protect the small producer. These prices, however, go into effect only at the end of the harvest season. Well before this, the poor farmers, who have no surplus funds, have already had to sell their crops in order to survive. Lacking transportation to transport their goods to market, they can only sell them to middlemen at very low prices. This system has kept large numbers of farmers in poverty, and has often resulted in their selling the land, also at very low prices.

16. Branford and Glock, *Last Frontier*, 64.

17. Branford and Glock, *Last Frontier*, 69-72; see also Schmink and Wood, *Contested Frontiers in Amazonia*, 59.

18. Dias Mendes, "Major Projects in Amazonia," 47.

19. The Pastoral Land Commission is an ecumenical agency supported mainly by the Roman Catholic Church with the goal of agrarian reform. It offers peasant farmers legal support and the technical services of agronomists, in addition to publishing annual reports on violence in rural areas. These annual reports are considered by both church and non-church people to be the most accurate sources of data on land problems in Brazil.

20. Traditionally, the harvesting and processing of the babaçu nuts has been a means by which women in Maranhão have supplemented the family income. The work is exhausting. It involves gathering the nuts, which grow on a palm tree, splitting open the hard shells with sticks and axes, and cutting the contents into small pieces. The nuts are then sold to be processed into oil. The grileiros, despite their lack of legal land titles, fence in the fields where the babaçu palms grow naturally. Then they usually demand that the women give them 50 percent of the nuts after processing. In recent years, the Catholic Church's Pastoral Land Commission has been organizing the nut harvesters and informing them of their legal rights.

21. De Toledo Sader, *Espaço e luta no Bico do Papagaio*, 64.

22. Branford and Glock, *Last Frontier*, 155, 168-79.

23. Although GETAT was officially established by a decree of President Figueiredo (Schmink and Wood, *Contested Frontiers in Amazonia*, 80), de Toledo Sader (*Espaço e luta no Bico do Papagaio*, 63) and Branford and Glock (*Last Frontier*, 154-55) suggest that Major Curió's influence was behind it.

24. The two priests were sentenced, under the National Security Law, to ten to fifteen years in prison, but were freed after eighteen months, in December 1983, when the law was changed because of nationwide demand for the release of political prisoners (Schmink and Wood, *Contested Frontiers in Amazonia*, 183). The story of Fathers Camio and Gouriou is told in detail in Ricardo Rezende Figueira, *A justiça do lobo* (Petrópolis: Vozes, 1986).

25. De Toledo Sader, *Espaço e luta no Bico do Papagaio*, 214-19.

26. De Toledo Sader, *Espaço e luta no Bico do Papagaio*, 211-24.

Chapter 2. Arame: The Town Named for Barbed Wire

1. Arame was at that time still part of the municipal district of Grajaú. Since unions are organized according to guidelines established by the government, only one rural union can be founded in each municipal district.

2. Since rice is an important cash crop for peasant farmers in Maranhão, this destruction of the rice was especially serious.

3. Reports from Maranhão newspapers (*Estado do Maranhão*, June 5, 1985; *O Imparcial*, June 5, 1985; *Jornal Pequeno*, June 6, 1985) confirm the occurrence of this violence and also mention death threats against one of the priests. One of the articles gives the names of the large landowners (actually, the term used in the article is *grileiros*, which means land robbers) who were known to have ordered the death of the priest and six peasants. These men were never charged with the crimes. Although most of the information for subsequent events in October 1985 came from my interviews with people in Arame in 1990 and 1992, it was also confirmed and supplemented by articles from newspapers written at that time.

4. On the front page of the newspaper *O Imparcial* (March 19, 1986) there was a photograph taken in the town of Arame with the caption: "Sandinistas are agitating in Maranhão." There were related articles in other local papers, such as *Estado do Maranhão* (March 19 and 20, 1986) and *Diário do Norte* (March 23, 1986).

5. "Não temos condições de chegar nem em Manaus, imagine em Managua." *O Imparcial*, March 23, 1986.

6. "See-judge-act," the method developed in French Catholic Action in the 1930s, provided the foundation of the approach used in the base communities.

Chapter 3. São Luís: The Great Aluminum Disaster

1. Barbara English, unpublished working paper on Alcoa in São Luís (written for schools in Maryland, 1984, photocopy). Information for this chapter is derived from, in addition to English's working paper, my ongoing acquaintance with Igaraú, a village in the interior of the island of São Luís, including one month of field research there in 1983 and return visits in 1990 and 1991; conversations with villagers, with a priest who worked in the parish of São Cristóvão from 1988 to 1992, with a lay parish worker, and with an environ-

mental activist in São Luís; in-depth interviews in August 1982 and November 1991 with Barbara English, a Sister of Notre Dame de Namur who had worked in the parish of São Cristóvão from 1969 to 1978 and was active in the resistance against the construction of the Alcoa plant until 1985.

2. According to English's working paper, the agreement signed on July 12, 1980, by representatives of the state government of Maranhão and of Alcoa provided for the ceding of a minimum of 3,700 hectares of land and the reserving of up to 10,000 hectares for the company's future use. One hectare is equal to approximately 2.7 acres. This area of 10,000 hectares, or 27,000 acres, constituted about 12 percent of the Island of São Luís and 50 percent of the industrial district.

3. A legal loophole for this transfer of property had been provided in 1976 by the federal government in the form of Directive 005, which permitted the circumventing of the requirement of legislative approval for transactions over 3,000 hectares, provided they "promoted the development of the region" (Schmink and Wood, *Contested Frontiers in Amazonia*, 64).

4. Raul Ximenes Galvão, "O gerenciamento costeiro e a ocupação do litoral," *Pau Brasil* (September/October 1985), 39.

5. There was one other village besides Igaraú that was not abandoned. The village of Coqueiro was not planned for demolition by the company, but the residents who stayed suffered the consequences of the pollution of the air and water.

6. "Alberto Soluciona o Problema de Igaraú," *O Imparcial*, June 27, 1990.

Chapter 4. Santa Rita: Where the Buffalo Roamed

1. As mentioned in chapter 1, peasant farmers who occupy and cultivate a plot of land for a year and a day gain the permanent right to use that land. These peasant farmers are called *posseiros*. Those who inherit this right are called *herdeiros*.

2. For a more detailed description of corporatism in relation to unions in Brazil, see chapter 10.

3. A newspaper article in *O Imparcial* (April 4, 1990) indicated that 256 farmers in Maranhão had received land titles from the governor and that some of these were for property in Santa Rita. Another article in the same paper on November 8, 1990, stated that farmers in Santa Rita received 139 more titles.

4. Luís Inácio Lula da Silva was the Workers' Party candidate for President of Brazil in 1989 and 1994. He was defeated in 1989 by a small margin by the right-wing candidate, Fernando Collor de Melo, who was later

impeached on charges of corruption. He was defeated again in 1994 by Fernando Henrique Cardoso, who was supported by a coalition of right-wing and centrist parties.

5. Data from a newspaper article in *O Imparcial*, May 12, 1989. Information on the buffalo problem is from newspaper articles and documentation on file at the regional office of the Pastoral Land Commission in São Luís and at the parish house in Santa Rita, as well as from interviews with union leaders and Father Osvaldo Fernandes Marinho. It was updated by information faxed to the author from the Pastoral Land Commission in February 1994.

6. *O Imparcial*, March 4 and April 27, 1989.

7. This incident was reported in *O Imparcial*, December 22, 1989.

8. *O Imparcial*, December 22, 1989.

9. Information on the conflict in Sítio Novo is from newspaper articles and documentation on file at the regional office of the Pastoral Land Commission in São Luís and at the parish house in Santa Rita, as well as from interviews with people in the village. It was updated by a five-page report sent to the author from the Pastoral Land Commission in January 1994.

Chapter 5. Northern Tocantins: Blood in the Parrot's Beak

1. See Ralph Della Cava, *Miracle at Joazeiro* (New York: Columbia University Press, 1970) for a detailed account of the events that led to the veneration of Father Cicero by rural people of northeast Brazil. See also Ribeiro de Oliveira, *Religião e dominação de classe*, 248-54. Ricardo Rezende Figueira, in *Rio Maria: canto da terra* (Petrópolis: Vozes, 1992), gives an account of a visit to a community of green-flag pilgrims, inspired by Father Cicero's prophecies, in the south of Pará. Unfortunately, this passage was omitted in the abridged English translation of the book (*Rio Maria: Song of the Earth* [Maryknoll, NY: Orbis, 1994]).

2. De Toledo Sader, *Espaço e luta no Bico do Papagaio*.

3. De Toledo Sader, *Espaço e luta no Bico do Papagaio*, 106.

4. There are seven parishes in the diocese of Tocantinopolis. However, only six of these are actually located within the Bico do Papagaio. The seventh, in the city of Tocantinopolis itself, is just south of that region.

5. De Toledo Sader, *Espaço e luta no Bico do Papagaio*, 203.

6. The information on the 1992 murder is from the annual report of the Pastoral Land Commission. The information on the subsequent threats is from my interviews with a parish priest and with one of the men being threatened.

7. "The Announced Death of Josimo Morais Tavares," by Pedro Tierra. Permission to reprint this excerpt was given by the poet. The translation is by Madeleine Adriance.

Chapter 6. Rio Maria: Tragedy and Hope in the Land of Canaan

1. The details of the planning of the murder of João Canuto by twenty landowners, including the victorious mayor of the town, are recorded in Rezende, *Rio Maria*.

2. Quoted in Rezende, *Rio Maria*, 229.

3. In this chapter, I have identified more people by name than in other chapters because they are already known in international solidarity networks and in the mass media, and would not be harmed by being named here. In the other chapters, most of the interviewees are not identified because the interviews were obtained with a promise of anonymity.

Chapter 7. Bye-Bye Brazil: Along the Transamazonic Highway

1. Information about changes in diocesan policy is from interviews with Sister Dorothy Stang and a regional coordinator for the CPT.

2. Comissão Executiva do Movimento pela Sobrevivência na Transamazônica, "Movimento pela Sobrevivência na Transamazônica: Viver, Produzir, Preservar" (1991, photocopy), 4.

3. Comissão Executiva do Movimento pela Sobrevivência na Transamazonica, "Movimento pela Sobrevivência," 5.

Chapter 8. Help and Hindrance: The Institutional Church

1. Four months after his resignation from the Franciscans, Boff appeared at the national gathering of base communities in Santa Maria (in the state of Rio Grande do Sul). Although he was not on the program, word got around that he was present in the crowd, and over a thousand people chanted his name until he went to the stage and addressed the gathering. His brief speech was punctuated with several bursts of applause and was followed by more applause. Countless people later went to speak with him individually, and several asked to have their pictures taken with him.

2. For an analysis of the process by which the Church uses innovation and orthodoxy to maintain its influence, see Mark R. Kowalewski, "Firmness

and Accommodation: Impression Management in Institutional Roman Catholicism," *Sociology of Religion* 54, no. 2 (1993), 207-17. See also Jean-Guy Vaillancourt, *Papal Power: A Study of Vatican Control over Lay Catholic Elites* (Berkeley: University of California Press, 1980).

3. Raimundo Caramuru de Barros, *Brasil: uma igreja em renovação* (Petrópolis: Vozes, 1968), 25-26.

4. The First General Conference of CELAM was held in Rio de Janeiro in 1955. Subsequent conferences in Puebla, Mexico, in 1979 and in Santo Domingo in 1992 will be discussed below.

5. For analyses of ecclesial change that focus on the Church's priority of preserving its influence over society, see Bruneau (*Political Transformation*) and Ivan Vallier, *Catholicism, Social Control, and Modernization in Latin America* (Englewood Cliffs, NJ: Prentice-Hall, 1970). For modified versions of this approach, see Adriance (*Opting for the Poor*) and Mainwaring (*Catholic Church and Politics in Brazil*).

6. See Hewitt, *Base Christian Communities*, 102-4.

7. See Alfred T. Hennelly, S.J. (ed.), *Santo Domingo and Beyond: Documents and Commentaries from the Historic Meeting of the Latin American Bishops' Conference* (Maryknoll, NY: Orbis, 1993).

8. Hennelly, *Santo Domingo and Beyond*, 121.

9. Hennelly, *Santo Domingo and Beyond*, 122. The emphasis on "legitimate channels" seems consistent with Pope John Paul II's preaching against the occupation of private property by landless peasants. Nevertheless, this document can still be used by those who advocate land occupations, because of the possibility of different interpretations of legitimacy.

10. Interview with Father Ricardo Rezende in Cambridge, Massachusetts, October 1993. Information for this section is derived from the interview, from the CPT's annual reports, and from a book authored by the organization, *CPT: pastoral e compromisso* (Petrópolis: Vozes, 1983).

11. Comissão Pastoral da Terra, *CPT*, 7.

Chapter 9. Base Communities: Link Between Religion and Agrarian Activism

1. The type of Catholic Action referred to here is the movement of youth groups, specialized according to occupational categories—Young Catholic Workers, Young Catholic Farmers, Young Catholic Students—begun in Belgium and France in the 1920s, as distinct from the earlier movement in Italy. French Catholic Action emphasized lay leadership and action on one's immediate social milieu. For descriptions of the relationship of Catholic Action to changes

in the Church, see Adriance (*Opting for the Poor*), Bruneau (*Political Transformation*), and Mainwaring (*Catholic Church and Politics in Brazil*).

2. The Basic Education Movement is described in Emanuel De Kadt, *Catholic Radicals in Brazil* (London: Oxford University Press, 1970).

3. Information on this development is derived from sections of my earlier book (*Opting for the Poor*) which were based on interviews conducted in Maranhão in May and June 1983. The pastoral innovations begun in São Luís in the 1950s are described on pp. 54-56 of that book.

4. This is evident in Hewitt's study of CEBs in São Paulo (*Base Christian Communities*), where people seem to depend on the priest to motivate them to action.

5. Carolina Clemens, *É bom lembrar: um pedacinho da história das CEBs no Maranhão* (São Luís, Maranhão: Equipe Provincial das CEBs do Maranhão, 1989).

6. Clemens, *É bom lembrar*, 9.

7. Some of the material in this section has previously appeared in Adriance, "Agents of Change," and has been reprinted with the permission of the *Journal for the Scientific Study of Religion*.

8. See Bruneau, "Base Christian Communities in Latin America"; Hewitt, "Strategies for Social Change"; Levine and Mainwaring, "Religion and Popular Protest."

9. For a more detailed analysis of these factors, see Adriance, "Agents of Change," 292-305.

10. There is much clearer evidence of differences between women and men in pastoral roles in Ruth Wallace, *They Call Her Pastor: A New Role for Catholic Women* (Albany: State University of New York Press, 1992).

11. Rezende, *Rio Maria*, 84.

12. When information is applicable to the parish in general, I am reporting the interview data in terms of numbers of parishes. When the information is more personal—the effect of the base community or of faith on one's own life—I am reporting the data in terms of numbers or percentages of individual interviewees.

Chapter 10. CEBs, Rural Unions, and the Struggle for Land

1. For a description of Vargas's Estado Novo regime and his elected presidential term, see Thomas E. Skidmore, *Politics in Brazil, 1930-1964: An Experiment in Democracy* (New York: Oxford University Press, 1967), 3-53, 81-142.

2. See James M. Malloy, "Authoritarianism and Corporatism in Latin America: The Modal Pattern," in *Authoritarianism and Corporatism in Latin America*, ed. James M. Malloy (Pittsburgh: University of Pittsburgh Press, 1977), 3-19.

3. For more details on the growth of the Peasant Leagues, based on interviews with Francisco Julião, see Adriance, *Opting for the Poor*, 33-40. A thorough treatment of the topic may be found in Fernando Antônio Azevedo, *As ligas camponesas* (Rio de Janeiro: Paz e Terra, 1982).

4. Irving Louis Horowitz, *Revolution in Brazil* (New York: E. P. Dutton, 1964), 22.

5. This analysis was derived from interviews with Francisco Julião (see Adriance, *Opting for the Poor*, 36-37).

6. Dom Antônio Costa, quoted in Adriance, *Opting for the Poor*, 41.

7. Itamar de Souza, *A luta da igreja contra os coroneis* (Petrópolis: Vozes, 1982), 58.

8. De Toledo Sader, *Espaço e luta no Bico do Papagaio*, 198.

9. Information from interviews with Francisco Julião (see Adriance, *Opting for the Poor*, 38-39).

10. In the case of the base communities along the Transamazonic Highway, I am considering the community association as a substitute for a union. The nearest union, which was started by base community members, is located 70 kilometers away in the city of Altamira.

11. ACR (Atuação Cristã no Meio Rural), which developed out of the Rural Catholic Action movement, was in some dioceses a source of lay leaders, many of whom organized base communities.

12. For a more detailed discussion of the social consequences of religious belief among Pentecostal Protestants and base community members, see Cecilia Mariz, *Coping with Poverty*. Carol Drogus has done a similar study focused specifically on women, "Religious Change and Women's Status in Latin America: A Comparison of Catholic Base Communities and Pentecostal Churches" (unpublished working paper, typescript). Ricardo Rezende (*Rio Maria*) presents numerous examples of the contrasts between Pentecostals and Catholics that emerge in the everyday life of a town in the Amazon.

13. This passiveness on the part of Pentecostals is not necessarily true in urban areas. For example, a candidate for mayor of Rio de Janeiro in 1992 was Benedita da Silva, a black woman from a poor neighborhood who is a member of a Pentecostal church, a community organizer, and a federal congressperson. In 1994 Benedita was elected to the national senate.

14. This table summarizes data from CPT annual reports for the four-year period from the beginning of 1990 to the end of 1993. Data for 1994, which will be published in May 1995, were not available at the time of this writing.

15. "Union leaders" refers either to officers or to members of the directorate, both of whom are elected by the membership.

16. The bishop, who is reported by the CPT to have received more than one death threat, is Dom Erwin Krautler, whose Prelacy of Xingu includes the area along the Transamazonic Highway included in this study. He is known by both CEB members and pastoral agents to be supportive of the land rights of peasant farmers. He is also the president of CIMI (Conselho Missionário Indígena), the church organization that focuses on the defense of the rights of indigenous people.

Chapter 11. Daughters of Judith: Women in the Land Struggle

1. See, for example, Sonia Alvarez, "Women's Participation in the Brazilian 'People's Church': A Critical Appraisal," *Feminist Studies* 16 (1990): 381-408; Alvarez, *Engendering Democracy in Brazil* (Princeton, NJ: Princeton University Press, 1991); Carol Drogus, "Reconstructing the Feminine: Women in São Paulo's CEBs," *Extrait des archives de sciences sociales des religions* 17 (1990): 63-74; Drogus, "Popular Movements." There is also some mention of the effect of base community participation on women in Hewitt (*Base Christian Communities*) and in Caipora Women's Group, *Women in Brazil* (London: Latin American Bureau, 1993).

2. There seems to be a tendency among a number of North American social scientists who study base communities to restrict their research to São Paulo. The danger in this is that they or their readers will generalize to the whole of Brazil from a case that is in many ways unique.

3. See Alvarez, "Women's Participation"; Alvarez, *Engendering Democracy in Brazil*; Drogus, "Reconstructing the Feminine"; Drogus, "Popular Movements."

4. Drogus, "Reconstructing the Feminine," 65.

5. Hewitt (*Base Christian Communities*) claims to have located middle-class groups in São Paulo that call themselves base communities. I have found no middle-class base communities in the north of Brazil.

6. For the general outline of questions, see the Appendix.

7. *Machista* is the adjective used in Brazil to mean sexist or patriarchal, in contrast to *macho*, which literally means male, without necessarily an ideological connotation. The noun corresponding to *machista* is *machismo*.

Chapter 12. Beyond the Amazon:
Religion and Social Change

1. Susan Goodwillie and Perdita Huston, "The NGO Revolution," *WorldPaper*, August 1992, 1.

2. Alternex, based in Rio de Janeiro, is part of the Associates for Progressive Communication, which links electronic networks in twelve countries. Alternex is also joined with the Internet.

3. See Marx and Engels, *On Religion*.

4. Vaillancourt, *Papal Power*. I have termed Vaillancourt's analysis "Gramscian" because it appears to build on Antonio Gramsci's insights into the Roman Catholic Church's capacity, throughout history, to adapt to changing social contexts. One of the ways the Church does so is by assisting a class that is beginning to gain power with the articulation of a unifying (or organic) ideology in a religious form. See Antonio Gramsci, *Selections From the Prison Notebooks* (New York: International Publishers, 1971).

5. Meredith McGuire, in *Religion: The Social Context*, 3d ed. (Belmont, CA: Wadsworth, 1992), 33, draws on Weber's theory to explain theodicies as "religious explanations that provide meaning for meaning-threatening situations." These may include death, disaster, disease, suffering, and poverty.

6. A phrase heard frequently in the Brazilian Catholic Church, with reference to base communities is *"novo jeito de ser igreja"* (new way of being church).

7. This conclusion could easily be derived from Hewitt, "Strategies for Social Change," 107-9.

8. Valle and Pitta, *Comunidades eclesiais católicas*, 63.

BIBLIOGRAPHY

Adriance, Madeleine. *Opting for the Poor: Brazilian Catholicism in Transition.* Kansas City: Sheed and Ward, 1986.

———. "Agents of Change: Priests, Sisters, and Lay Workers in the Grassroots Catholic Church in Brazil." *Journal for the Scientific Study of Religion* 30 (1991): 292-305.

———. "Base Communities and Rural Mobilization in Northern Brazil." *Sociology of Religion* 55, no. 2 (1994): 163-78.

Alvarez, Sonia E. "Women's Participation in the Brazilian 'People's Church': A Critical Appraisal." *Feminist Studies* 16, no. 2 (1990): 381-408.

———. *Engendering Democracy in Brazil.* Princeton, NJ: Princeton University Press, 1991.

Azevedo, Fernando. *As ligas camponesas.* Rio de Janeiro: Paz e Terra, 1982.

Baldissera, Adelina. *CEBs: Poder, nova sociedade.* São Paulo: Paulinas, 1988.

Boff, Clodovis. *Comunidade eclesial, comunidade política.* Petrópolis: Vozes, 1978.

———. *Como trabalhar com o povo.* Petrópolis: Vozes, 1982.

Boff, Leonardo. *Church, Charism and Power: Liberation Theology and the Institutional Church.* New York: Crossroad, 1986.

Branford, Sue, and Oriel Glock. *The Last Frontier: Fighting over Land in the Amazon.* London: Zed Books, 1985.

Brown, Robert McAfee. *Gustavo Gutierrez: An Introduction.* Maryknoll, NY: Orbis, 1990.

Bruneau, Thomas. *The Political Transformation of the Brazilian Catholic Church.* New York: Cambridge University Press, 1974.

———. "Basic Christian Communities in Latin America: Their Nature and Significance." In *Churches and Politics in Latin America*, edited by Daniel H. Levine. Beverly Hills: Sage, 1980, 225-37.

———. *The Church in Brazil: The Politics of Religion.* Austin: University of Texas Press, 1982.

Burdick, John. *Looking for God in Brazil: The Progressive Catholic Church in Urban Brazil's Religious Arena.* Berkeley: University of California Press, 1993.

Caipora Women's Group. *Women in Brazil.* London: Latin American Bureau, 1993.

Caramuru de Barros, Raimundo. *Brasil: uma igreja em renovação.* Petrópolis: Vozes, 1968.

Cleary, Edward L. *Crisis and Change: The Church in Latin America Today.* Maryknoll, NY: Orbis.

Cleary, Edward L., and Hannah Stewart-Gambino, ed. *Conflict and Competition: The Latin American Church in a Changing Environment.* Boulder, CO: Lynne Rienner, 1990.

Clemens, Carolina. *É bom lembrar: um pedacinho da história das CEBs no Maranhão.* São Luís, Maranhão: Equipe Provincial das CEBs do Maranhão, 1989.

Comissão Executiva do Movimento pela Sobrevivência na Transamazônica, "Movimento pela Sobrevivência na Transamazônica: viver, produzir, preservar." 1991 Photocopy.

Comissão Pastoral da Terra. *CPT: pastoral e compromisso.* Petrópolis: Vozes, 1983.

———. *Espinhoso caminho para a liberdade: conflitos no campo—1990.* São Paulo: Edições Loyola, 1991.

———. *Terra, agua e paz—viver é um direito: conflitos no campo—Brasil/1991.* São Paulo: Edições Loyola, 1992.

———. *Luta e sonho na terra: conflitos no campo—Brasil/1992.* São Paulo: Edições Loyola, 1993.

———. *Conflitos no campo—Brasil, 93.* Goiânia: Comissão Pastoral da Terra, 1994.

Cox, Harvey. *The Silencing of Leonardo Boff: The Vatican and the Future of World Christianity.* Oak Park, IL: Meyer Stone, 1988.

Cussianovich, Alejandro. *Religious Life and the Poor: Liberation Theology Perspectives.* Maryknoll, NY: Orbis, 1979.

De Kadt, Emanuel. *Catholic Radicals in Brazil.* London: Oxford University Press, 1970.

Della Cava, Ralph. *Miracle at Joazeiro.* New York: Columbia University Press, 1970.

De Oliveira Filho, Moacyr. *Rio Maria: terra da morte anunciada.* São Paulo: Editora Anita Garibaldi, 1991.

De Souza, Itamar. *A luta da igreja contra os coroneis.* Petrópolis: Vozes, 1982.

De Souza Martins, José. *Caminhada no chão da noite: Emancipação política e libertação nos movimentos sociais do campo.* São Paulo: Editora Hucitec, 1989.

———. *Os camponeses e a política no Brasil.* 4th ed. Petrópolis: Vozes, 1990.

De Toledo Sader, M. Regina C. "Espaço e luta no Bico do Papagaio." Ph.D. diss., University of São Paulo, 1986.

Dias Mendes, Armando. "Major Projects and Human Life in Amazonia." In *Change in the Amazon Basin, Volume I: Man's Impact on Forests and Rivers,* edited by John Hemming. Manchester, UK: Manchester University Press, 1985, 44-57.

Drogus, Carol. "Reconstructing the Feminine: Women in São Paulo's CEBs." *Extrait des archives de sciences sociales des religions* 17 (1990): 63-74.

———. "Popular Movements and the Limits of Political Mobilization at the Grassroots in Brazil." In *Conflict and Competition: The Latin American Church in a Changing Environment,* edited by Edward L. Cleary and Hannah Stewart-Gambino. Boulder, CO: Lynne Rienner, 1992, 63-86.

———. "Religious Change and Women's Status in Latin America: A Comparison of Catholic Base Communities and Pentecostal Churches." Photocopy, working paper.

English, Barbara. Unpublished working paper on Alcoa in São Luís, prepared for Maryland schools. 1984. Photocopy.

Freire, Paulo. *Pedagogy of the Oppressed.* New York: Seabury, 1970.

Foweraker, Joe. *The Struggle for Land: A Political Economy of the Pioneer in Brazil from 1930 to the Present Day.* Cambridge: Cambridge University Press, 1981.

Goodwillie, Susan, and Perdita Houston. "The NGO Revolution." *WorldPaper* (August 1992): 1-2.

Gramsci, Antonio. *Selections from the Prison Notebooks.* New York: International Publishers, 1971.

Greeley, Andrew. *American Catholics since the Council: An Unauthorized Report.* Chicago: Thomas More Press, 1985.

———. *Virgin and Martyr.* New York: Warner, 1986.

Grindle, Merilee S. *State and Countryside: Development Policy and Agrarian Politics in Latin America.* Baltimore: Johns Hopkins University Press, 1986.

Gutierrez Gustavo. *A Theology of Liberation.* Maryknoll, NY: Orbis, 1973.

Hennelly, Alfred T., ed. *Santo Domingo and Beyond: Documents and Commentaries from the Historic Meeting of the Latin American Bishops' Conference.* Maryknoll, NY: Orbis, 1993.

Hewitt, W. E. "Strategies for Social Change Employed by Brazilian CEBs in the Archdiocese of São Paulo." *Journal for the Scientific Study of Religion* 25, no. 1 (1986): 16-30.

———. *Base Christian Communities and Social Change in Brazil.* Lincoln: University of Nebraska Press, 1991.

Horowitz, Irving Louis. *Revolution in Brazil.* New York: E. P. Dutton, 1964.

Huizer, Gerrit. *The Revolutionary Potential of Peasants in Latin America.* Lexington, MA: D. C. Heath, 1972.

Ianni, Octavio. *Ditadura e agricultura: o desenvolvimento do capitalismo na Amazônia (1964-1978).* Rio de Janeiro: Civilização Brasileira, 1979.

Ireland, Rowan. *Kingdoms Come: Religion and Politics in Brazil.* Pittsburgh: University of Pittsburgh Press, 1992.

Kleinpenning, Johan M. G., and Sjoukje Volbeda. "Recent Changes in Population Size and Distribution in the Amazon Region of Brazil." In *Change in the Amazon Basin, Volume II: The Frontier after a Decade of Colonisation,* edited by John Hemming. Manchester, U.K.: Manchester University Press, 1985, 6-36.

Kowalewski, Mark R. "Firmness and Accommodation: Impression Management in Institutional Roman Catholicism." *Sociology of Religion* 54, no. 2 (1993): 207-17.

Levine, Daniel H., ed. *Churches and Politics in Latin America.* Beverly Hills, CA: Sage, 1980.

Levine, Daniel H., and Scott Mainwaring. "Religion and Popular Protest in Latin America: Contrasting Experiences." In *Power and Popular Protest: Latin American Social Movements,* edited by Susan Eckstein. Berkeley, CA: University of California Press, 1989, 203-40.

Libânio, João B. "Igreja, povo que se Liberta: III Encontro Intereclesial de Comunidades de Base." *Síntese* 5, no. 14 (1979): 93-110.

McGuire, Meredith. *Religion: The Social Context.* 3d ed. Belmont, CA: Wadsworth, 1992.

Maduro, Otto. *Religion and Social Conflicts.* Maryknoll, NY: 1982.

Mainwaring, Scott. *The Catholic Church and Politics in Brazil: 1916-1985.* Stanford, CA: Stanford University Press, 1986.

Malloy, James M., ed. *Authoritarianism and Corporatism in Latin America.* Pittsburgh: University of Pittsburgh Press, 1977.

Mariz, Cecilia. *Coping with Poverty: Pentecostals and Christian Base Communities in Brazil.* Philadelphia: Temple University Press, 1994.

Marx, Karl. *Selected Writings in Sociology and Social Philosophy*. New York: McGraw-Hill, 1982.

Marx, Karl, and Friedrich Engels. *On Religion*. New York: Schocken Books, 1964.

May, Roy H., Jr. *The Poor of the Land: A Christian Case for Land Reform*. Maryknoll, NY: Orbis, 1991.

Navarro, Zander. "Democracia, cidadania e representação: os movimentos sociais rurais no estado do Rio Grande do Sul, Brasil, 1978-1990." Paper presented at the International Congress of Americanists, Tulane University, New Orleans, LA, July 7-11, 1991.

Novak, Michael. "Why Latin America Is Poor." *Forbes*, April 17, 1989, 76.

―――. "Subverting the Churches." *Forbes*, January 22, 1990, 94.

Pace, Richard. "Social Conflict and Political Activism in the Brazilian Amazon: A Case Study of Gurupá." *American Ethnologist* 19, no. 4 (1992): 721-32.

Paige, Jeffery M. *Agrarian Revolution: Social Movements and Export Agriculture in the Underdeveloped World*. New York: Free Press, 1975.

Paiva, Vanilda. *Igreja e questão agrária*. São Paulo: Edições Loyola, 1985.

Puleo, Mev. *The Struggle Is One: Voices and Visions of Liberation*. Albany, NY: State University of New York Press, 1994.

Rezende Figueira, Ricardo. *A justiça do lobo: posseiros e padres do Araguaia*. Petrópolis: Vozes, 1986.

―――. *Rio Maria: canto da terra*. Petrópolis: Vozes, 1992. Abridged translation, *Rio Maria: Song of the Earth*, Orbis Books, Maryknoll, NY, 1994.

Ribeiro de Oliveira, Pedro A. *Religião e dominação de classe: gênese, estrutura e função do catolicismo romanisado no Brasil*. Petrópolis, Brasil: Vozes, 1985.

―――. "Comunidade, igreja e poder: em busca de um conceito sociológico de 'igreja'." *Religiaõ e Sociedade* 13, 3 (1986).

Rios, Radames. "Multinationals Given Free Reign in Brazilian Amazon." *Latinamerica Press*, 2 December 1982: 3-4.

Schmink, Marianne, and Charles H. Wood. *Contested Frontiers in Amazonia*. New York: Columbia University Press, 1992.

Scott, James C. *The Moral Economy of the Peasant*. New Haven: Yale University Press, 1976.

―――. *Weapons of the Weak: Everyday Forms of Peasant Resistance*. New Haven: Yale University Press, 1985.

Skidmore, Thomas E. *Politics in Brazil, 1930-1964: An Experiment in Democracy.* New York: Oxford University Press, 1967.

————. *The Politics of Military Rule in Brazil, 1964-85.* New York: Oxford University Press, 1988.

Vaillancourt, Jean-Guy. *Papal Power: A Study of Vatican Control over Lay Catholic Elites.* Berkeley: University of California Press, 1980.

————. "Penser et concrétiser le développement durable." *Ecodécision,* Winter 1995: 24-29.

Valle, Rogério, and Marcelo Pitta. *Comunidades eclesiais católicas: resultados estatísticas no Brasil.* Petrópolis: Vozes, 1994.

Vallier, Ivan. *Catholicism, Social Control, and Modernization in Latin America.* Englewood Cliffs, NJ: Prentice-Hall, 1970.

Wallace, Ruth. *They Call Her Pastor: A New Role for Catholic Women.* Albany: State University of New York Press, 1992.

Weber, Max. *The Protestant Ethic and the Spirit of Capitalism.* New York: Charles Scribner's Sons, 1958.

————. *The Sociology of Religion.* Boston: Beacon Press, 1963.

Ximenes Galvão, Raul. "O gerenciamento costeiro e a ocupação do litoral." *Pau Brasil,* September/October 1985.

Newspaper articles cited are from the following:

Diário do Norte

Estado do Maranhão

Jornal Pequeno

Latinamerica Press

O Imparcial

INDEX

Afro-Brazilian religions, 165, 167. *See also* syncretist religions
agrarian reform, 84, 109, 110; bishops' position on, 107
Alcoa, 41, 46-50, 183-184n.1,2
aluminum refining: environmental threat, 44-45, 48, 49
Alvarez, Sonia, 142-143
Amazônia, Legal, 14, 17, 21, 23, 27
Amnesty International, 73, 85
Arame, 5, 27-40
Arns, Cardinal Paulo Evaristo, 101
Azevedo, Fernando, 189n.3

base communities (base Christian communities, base ecclesial communities, *comunidades eclesiais de base*, CEBs), 3-4, 28-29, 35-37, 42, 45, 50-51, 53-56, 65-68, 77, 78-79, 81-82, 89-90, 106-107, 110, 113-139, 163-164; and Bible study, 4, 33, 42, 67, 124; and critical reflection, 4, 124; initial organization of, 117-119; origins of, in Maranhão, 113-116; roles of religious sisters and priests in organizing, 116-122; rural-urban differences, 114-115, 165-167; in São Paulo, 106, 165-166; and social activism, 4, 62, 113-139; support for, or lack of support for, from bishops, 3, 5, 55; and women, 141-156
Basic Education Movement, 81, 113, 188n.2
Bible courses, 4
Bico do Papagaio, 63-74, 97
Boff, Leonardo, 9, 101, 180n.24, 186n.1

Bruneau, Thomas C., 3, 179n.22
buffalo, 53, 57-59
Burdick, John, 165, 166, 180n.25

Câmara, Bishop Helder, 101, 103, 105
Camio, Father Aristide, 23, 182n.24
Canuto, João, 76, 186n.1
Canuto, Luzia, 84
Canuto, Orlando, 83-84
Carajás Hills, 16, 20, 23
Cardoso Sobrinho, Bishop José, 105
Catholic Action, 54, 113, 183n.6, 187n.1
cattle projects, 14-15; 181n.5
CEBs. *See* base communities
Cicero, Father, 64, 185n.1
CNBB. *See* National Conference of the Brazilian Bishops
colonization, 17-19, 87-88, 164; failure of, 18
Committee for the Defense of the Island, 45, 49
Communism, accusations of, 22, 31, 44
Communist Party of Brazil (*Partido Comunista do Brasil*, PC do B), 76, 81-82
corporatism, 126-127, 129, 184n.2
CPT. *See* Pastoral Land Commission
Curió, Major (Sebastião Rodrigues de Moura), 23, 80
Cussianovich, Alejandro, 3

Da Mota, Bishop João José, 41-42, 43, 53, 114
death threats, 58, 61, 71, 84, 93, 137

decision-making by lay people 38, 42
Delgado, Bishop José, 114
Democratic Rural Union (*União
    Democrática Rural*, UDR), 58
De Souza Martins, José, 179-180n.22
De Toledo Sader, M. Regina C., 64, 65
Drogus, Carol, 142-143

English, Sister Barbara, 42, 44, 47
environmental issues, 15, 44-45, 93-
    94. *See also* aluminum refining,
    hazardous waste, pollution, rain
    forest
eviction of peasant farmers, 20-21,
    60-61, 64-65, 76-77; resistance to,
    57, 60, 65, 66, 133-134, 147
Executive Land Administration of
    Araguaia-Tocantins (*Gerência
    Executiva de Terras de Araguaia-
    Tocantins*, GETAT), 22-24, 182n.23;
    official objectives, 22-23; relation-
    ship to rural violence, 23-24

Father Josimo Human Rights
    Commission, 73, 74
Fragoso, Bishop Antônio, 114

Geisel, President Ernesto, 20
GETAT. *See* Executive Land
    Administration of Araguaia-
    Tocantins
Goulart, President João, 128
Gouriou, Father François, 23, 182n.24
Gramsci, Antonio, 191n.4
Greeley, Andrew, 2, 177n.3
grilagem. See land robbing
gunmen, 22, 30-31, 76, 85, 93
guerrilla activity, accusations of, 23,
    31
Gutierrez, Gustavo, 2, 9

Hanrahan, Bishop Patrick Joseph
    (Dom José), 79-80

hazardous waste, 45, 46, 49
Hewitt, W. E., 3, 106, 165, 188n.4

Igaraú, 46-49
INCRA. *See* National Institute for
    Colonization and Agrarian
    Reform
infrastructure, 16; lack of, 33
institutional church support for peas-
    ant struggles, 65, 74, 80-81

John XXIII, Pope, 103
John Paul II, Pope, 116
Josimo, Father, *See* Morais Tavares,
    Father Josimo
Julião, Francisco, 13, 127, 189n.3

Koopmans, Father John Joseph, 48,
    49
Krautler, Bishop Irwin, 88, 90,
    190n.16
Kubitschek, President Juscelino, 127

land, expropriation of, 32, 78, 93, 138-
    139
land occupations, 29-30, 76-78, 131-
    135
land pilgrimage, 37, 109-110
land robbing (*grilagem*), 21, 22, 56-57
LeMoal, Michel, 89
Levine, Daniel, 178n.6
Libânio, João B., 3
liberation theology, 2, 101, 121, 143
Lula (Luís Inácio Lula da Silva),
    184n.4

Maduro, Otto, 6, 161-162
Mainwaring, Scott, 178n.6
Marinho, Father Osvaldo Fernandes,
    57-61
Mariz, Cecília Loreto, 165, 189n.12
Marx, Karl, 6, 161

Marxism, 2-3
McGuire, Meredith, 191n.5
Medellín Conference (Second General Conference of the Latin American Bishops), 103, 106-107, 163
Médici, President Emílio Garrastazú, 17
Migration of peasant farmers, 16
Military Police: role in evicting peasant farmers, 22, 76, 92; working together with hired gunmen, 76, 83
military regime, 13-24, 30-31
mining projects, 15, 16, 41
Morais Tavares, Father Josimo, 70-73
Movement for Survival on the Transamazonic, 93-95
Movement of the Landless, 110-111, 171
multinational corporations, tax breaks for, 16
murders of activists and church people, 1, 71, 73, 75, 76, 81, 83-84, 137

National Conference of the Brazilian Bishops, (Conferência Nacional dos Bispos do Brasil, CNBB), 102, 164
National Institute for Colonization and Agrarian Reform (Instituto Nacional de Colonização e de Reforma Agrária, INCRA), 17, 19-20
National Security, Doctrine of, 13
Nicola (lay missionary) 68-69, 74
non-governmental organizations (NGOs), 159-160
northeast region of Brazil, 16, 17
Notre Dame de Namur, Sisters of 42, 90
Novak, Michael, 2

Pastoral Land Commission, (Comissão Pastoral da Terra, CPT), 73-74, 78, 82-83, 103, 107-112, 164-165, 170, 175, 182n.19; administra-

tive structure, 108-109; functions, 109-111; impact on the lives of peasant farmers, 111-112; and land occupations, 110; origin, 107-108; support of rural unions, 126
PC do B. See Communist Party of Brazil
Peasant Leagues, 127, 189n.3
Pentecostals, 9, 135-136, 165, 189n.12
Pirotta, Father Luís, 28
Pitta, Marcelo, 178n.10
Ponte, Bishop Paulo, 48, 58-59
pollution, 44-45, 48, 49
preferential option for the poor, 102-106
Protestantism. See Pentecostals
Puebla Conference (Third General Conference of the Latin American Bishops), 106

rain forest, burning of, 15, 87
Recife, Archdiocese of Olinda and, 105
religious authority, 38-39, 43-44
Rezende, Father Ricardo, 83, 84-85, 107, 180-181n.3
Ribeiro de Souza, Expedito, 84, 86
Rio Maria, 75-86
Rio Maria Committee, 85-86
rural mobilization (defined), 7

Santa Rita, 53-62
Santo Domingo Conference (Fourth General Conference of the Latin American Bishops), 106-107
São Luís, Archdiocese of, 41, 53, 114
São Paulo, Archdiocese of, 105-106, 114-116
Sarney, President José, 21
Spreafico, Bishop Serafim, 34
Stang, Sister Dorothy, 89-90
STR's. See Unions of Rural Workers
syncretist religions, 9. See also Afro-Brazilian Religions

SUDAM. *See* Superintendency for the Development of the Amazon
Superintendency for the Development of the Amazon (*Superintendência do Desenvolvimento da Amazônia,* SUDAM), 13-16, 20; and cattle ranches, 14-15, 181n.5; and the burning of the rain forest, 15; tax breaks, 14-15

Tierra, Pedro, 72
Transamazonic Highway, 17-18, 87

UDR. *See* Democratic Rural Union
unions of rural workers (*sindicatos dos trabalhadores rurais,* STR's), 29, 36, 68-70, 81-83, 125-131, 135-136; participation by base community members, 55, 69-70, 82, 130-131; patterns of emergence, 129-130; takeover by base community members, 55, 129

Vaillancourt, Jean-Guy, 162, 191n.4
Valle, Rogério, 178n.10
Vargas, President Getúlio, 126-127
Vatican, 9, 162
violence, 23-24, 30, 72-73, 75-76, 83-85, 92, 109, 137-138, 148. *See also* death threats, murders of activists and church people
Volkswagen, 180-181n.3

Wallace, Ruth, 188n.10
Weber, Max, 6, 10, 161
women: in base communities, 33, 56, 141-149; changing consciousness, 141-142, 145-146, 154-156; in the land struggle, 32, 56, 147; men's attitudes toward, 56, 146, 149-152; as mothers, 142-143, 153-154

Xingu, Prelacy of, 88-90

Zannoni, Father Claudio, 28
Zuffellato, Father Gian, 28